Technology Scorecards

Technology Scorecards

Aligning IT Investments with Business Performance

SAM BANSAL

WILEY

John Wiley & Sons, Inc.

ree paper. ⊗

Published by John Wiley & Sons, Inc., Hoboken, New Jersey.
Published simultaneously in Canada.

For general information on our other products and services, or technical support, please
contact our Customer Care Department within the United States at 800-762-2974, outside
the United States at 317-572-3993 or fax 317-572-4002.

Wiley also publishes its books in a variety of electronic formats. Some content that
appears in print may not be available in electronic books. For more information about
Wiley products, visit our Web site at http://www.wiley.com.

Library of Congress Cataloging-in-Publication Data

Bansal, Sam, 1940-
    Technology scorecards : aligning it investments with business
performance / Sam Bansal.
        p. cm.
    Includes bibliographical references and index.
    ISBN 978-0-470-46456-4 (cloth)
    1. Strategic planning.   2. Business logistics.   3. Performance
technology.   I. Title.
    HD30.28.B3644 2009
    658.4'012–dc22

                                                            2008052098

Printed in the United States of America

10 9 8 7 6 5 4 3 2 1

Disclaimer

This publication contains references to the products of SAP AG. SAP, R/3, xApps, xApp, SAP NetWeaver, Duet, PartnerEdge, ByDesign, SAP Business ByDesign, and other SAP products and services mentioned herein are trademarks or registered trademarks of SAP AG in Germany and in several other countries all over the world.

Business Objects and the Business Objects logo, BusinessObjects, Crystal Reports, Crystal Decisions, Web Intelligence, Xcelsius and other Business Objects products and services mentioned herein are trademarks or registered trademarks of Business Objects in the United States and/or other countries.

SAP AG is neither the author nor the publisher of this publication and is not responsible for its content, and SAP Group shall not be liable for errors or omissions with respect to the materials.

Contents

Acknowledgments

The author is indebted to SAP AG for the knowledge gained on Advance Planner & Optimizer (APO), Supply Chain Management (SCM), and Product Life Cycle Management (PLM) while in tenure over there. Most of the information presented in these areas is based on the author's own practice and knowledge of the SAP domain. To the best of the author's knowledge, nothing discussed is of a confidential nature.

I also wish to acknowledge all those friends, relatives, colleagues, and associates without whose help, advice, and encouragement this book would have still remained in my head. Specifically, some people I want to thank for their help are:

Amrish Goyal, my friend, for his constant encouragement to complete this work.

Sneh Agarwal, my wife, for her continued enthusiasm and for encouraging me when I did not feel up to completing this work.

Sahil Bansal, my son, for editing the preface and sowing the seeds of confidence in this effort.

Suresh Mehta, my friend; as a CIO and project manager, he critiqued the preface and introduction with a high degree of enthusiasm.

Sanjay Jain, my friend and colleague, for his endorsement blurb. Sanjay has always encouraged and advised me on various issues. His review and critique of the entire book has proven invaluable. A professor at George Washington University, Sanjay is a subject matter expert.

Ajay Agrawal, my friend and erstwhile colleague, for his implicit faith in my claim that a high percentage of software projects fail the first time. His belief gave me the confidence to begin this project.

Mike O'Brien, my friend, mentor, and client, for his kind encouragement and for agreeing to review the book and give me an endorsement.

Mike Petrucci, my friend, mentor, and client, for agreeing to give me an endorsement.

Acronyms and Abbreviations

APO: Advanced planner and optimizer
Avg: Average
BBP: Business blue print
BCD: Business case development
BPR: Business process reengineering
CAD: Computer-aided design
CAE: Computer-aided engineering
CAM: Computer-aided machining
CAPE: Computer-aided process engineering
CAPP: Computer-aided process planning
CIM: Computer-integrated manufacturing
CIMing: Usually means tasks related to computer-integrated manufacturing
Collabn: Collaboration
Config
   Mgmt: Configuration management
CPG: Consumer packaged goods
CPM: Collaborative project management
CRM: Customer relations management
CSF: Critical success factors
DDC: Direct digital control
DFA: Design for assembly
DFM: Design for manufacturing
EH&S: Environment, health, and safety
Env: Environment
ERP: Enterprise resource planning
fabs: Fabrication units; usually refers to chip-making plants
FI: Finance
iPPE: Integrated product and process engineering
IT: Information technology
KPI: Key performance indicator
LCM: Life cycle management
MES: Manufacturing execution system

MM: Materials management
mySAP: SAP's software product begun in 1999
mySAP
  SCM: SAP's Supply Chain Management
OA: Opportunity assessment
PM: Project manager, also program manager
Psft: Peoplesoft
R3:   SAP software system
SAP: Software Application Products (usually refers to SAP Ag of Germany)
SCM: Supply chain management
SD: Sales and distribution
SEM: Strategic enterprise management
SIS: Semiconductor integration services; also strategic international services
SKU: Stock keeping unit
SOA: Supply chain opportunity assessment
Sr: Senior
SRM: Sourcing relations manager
SWOT: Strength, weakness, opportunity, threat
WBDS: Work break-down structures
WF: Work flow
WFM: Work flow modeling

PART I

Introduction

CHAPTER 1

Why Projects Fail, Scorecards, and How This Book Is Organized

Today's Environment

Since the dot-com bust in the year 2000, information technology (IT) and IT people have been under an unprecedented squeeze. Today's high-tech industry has come close to being a $10 trillion behemoth, of which software is fully more than 25%. There was a time when software was a forgotten appendage to the mighty mainframe, but such is not the case anymore. Now software, even if only 25% of the total content, is the tail that wags the dog.

As paradigm after paradigm is changing in the high-tech landscape of our world, software is increasing in importance and is contributing more business benefits than ever before. But this is not enough.

It seems the honeymoon days for IT are over. The free rein that chief information officers (CIOs) enjoyed not too long ago are gone. Instead, we find ourselves in the midst of very tight operating conditions. In today's software environment, CIOs must:

- Reduce total cost of ownership.
- Increase value to the corporation.
- Contribute to improve bottom and top line.

And the normal things that CIOs were expected to do in addition to the top-level goals continue:

- Decrease complexity in increasingly heterogeneous environment.
- Contribute to creating a real, real-time enterprise.
- Manage resources.
- Do a lot with the little that is available.
- Produce miracles without budget growth.

The champions of IT, the CIOs and their staffs, try to deal with these issues while the project world is delivering the other messages:

- New technologies are being introduced at a more rapid rate than before.
- There are too many vendors to choose from.
- All claim to have practically the same offerings, so it is difficult to differentiate among them.
- So-called neutral consultants are too eager to take your money without contributing much value.
- Requirements are not understood. Promises are made to be broken later.
- And to make matters worse, when projects are finished, chief executive and chief financial officers complain that:
  - Expectations are not met.
  - Too much money was spent for too little return.
  - They want to sue the vendor because it failed to deliver as promised.

When a new technology is first implemented by a group of trailblazer companies, success is far from guaranteed. Success and satisfaction are seldom found in this group of companies. However, as the technology gets old and commonplace, the success rate generally goes up. In fact, the larger the company and larger the project, the more likely project failure is. The frank reality is that larger projects (more than $3 million in application spend) routinely need harsh turn-around measures, or they get stalled and eventually killed by the weight of their own bureaucracy.

A survey published in 2001 in *Chaos News Letter*[1] has shed light on companies' success by taking the cumulative cost of failure, estimated by the Standish Group at $145 billion, and by the Meta Group figure at $180 billion. This amount, they believe, is the amount lost each year in the United States due to failed or challenged projects. The *Chaos* report is full of grim numbers, such as "for every 100 projects, there are 94 restarts" and "only 9% of projects for large companies come in on-time and on-budget." However, the 2004 *Chaos* report,[2] entitled "CHAOS Chronicles," found a total project costs to be $255 billion, of which a total failure cost was estimated to be $110 billion. While this is an improvement over the previous estimates, it is still a large cost of failure. And compare failure or success of a project from the perspective of the stake holders as defined by the chief stakeholders who believe that their IT investments did not give them the desired returns from their perspective.

The question is: What are the promises of technology, and how can technology deliver on those promises?

Human nature is such that first we create problems, then we search for reasons behind them, and then we try to solve them. So, having seen the current complex and heterogeneous landscape of systems, let us examine briefly the reasons for widespread failures of software projects.

A cautionary note about failure is that systems may not necessarily have failed; in the eyes of the stakeholders, however, they may not have fulfilled expectations.

Why Projects Fail

These are the messages we are getting from the media:

- Enterprise software at X Company failed to perform.
- SCM software from Y vendor failed to perform.
- Company Z is suing the vendor A for noncompliance.
- Consulting Group A was thrown out of Company B.

Here are some basic causes of these problems:

- Strategic alignment did not match the business goals.
- There were communication breakdowns.
- Up-front buy-in was not obtained.
- User involvement was inadequate.
- There were poor user inputs.
- Stakeholder conflicts existed.
- The requirements were vague.
- User requirements were not firmly nailed down.
- User requirements may have changed midway.
- Poor cost and schedule estimates existed.
- Skills did not match the job.
- There were hidden costs of going "lean and mean."
- There was a failure to plan properly.
- Poor architecture existed.
- Failure warning signals came late.
- Company financials may have changed.
- Project manager may not have been skilled.
- The project team may have been unacceptable to management.
- The champion and executive sponsor was transferred, or left the company, or was not there.

Additional problems encountered in the field include:

- Value is not understood.
- Vendors bid without understanding the requirements well.
- Goals are not clearly and succinctly defined.
- Key performance indicators (KPIs) are neither defined nor understood.
- Change management was not practiced.
- Risk planning was not done properly.
- Most projects get initiated as automation of as-is without due business process reengineering (BPR) or to-be views.
- The quality of external consulting was poor.

It is not my intention to discuss the causes and cures here. Suffice it to say that the literature provides plentiful basic causes. The additional causes, just enumerated, constitute the main theme of this book. They will form the key factors to unleashing the quantum improvements in cost, value, and productivity. They will form the bulk of the chapters in Part II which will deal with the technologies—their features and benefits—and in Part III the complete step-wise approach to get the projects to succeed will be discussed.

Are we investing too much money in information technology and information systems? This is a question many of today's CEOs and boards of directors ponder. Until recently, companies have made major investments in IT, trusting that this measure alone would increase productivity. Now decision makers are increasingly questioning whether IT projects actually create value.

Jurgen H. Daum, writing about adding value through IT investments,[3] cited statistics from a survey conducted by *CFO Magazine*: Only 14% of executives state that their companies' IT investments achieved the expected return on investment (ROI), whereas 74% were unsure of whether they had spent too much money on IT in the past three years. Similarly, in June 2007, as I was talking with Ajay Agrawal, a vice president of a financial services company, he mentioned that most IT projects fail the first time they are attempted. Clearly, doubts are being raised about the benefits of IT investments, and managers are becoming more careful about giving the go-ahead to IT budgets.

These reservations are apparently warranted. According to a study published by the Gartner Group in October 2008,[4] of the $570 billion that flowed into IT investments worldwide, a high percentage was spent in vain. My estimate of this wasted spending is around $246 billion. Figure 1.1 summarizes the basic reasons for the failure.

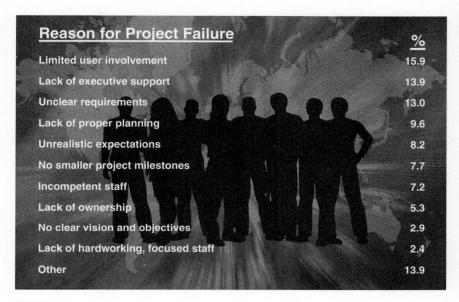

FIGURE 1.1 Why Projects Fail

Numerous studies prove this failure in IT project in particular. One important study, however, set out to understand what the projects that did succeed contribute to business performance. The survey results are discussed in the next section.

Harry's Survey

I collaborated with Harry Sakamaki of SITA Corporation to conduct a survey of companies in the United States to provide bottom-line KPIs. We selected 16 companies in the manufacturing sector representing a mix of small- to midsize and some large companies. We solicited data from their CEOs, heads of IT, and their staff. Figure 1.2 gives the highlights of this survey.

In Figure 1.2, rows 1–14 that are in the smallest type size give the KPIs with respect to systems infrastructure; KPIs in rows 15–25 represent the same of the business performance but specifically of the supply chain; the ones in rows 26–34 are the KPIs of the business performance representing the bottom lines. The improvements shown in the extreme right column are the improvement percentages of each row. Do not add these percentages; they must be looked at as the individual performance improvements.

Row No	Key Performance Indicator	Best practice improvement
1	**Systems Infrastructure**	
2	Rely on enterprise resource planning (ERP) system to provide analytical/business intelligence information	3%
3	Utilize additional applications such as SAP SEM, Oracle OFA, PeopleSoft EPM, Hyperion or Cognos tools	10%
4	Use spreadsheets and manual processes to provide information	5%
5	Utilize balanced Score Card/metrics	10%
6	Utilize daily key measures	5%
7	Enterprise-wide standard management reporting exists	3%
8	Analytics and business intelligence are integrated into the entire enterprise	
9		
10	Fully integrated ERP system	3%
11	Limited numbers of ERP/legacy systems with modest integration	10%
12	Disparate information systems with multiple ERP systems and applications	5%
13	Utilize balanced Scorecard and SCOR Card metrics	10%
14	No ERP; use legacy system	5%
15	**Business Performance/Supply Chain Performance**	
16	Increase in customer fill rate	3%
17	Increase in on-time delivery to request	10%
18	Increase in on-time delivery to commit	5%
19	Days Sales Outstanding (DSO) via increasing invoice accuracy etc.	10%
20	Increase in sales via better forecasting and production planning	5%
21	Reduce excessive inventory carrying cost	3%
22		
23	Total days of raw material	3%
24	Total days of work in process	10%
25	Total days of finished goods	5%
26	**Bottom Line Business Performance**	
27	Product margin improvement via increase in yield, better production planning, increase in machine uptime, etc.	3%
28	Production yield improvement by improvement plant scheduling, reducing scrap, etc.	10%
29	Production cost reduction	5%
30		
31	Reduction in head count (full-time equivalent basis)	3%
32	Cost of goods sold (COGS)	10%
33	Cash flow	5%
34	Profit	10%

FIGURE 1.2 Harry's Survey Summary

Highlights from Figure 1.2 are that bottom-line performance improvements are in the 3% to 10% range. This is a very low number. In fact, it is lower than the earlier number, which said that fully 75% of firms do not fulfill stakeholders' expectations. Whether the figure is 3% to 10% or 25%, it is clear that the success rate as measured by performance improvement is very low. I have tacitly recognized the sad state of affairs of low returns for a long time. My conversations in the field always confirmed that some regular culprits will raise their ugly heads whenever one's guard is down. When I pondered why I often succeeded in delivering values via projects yet sometimes did not, a pattern emerged. This pattern was based on the best practices I employed by design or sheer luck. This is what I want to share with you. The rest of this chapter describes the scorecards and how the major parts of this book are organized. After reading the next section, you will understand the technologies and how to create scorecards that are based on aligning investments and can drive the achievement of business performance.

Scorecards and SCOR Cards

Scorecarding technology has been around since early 1980s. First there was the Balanced Scorecard methodology, where nonfinancial processes are measured based on their impact on company performance. The term *SCOR card* is based on the supply chain operations reference model that was introduced in the mid-1990s for measuring, monitoring, and thereby driving the performance of supply chains. In my practice, I used SCOR cards very successfully. However, I grew into SCOR cards using the Balanced Scorecard. The main difference between the two is that the SCOR card is geared more specifically around the KPIs of the supply chain operations whereas regular scorecards can be applied to all enterprise operations. And best of all, I could use either scorecard to impact the development of strategy to align the IT investments with business performance. An example of the potential power of scorecards comes from a conversation I had with the president of a major automotive company in India. I had redesigned his supply chain and presented him with his company's scorecard. It would drive the implementation and huge reduction in his inventory cost. Upon hearing my presentation and reviewing the scorecard, he said, "Sam, I will hang it right behind my chair in my office so that every time any of my staff comes to see me, they see where we are, where our goals are, and who we have to beat to become the best-in-class business." The scorecard had all of that information in it. Part II of this book describes knowledge essential to creating scorecards. Part III presents case examples that show how scorecards can be developed and can drive the development of a realistic strategy that then can be used to implement the IT investments and exploit the business benefits (i.e., the business performance).

Promise of Technology: Functionality, Key Performance Indicators, and Business Benefits

Part II explains the concepts behind the value drivers in the value chains from which KPIs can be extracted; they become the basis of functionality required and finally the planning for implementation and development of a business case to benefits exploitation. Thus Part II shows practitioners and stakeholders what is practical to get from the technology. It is divided in three chapters:

> Chapter 2 Strategic Enterprise Management
> > This chapter examines the functionality of strategic enterprise management (SEM) in detail and discusses its benefits
> Chapter 3 Supply Chain Management
> > This chapter examines the functionality benefits and KPIs of supply chain management (SCM). SCM impacts the bottom line the most. A 50% improvement in SCM can increase the net before taxes by as much as 100%.
> Chapter 4 Product Life Cycle Management
> > This chapter examines the functionality, benefits and KPIs of product life cycle management (PLM). This is the application that impacts the top line the most.

Deliver on Promises: Scorecard Methodology to Align Investments to Business Performance

Part III describes scorecard methodology to align IT investments with business performance. The chapters describe all the areas and activities that have to happen to estimate the benefits and exploit them so that the promises are fulfilled. Note the activities are far more than mere project management. My 44 years of field experience in the management of large and complex projects serves as the basis for this part.

> Chapter 5 Strategy
> > Enterprise Strategy
> > > This chapter is about developing IT strategy that is responsive to business strategy. IT strategy formulation or

synchronizing it with the enterprise strategy is based on business goals and strengths, weaknesses, opportunities, and threats (SWOT) analysis. This chapter is the driver for KPI, benchmarking and SCOR carding, as-is and to-be modeling, and business blueprinting. It drives planning for all the activities in the realization phase, such as solution architecting, gap analysis, roll-out planning and configuring, as well as the planning for change, quality, risk, and test management, training, performance measurement, and performance tracking.

Key Performance Indicators

Key performance indicators are the measure of a business goal. Unlike most projects, which concentrate on IT-oriented KPIs, these are the business goals as extracted from the key stakeholders of the project. Remember however that there are KPIs that are action/independent variables that impact the business goals or dependent KPIs.

Benchmarking

Here the comparison is done with the best in class and average in class and the targets the company chooses for KPI (business goal) improvements.

Value/Benefits Estimating

This section provides a succinct calculation of the value contribution as derived from the SCOR card.

Business Process Reengineering

Here the workflow modeling of the as-is and to-be views of the enterprise and processes is covered.

Chapter 6 Realization Phase

Solution Architecting

Translating the business blue print to the hardware, software and network structures creates solution architecture. This solution is entirely IT-centric.

Gap Analysis

This activity pertains to determining whether there is difference between the business requirement and the selected vendors' technology functionality.

Roll-Out Planning

Various alternatives for rolling out solutions are considered. This planning is very important for a global project.

Configuration Planning

This section defines the activities of configuring processes and the ways to plan.

Chapter 7 Human Factors
    Project Management
        Here various models of project management are presented along with the characteristics of an ideal project manager. Critical success factors and how to do them are given. Also presented are the burning issues of the day in this discipline.
    Project Champions
        Project champions are the most essential people, the invisible reasons for a project's success. This section discusses how to work with them and get them interested in the project.
    Business Case Development.
        This section discusses all the human and political aspects of taking the business case to the stakeholders and the board to sell the project.
Chapter 8 Umbrella Considerations
    Change Management
        This section demonstrates how to rigorously manage the change. Most projects fail because they were not done well enough to proactively manage the change that promotes success.
    Implementation Time Risk Analysis and Mitigation of Risk in Enterprise Systems.
        This section shows how to estimate and eliminate risk in the various phases of the project. Recovery models are also given.
    Quality Management
        This section discusses quality as applied to software and explains how to establish and enforce the quality regimen.
    Communications Management
        This section describes how to plan and enforce the proactive communication system.
    Test Plan and Test Procedures
        Here we discuss various aspects of the test plan, test procedure, and test methodology through the entire life cycle of the project. This section includes validation and reviews.
    Training
        This section explains who to train and how much to train. Without a successful graduation from a training program, the project will not succeed.

Chapter 9 Performance Measurement
This chapter explains how to do ongoing measurement and track the KPIs. It discusses where and when KPIs should be presented to the stakeholders in order to continue to buy their support.
Chapter 10 Summary
This chapter provides the overall summary of the book.

Bibliography

"Danger Signs on the Road to Success," *Chaos News Letter,* August 17, 2001.

Daum, Jurgen H. "Strategy—A Holistic Approach: Adding Value Through IT Investments," Sapinfo.net.

Gartner Group. "Most Business-Launched Virtual Worlds Fail," May 16, 2008, www.informationweek.com/news/personal_tech/virtualworlds/showArticle.jhtml?articleID=207800.

Gartner Group. "90 Per Cent of Corporate Virtual World Projects Fail," May 15, 2008, www.gartner.com/it/page.jsp?id=670507.

Gonsalves, Antone. "Gartner Backtracks on Earlier IT Spending Growth," *Information Week,* October 13, 2008.

Krigsman, Michael. "Why IT Projects Fail," August 10, 2007, www.softwaremag.com/L.cfm?doc=newsletter/2004.zdnet.com/projectfailures/?p=329.

PM Hut Admin. "Why Do Projects Fail?" August 30, 2008, www.pmhut.com/why-do-projects-fail.

Standish Group. "Project Success Rate," *Software Magazine,* January 15, 2004.

PART II

Promise of Technology

This part serves as an introduction to three chapters: Chapter 2, Strategic Enterprise Management, Chapter 3, Supply Chain Management, and Chapter 4, Product Life Cycle Management. These chapters cover the promises of technologies and explain the broad functionality of each application. Also included is a description of the key performance indicators (KPIs) of each area, organized as KPIs that act as the value drivers and KPIs that measure the driven values. Taken together, these chapters provide a substantive knowledge base that will give the reader knowledge of how a bottom-line improvement can be achieved and what technology can be used as an enabler. Figure IIA describes the interrelationships between these concepts.

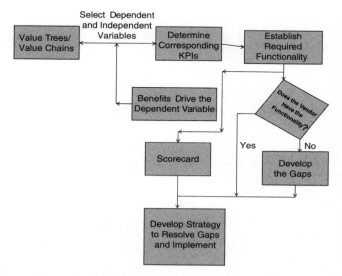

FIGURE IIA Overview of Development of Scorecard and Strategy

CHAPTER 2

Strategic Enterprise Management

Introduction

Chief financial officers and chief information officers have long struggled to satisfy the strategic information requirements associated with managing in an organized, structured, and efficient manner. The promise of integrated enterprise resource planning (ERP) systems to fulfill these requirements has been only partially realized. Companies have reduced cycle times and costs while increasing service and customer satisfaction levels. Yet many fundamental strategic questions about customer, channel, segment, service and product profitability, and the financial and nonfinancial performance of key business segments remain unanswered. Strategic Enterprise Management (SEM) deals with the higher-level tasks to:

- Measure business performance against simulations, targets, and benchmarks, using a Balanced Scorecard, value drivers, and management. Balanced Scorecard is a performance measurement technique; the SCOR card is similar but applies to the supply chain domain and is based on the supply chain operations reference model.
- Automate and accelerate the entire business consolidation process.
- Control and monitor business using value-based management principles.
- Change static operational planning cycles into continuous, rolling forecasts.
- Integrate business strategy with operations, planning, and employee goals and incentives.

SEM is a suite of tools designed to enable advanced cost management and performance measurement capabilities while allowing managers to focus explicitly on driving increased shareholder value.

SEM affords companies the opportunity to efficiently and systematically measure the performance of key business processes and the value they contribute to the business. SEM unlocks the complex array of data populated within the ERP environments, offering companies an effective way to utilize the full capabilities of these applications. Specific benefits include:

- Improved strategic decision making
- Improved tactical decision making
- Increased organizational alignment

At the core of SEM is the principle that whatever is not automated but needs to be automated should follow a rigid discipline consisting of the following rules:

- Focusing on value propositions and the development of a business case
- Establishing clear objectives
- Facilitating return on investment estimates
- Considering continuous improvements to ensure stabilization and user satisfaction to ensure the most cost-effective approach through onsite/ offshore deployment

The goal of Strategic Enterprise Management is the (re)definition and implementation of strategic goals and visions based on economic constraints gearing toward a competitive advantage of the corporation, while constantly improving and questioning strategic decisions. SEM also keeps future developments in mind. Because of the rapidly changing markets, it is very important that strategic decision processes are continuously accelerated and improved.

Core Activities with Strategic Enterprise Management

Strategy Definition

A future strategy cannot be implemented and validated immediately. Therefore, thorough planning is mission critical. Initially, the strategy is created, communicated, and discussed by using easy-to-understand graphical models. Simulation technology can be used for validation. Finally, the clear communication of the strategy is a key success factor for the implementation. This communication can be done by publishing the strategy to all relevant stakeholders and then deriving measurable performance indicators based on the abstract goals and visions.

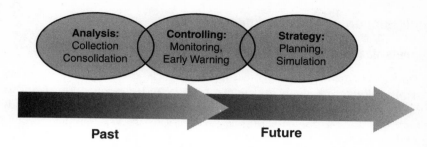

FIGURE 2.1 Direction of Strategic Enterprise Management

Controlling

In addition to monitoring performance indicators, one main goal of controlling a process or the entire enterprise is to define and monitor early-warning indicators that look ahead of the current situation. All controlling results play an important role in redefining the corporate strategy.

Analysis

Data from past business processes are collected and consolidated. In some cases, this is required by law; even if it is not, data collection can help tremendously in evaluating and redefining corporate strategies. (See Figure 2.1.)

How to Create a Strategy

Initially an external consultant and corporate management carry out a strength, weakness, opportunity, threat (SWOT) analysis. During the analysis, the strengths, weaknesses, opportunities, and threats of the enterprise are identified.

Based on the SWOT analysis, the main areas of interest are identified and are further investigated. The analysis results in a redefinition of the areas identified, which are described by means of various models. The models for a process road map show process structures and interfaces as well as organizational units that are involved. In addition, critical performance indicators are identified. The strategic decision process may also be subject to redesign in order to implement faster decision processes and improve the support for strategic decisions.

All models created in this stage are communicated between the various stakeholders.

Tools Supporting Strategic Enterprise Management

Business Management Tools

Business management tools consisting of models embodying cause effect variables along with goals and limits, reports and dissemination methods support by creating meaningful and consistent corporate models. The models are the starting point for ongoing discussion, analysis, simulation, and optimization. In many cases, the tools support the publication of the models.

Portal Solutions

The best corporate strategy is worthless if no one knows about it and if the enterprise is not aligned with the strategy. Corporate portals can support you in publishing strategies and in delivering user-specific content. These portals also act as a single access point to all relevant corporate information, which helps to reduce the strategic decision life cycle.

Analytical Tools

Ideally, every strategic decision is based on up-to-date corporate information. Business Intelligence solutions can offer a highly valuable advantage to corporate management during the process of strategy (re)definition.

Collaboration Services

Especially in larger corporations, strategic decisions are based on complex and labor-intensive decision processes. Collaboration services can help to provide the common ground for these processes.

SEM enables companies to execute strategies quickly and successfully and to manage business performance throughout the entire organization. It supports integrated strategic planning, performance monitoring, business consolidation, and effective stakeholder communication, thereby enabling value-based management.

The listed business goals and objectives can be achieved through the implementation of these collaboration processes:

- Improve customer service.
- Offer 24×7 customer self-service.
- Personalize customer interaction.
- Raise competitive barriers to entry.
- Improve product/service quality.

- Improve forecast accuracy.
- Increase revenue.
- Extend market share.
- Develop new markets.
- Improve the sales lead generation and process.
- Reduce time to market and volume.
- Provide efficient campaign planning and management.
- Gain market share.
- Lower working capital requirements.
- Improve capacity utilization.
- Reduce operating costs.

Figure 2.2 is an architectural presentation of an SEM.

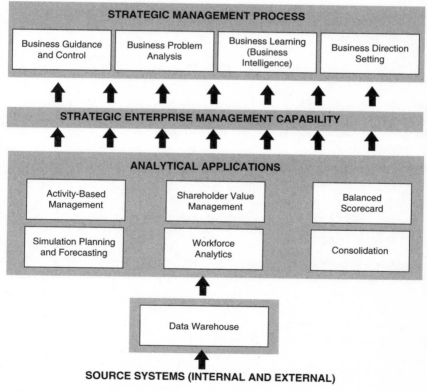

FIGURE 2.2 Architecture of an SEM

Essential Support from SEM Application Modules

Stakeholder Relationship Management

Stakeholder relationship management communicates strategies and investor information to major stakeholders and collects information and feedback via the Internet.

Strategy Management

Strategy management communicates strategies and objectives throughout the entire organization, using the Balanced Scorecard. It also supports value-based management, management by objective (MBO), and strategic initiatives.

Performance Measurement

Performance measurement monitors the performance of strategic key success factors and integrates external and internal benchmarks into the Balanced Scorecard and the Management Cockpit.

Strategic Planning and Simulation

Strategic planning and simulation supports strategic and business performance management through scenario planning, dynamic simulation, and integration of strategic and operational planning.[1]

Business Consolidation

Business consolidation consolidates actual and plan data supporting all aspects of legal and management consolidation.

Enterprise Management

Enterprise management integrates business processes and provides predefined, closed-loop business scenarios and predefined metrics to measure the effectiveness of business operations and enable immediate corrective action. Analytical applications (analytics) are built on consistent data stored in the data warehouse and are based on a variety of business areas. Business analytics are discussed in the next sections.

These business goals and objectives can be achieved through the implementation of these processes:

- Improve customer service.
- Offer better service levels.

- Improve product/service quality.
- Improved quality and accuracy.
- Increase revenue.
- Maximize profitability by customer.
- Enable cross-sell/up-sell capability.
- Improve customer retention and loyalty.
- Improve sales lead generation and process.
- Gain market share.
- Provide efficient campaign planning and management.
- Reduce time to market and volume.
- Lower working capital requirements.
- Improve cash management, minimize borrowing.
- Increase visibility to vendor/supplier inventory.
- Reduce inventory carrying costs.
- Improve capacity utilization.
- Reduce material and component obsolescence.
- Lower work-in-process inventory.
- Lead to fewer returns, more efficient process.
- Lead to lower-cost procured goods and services.
- Manage fixed assets.
- Optimize capital equipment and asset utilization.
- Reduce operating costs.

Business Analytics

Customer Relationship Analytics

Customer relationship analytics measures and optimizes customer relationships and include applications such as profitability analysis, market exploration, and customer-retention analysis. Customer relationship analytics allows you to analyze customer requirements systematically, enabling you to increase customer loyalty or acquire new customers by applying the results of your analysis and executing them in your customer management system.

E-Analytics

E-analytics analyzes the online customer experience, allowing companies to maximize their return on Web site investments, build one-to-one relationships with customers over the Internet, and improve competitiveness in the e-business and e-market world.

Supply Chain Analytics

Supply chain analytics measures and optimizes the value chain by supporting collaborative planning and forecasting, procurement analytics, and production efficiency analytics.

Financial Analytics

Financial analytics allows for business planning and forecasting, activity-based cost and profitability management, and working capital as well as investment management.

Human Resource Analytics

Human resource analytics analyzes and evaluates an organization's workforce by supporting workforce planning and forecasting, benchmarking and reporting, and by aligning the personal scorecard to MBO goals.

Product Life Cycle Analytics

Product life cycle analytics measures and optimizes the life cycle of a product by supporting product portfolio management and various aspects of life cycle cost management.

Business Intelligence and Decision Support

Business intelligence integrates all your corporate information so you can turn information into insight, insight into action, and action into improved business operations.

Flexible Reporting

Flexible reporting provides reporting and analysis scenarios and enables users to evaluate information across company boundaries. It consists of decision support tools, such as query, reporting, and multidimensional analysis for collaborative decision making, including data exploration and data visualization tools.

Information Dissemination and Sharing

Information dissemination and sharing enable users to organize and share information according to their specific role and information needs within the enterprise portal. It combines structured and unstructured information, internal enterprise information with external data, and allows executives, knowledge workers, and business partners to use the Internet, intranet, or mobile devices to browse the enterprise's data warehouse and business intelligence.

Performance Monitoring

Performance monitoring provides a complete view of all corporate business operations and information needed to make profitable decisions, set strategy, and measure the results of business tactics.

Planning and Simulation[1]

Planning and simulation link strategy with goals and simulate the impact of changes.

Ad Hoc Analysis

Ad hoc analysis allows users with specific information needs to create ad hoc queries, analyze data via a standard Web browser, and adjust strategy to meet changing markets and make immediate decisions.

Collaborative Decision Support

Collaborative decision support allows decision makers to collaborate, add comments to reports and key figures, and automate approval processes so that they can participate in decision making within the wider context of the enterprise.

Data Collection and Integration

Companies need to collect, organize, and analyze data quickly and efficiently to meet changing market needs. Data collection and integration enable the integration of data from multiple sources used to support the decision-making process based on a unified data model.

Content Management and Collaboration

Content management and collaboration help companies identify, manage, and share information.

Key Performance Indicators

Detailed key performance indicators (KPIs) given in Chapters 3 and 4 form the universe of KPIs applicable for SEM. The subset of these KPIs should be chosen based on the wishes and direction of management with respect to what they want to monitor and what they want to modulate for the desired result.

Case Example

Some time ago, in my work as a chief information officer, I oversaw the implementation of a full suite of enterprise software. Once the implementation was finished, I went to the executive team and requested a role related directly to the product and management of business processes. I was assigned an interesting task. It was not what I had requested, but it evolved precisely into product definition and product management, based on modeling and simulation. Before describing this role and how it evolved, a little bit of information about the company and product is useful.

This semiconductor company manufactured electronic packages, which are used as chip carriers. Its customers were the likes of Intel and Motorola.

My boss told me to study the requirements of the end users—in other words, the requirements of our customers' customers (e.g., Intel's customers, such as Dell or HP). In that context, the requirements were driven not only by Dell or HP but by those of their end users. Our company would have to furnish the packages to meet these new requirements in the future.

Based on a review of some published literature, I could determine impending requirements that we would have to be responsive to. However, the translation from one stage to the next was very much a guessing game, and this did not satisfy me. So I began toying with the idea of building a model that could predict the impact of end user requirements on the product characteristics of packages that we would have to manufacture. After I completed, tested, and verified the predictability and accuracy of this model, I was asked to include the impact of design features on manufacturing cost. With this model we could simulate the effect of design assumptions on product characteristics and product cost. Ultimately this cost performance study could be used with various input (customer requirements) scenarios to start new product initiatives or stop some that were already underway.

I call this model SLAM, for System Level Architectural Model. It includes detailed items such as concept, scope, concept chaining, physical model, model architecture, simplifying assumptions, model statistics, salient features, range of usage, and implementation. SLAM was developed as a software tool. It is comprised of 76 highly complex mathematical equations derived from the fields of device physics, material science, very large scale integration technology (VLSI), and design sciences. It has 76 independent variables (design rules, design requirements) and 76 dependent variables (product characteristics) in the performance domain alone. It can be categorized in the general domains of computer-aided design, computer-aided engineering, concurrent engineering design for manufacturing, predictive engineering, or computer aided product engineering (CAPE). This tool is a system-level, early-stage architectural design aid. Its area of application lies in electronic systems. It can be applied in the design of chips, their packages, printed circuit boards, and entire systems such as personal computers, work stations (WSs), servers, and all the way up to the supercomputers.

SLAM was used to develop a new paradigm of cost performance studies, described in Figure 2A.

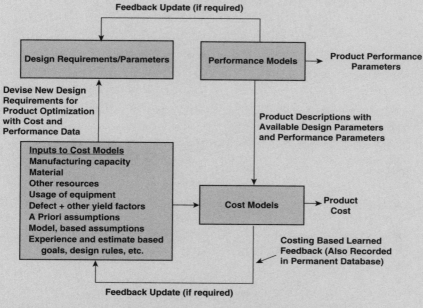

FIGURE 2A Virtual Reality, Model, and Assumption-Based Simulations

(Continued)

(Continued)

In Figure 2A, the needs (input requirements) are fed to the performance models (SLAM). These models use design rules (input requirements) and produce performance parameters (output variables). Performance parameters are then input to the cost models along with the manufacturing rules and the like, and cost is in turn computed. The result is cost and performance information available simultaneously for a set of design rules (input requirements). Cost or performance can be optimized iteratively, in a closed-loop feedback manner. The interesting thing is that this can happen long before detailed design of the product or even the physical manufacturing process to produce electronic packages has been accomplished. It is done at an early architectural stage and with few details on hand. This model was used extensively[2] in the management of the business with high predictability and accuracy, as testing by outside agencies confirmed. Specifically, this tool set has been used in these areas:

- Printed circuit board manufacturing
- Product line management
- Electronic forecasting
- Business plan and marketing management
- Business development
- New materials invention
- Research and development strategy formulation

In each of these cases, there was a need to know certain facts without the detailed knowledge. These details usually come from having done a detailed design of the product, material, process or the technology, depending on the case in hand. The needed predesign stage knowledge—both design rules (input variables) and product characteristics (output variables)—to iterate successfully included:

- Product footprint
- Number of planes
- Delay
- Wirability
- Power
- Trade-off of cost with performance parameters
- Cost/performance comparison of competing technologies

This effort was well received. It seemed to fulfill a long-felt need of various personnel who needed to know cost performance of new products, processes, technologies, and materials. People need this kind of information at very early stages in the life of new products. If they have it, fact-based decision making can take place, saving time, money, and costly mistakes. Working on SLAM was very fulfilling to me personally. The encouraging results reconfirmed my belief that model-based industrial virtual realities can be created successfully and be commercially useful.

Bibliography

Fahey, Liam. *Competitors*. New York: John Wiley & Sons, 1993.

Bansal, Sam. "Cost Estimation of Electronic Systems-Technical Cost Modeling," Paper presented at Pemas 94 conference, Penang, Malaysia, May 1994.

Bansal, Sam. "Practical Applications of Models and Their Benefits, Evolution of a New Paradigm," *Journal of International Federation of Automatic Controls* (October 1994).

Bansal, Sam. *Simulation in the Life Cycle of Manufacturing Systems*. Paris, France: Inria, 1995.

Bansal, Sam. "Trends and Methodologies in Business Consulting—KPI-based Performance Improvement," Paper presented at the International Federation of Automatic Controls, Barcelona, Spain, July 2002.

Strategic Enterprise Management—Unlocking the Potential of ERP. CSC India, May 2006.

CHAPTER 3

Supply Chain Management

Introduction

Advanced planning and scheduling (APS) is a new technology, a revolutionary breakthrough, and the greatest innovation since the assembly line. It aims to do optimized planning and scheduling of all the manufacturing resources and personnel, keeping in view the constraints (i.e., man, machine, material, and time). It may surprise you to learn that companies have benefited from APS techniques for over 30 years. APS is a collection of well-established solution methods made more accessible and effective by incremental improvements in a wide range of technologies. Thus, an experience base exists that companies trying to implement APS can draw on. In the 1990s, the APS market boomed and products proliferated. Consumer packaged goods companies like Procter & Gamble, Colgate, and Gillette started to use more APS at that time. Although there were some early adopters in this market segment, this industry as a whole was slower in using APS techniques. This is true of the paper industry as well, despite its sophisticated approaches for trimming paper and leftover materials.

A number of companies that had been able to implement relatively simple tools for manufacturing scheduling discovered they needed a more sophisticated approach to the number of SKU (stock keeping unit) and location combinations in their distribution networks and for their forecasting capabilities. The simple tools used to generate revenue forecasts choked on the number of SKU and location combinations needed to provide the level of detail required for operational decisions.

The early 1990s also saw the introduction of new programming languages, such as embedded SQL capabilities, which allowed APS tools to interact more dynamically with relational databases. The availability of increased amounts of computer horsepower at decreasing costs led to new solution methods and expanded the size and complexity of the problems being addressed. Genetic algorithms became available that enabled multiple solutions to be finalized at once, combining the best features of

existing solutions to create new ones. People started using simulated annealing, which lets a solution get worse in the hope that this will create
pathways to even better solutions. Production tools with millions of decisions variables were developed (although if you create an application of
this size, you probably are making your life more difficult than it has to be).

The 1990s also saw a proliferation of APS vendors across a wide range
of industries. I2 and Fastman (Premier's previous name) made inroads with
electronic assembly, metals, and discrete manufacturing. I2's most dramatic
impact on the APS space was the introduction of brand-oriented marketing
and sales strategies to what had previously been a technology-driven niche
market, and soon the company was in a race with Manugistics for revenue growth. The reaction of the marketplace to I2, Manugistics, and others
caught the attention of the large consulting firms. They started allocating resources to products based on market success and client preferences, kicking
off a slew of relationships.

APS has presented two major challenges to the larger consulting firms:
the need for application and domain expertise. APS requires depth of
application expertise. The personnel development policies at many of these
firms were traditionally focused on producing information technology gen-
eralists who could manage and bring in major engagements. Annual staff
turnover of 25% or more also hindered development of technical depth.
In addition, rigid application of standard project methodologies can be a
very ineffective way to implement APS. Domain expertise still is needed to
determine how to use the project methodology effectively. The mid-1990s
also saw vendors move user interfaces to a Microsoft Windows environment
via client-server architecture or move entire applications to a Windows NT
environment. In addition to providing more intuitive user interfaces and reporting capabilities, this moved APS applications into an environment where
low-cost computer horsepower was increasing at an amazing rate. At this
time, semiconductor companies also began to use APS. These companies
are extremely aggressive in changing production technology and have products with extremely short life cycles. Changing production technologies and
short product life raise challenges to provide the knowledge base required
for APS applications, particularly at the scheduling level. Initial use of APS
techniques paralleled that in the process industry, as such companies as
Harris Semiconductor, IBM, Intel, and Texas Instruments started by developing internal solutions, with mixed results. APS also captured the attention
of the enterprise resource planning (ERP) vendors. Among the majors, first
came Peoplesoft, then SAP, soon to be followed by Oracle and others.

SCM Domain

The supply chain management technology of many vendors has become
a comprehensive tool set that provides solution not only for supply chain

planning but also for supply chain execution, coordination, and collaboration. This chapter is based on my own practice at SAP, papers I published during my tenure on the subject and SAP Solution Maps. Hence there are heavy references of SAP APO & SAP SCM functionality. All products are SAP's and where applicable the trademarks of SAP are owned by them all over the world. Figure 3.1 shows the support provided by each of these technologies.

Figure 3.2 depicts how this functionality is placed in a full-service systems landscape.

These acronyms are used in Figure 3.2:

APO: Advanced Planner and Optimizer
ERP: Enterprise resource planning
MES: Manufacturing Execution System

Figure 3.3 shows all the support available from the Advanced Planner and Optimizer (APO) technology.

Limited details of Supply Chain Execution, Supply Chain Coordination, and Supply Chain Collaboration will be provided in this chapter. However, Figure 3.3 presents the pertinent details of advanced planning, scheduling, and optimization, forming the basis of the simulation technology as applied to this domain.

Supply Chain Planning	Supply Chain Design	Demand Planning	Supply Planning	Distribution Planning	Production Planning	Transportation Planning

Supply Chain Execution	Materials Management	Manufacturing	Order Promising and Delivery	Warehouse Management	Transportation Execution	Foreign Trade/Legal Services

Supply Chain Coordination	Supply Chain Event Management	Supply Chain Performance Management	Fulfillment Coordination

Supply Chain Collaboration	Supply Chain Portal	Collaboration Processes	Supply Chain Integration

FIGURE 3.1 Supply Chain Management Architecture

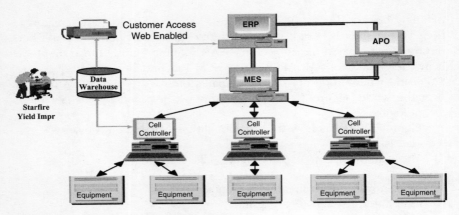

FIGURE 3.2 Systems Landscape Architecture

Advanced Planner and Optimizer

The APO technology, most of whose functionality is given in Figure 3.3, is architecturally given in Figure 3.4.

These acronyms are used in Figures 3.3 and 3.4:

BW: Business warehouse
OLTP: Online transaction processing
R/3™: SAP's enterprise resource planning (ERP)
SC: supply chain

The supply chain planning layer of Figure 3.4 is shown by the top right-hand block of Figure 3.3. However, APO's Solvers (algorithms) contain

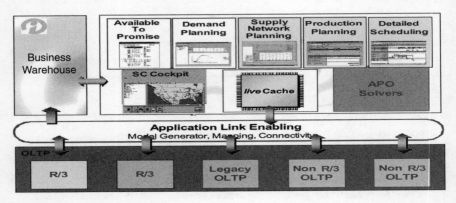

FIGURE 3.3 APO Functionality
Source: © Copyright (2009). SAP AG. All rights reserved.

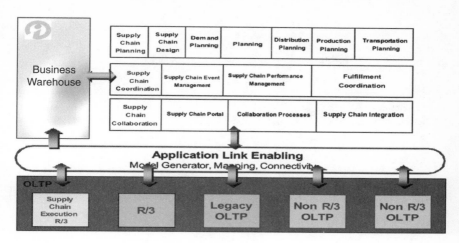

FIGURE 3.4 SCM and APO Architecture

Source: © Copyright (2009). SAP AG. All rights reserved.

the optimization models whereas live Cache contains the data sets for the Solvers to work on. The live Cache communicates with BW as well as other OLTP systems to get up-to-date data to operate on. The BW provides the data sets for results and reports. More on these aspects is given in the section entitled Solvers, Algorithms, and Simulation.

Figures 3.4 and 3.5 show the relationship of all the SCM modules. In Figure 3.4, the detailed top right-hand side of the block of Figure 3.3 is replaced by three blocks of SCM modules, called Supply Chain Planning, Supply Chain Coordination, and Supply Chain Collaboration. These are more advanced functionalities. Notice that the Supply Chain Execution block is given in the bottom left-hand side in Figure 3.4. This block replaces one of the R/3s that previously had a copy of ERP, illustrating the fact that this functionality is of a legacy nature.

Figure 3.6 presents the process flow for the full SCM functionality.

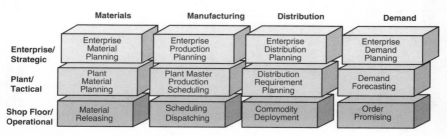

FIGURE 3.5 Basics of SCM Functionality

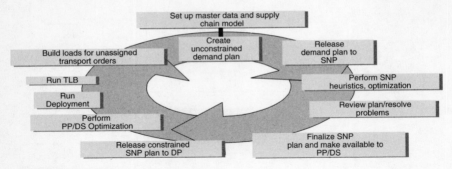

FIGURE 3.6 Workflow in SCM

Source: © Copyright (2009). SAP AG. All rights reserved.

These acronyms are used in Figure 3.6:

DP: Demand planning
PP/DS: Production planning and detailed scheduling
SNP: Supply network planning
TLB: Transport load builder

In the field of SCM, the battle cry is for "adaptive and collaborative supply chain management." Figure 3.7 illustrates a natural gap between the plans and actual situations as they exist at every step of the process. This gap is what needs to be controlled and driven to zero.

Solvers, Algorithms, and Simulation

Figure 3.3 shows APO functionality. It is supported heavily by Solvers, which are shown in Figure 3.8. Solvers are advanced algorithms based on optimization models that are built mostly with deterministic simulations.

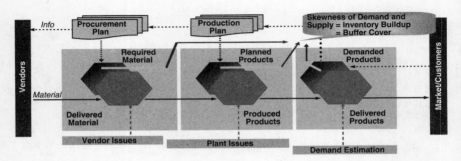

FIGURE 3.7 Supply Chain Paradox

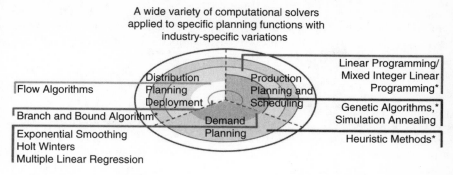

FIGURE 3.8 Solvers and Algorithms

Source: © Copyright (2009). SAP AG. All rights reserved.

The entire suite of Supply Chain Planning modules provides support for deterministic simulation technology in optimization, scheduling forecasting, and scenario analysis. Transactional simulations are done for scenario analyses. Figure 3.8 presents various algorithms that have gone to support the Solvers. Discrete event-based simulation is not used explicitly in APO, but the concepts are applied in deterministic framework for development of schedules in some of the algorithms. Perhaps that is why APO delivers more deterministic results. It is worth mentioning that:

- Distribution planning is based on flow algorithms.
- Deployment functionality is based on branch and bound algorithms.
- Demand planning sub-modules use exponential smoothing, heuristics, Holt winters and multiple regression analysis methodologies.
- Production planning modules use linear programming and mixed integer linear programming.
- Detailed scheduling modules are based on genetic algorithm and simulated annealing-based optimization technology.

So many Solvers are used because no one algorithm performs equally well for all classes of problems. Thus, the use of simulated annealing, which provides a better quality of solution, is computer memory intensive. To solve this problem, genetic algorithms are used.

Supply Chain Management Detailed

Supply Chain Planning

Supply chain planning technology is based on Solvers, algorithms, and simulation. However, it must be mentioned up front that the optimization models used here focus primarily on deterministic simulation themes. Scenario planning and scenario analyses are used extensively, and all the tools and facilities are available if discrete event simulation modeling needs to be done at some point in the project life cycle.

Supply Chain Design

SUPPLY CHAIN COCKPIT   Supply Chain Cockpit (SCC), an SAP Advanced Planning and Optimization application, consists of a highly intuitive, graphical interface that acts as the top enterprise planning layer covering all planning areas, such as manufacturing, demand, distribution, and transportation. All employees in the Plan→, Source→, Make→, Deliver cycle of supply chain management can use it to their advantage. As the gateway to APO, the SCC makes dealing with a vast supply chain easier and more manageable. SCC allows you to:

- Create individual work areas so several planners can work simultaneously on different parts of a supply chain.
- View the supply chain from all angles, down to the smallest detail, to minimize the complexity of the relationships among supply chain components.
- Retrieve information from the APO system through queries.
- Measure supply chain performance with key performance indicators that are stored in the Business Information Warehouse.
- Respond immediately and accurately to new developments by tracking alert situations.
- Retain flexibility in your decision-making process.
- Provide access to a rich collection of data for doing discrete event simulation.

The SCC can be configured to suit conditions within a wide variety of industries and business situations

STRATEGIC PLANNING   Strategic planning is the key element in a company's long-term success, and it has a critical impact on its future. Fast-changing market demands and short product life cycles force enterprises to continuously evaluate and optimize their supply chains. Companies have to use marketing and financial plans as a basis for deciding on the sourcing, production, and distribution of products to meet customer requirements at competitive costs. As strategic decisions are linked to costs, it is difficult to change them at short notice. It is, therefore, vital that companies make their long-term decisions carefully, achieving a cost-effective and profitable solution to guarantee the company's effectiveness.

These features support strategic planning problems:

- **Network definition.** Networks used in Demand Planning, as well as in Supply Network Planning, reflect a company's supply chain. A network can be used for feeding into simulation models. Planning can be executed based on this network. Every part of the supply chain (such as locations, transportation lanes, resources, products, and production process models) can be modeled using the Supply Chain Engineer, which allows you to place locations on a map and link them with the corresponding transportation lanes. The direction of the lanes determines the product flow. Using the Supply Chain Engineer, you can drill down to all elements belonging to the supply network. Further, you can request information about single or combined elements in the network. For example, you can see which products belong to a particular location. Products can also be added to this location or to modify the location's master data.
- **Alerts.** The Alert Monitor is a stand-alone component of APO that enables a unified approach to monitor planning situations. It notifies you of any critical situation occurring in one of the APO applications, such as Demand Planning and Supply Planning, Production Planning, and Detailed Scheduling, or Transportation Planning and Vehicle Scheduling. Alerts are displayed in various ways, either directly in the Supply Chain Cockpit, in the cockpits control panel, in the application, or through e-mail. Using a series of event triggers and alarm conditions, the Alert Monitor can automatically identify problems in the supply chain. It can also monitor material, capacity, transportation, and storage constraints. In addition, it can handle metrics such as delivery performance, cost flow, and throughput. It reports exceptions, including orders that exceed forecasts or orders that fall short of forecast, and therefore may lead to excess inventory if production is not adjusted accordingly. Based on this monitoring process, you can readjust plans whenever needed.

Demand Planning

STATISTICAL FORECASTING   Statistical or univariate forecasting predicts future demand based on historical data. As opposed to causal forecasting, in statistical forecasting other factors are not taken into account. Univariate forecasting provides methods that recognize the time series patterns that follow as a basis for the forecast. Constant demand varies very little from a

stable mean value. Trend demand falls or rises constantly over a long period
of time with only occasional deviations. Seasonal demand has periodically
recurring peaks that differ significantly from a stable mean value. Seasonal
trends have periodically recurring peaks and troughs, but with a continual
increase or decrease in the mean value. Intermittent demand is sporadic. If
there is no change from previous years, no forecast is carried out; instead,
the system copies the actual data from the previous year.

CAUSAL FORECASTING   Multiple linear regression (MLR) enables you to include causal variables (e.g., climatic conditions, price, advertising) in the
forecasting process. MLR investigates the historical influence of these variables on demand to produce a forecast. Simulation scenarios can be set up
for causal variables to show possible developments, taking possible risks
and opportunities into account.

COMPOSITE FORECASTING   This function combines forecasts from different
individual forecasts (statistical or causal forecasts) for a particular brand,
product family, or product. Each individual forecast is based on the same
historical data but uses a different technique. The underlying objective is
to take advantage of the strengths of each method to create a single one-
number forecast. You can average the forecasts, giving each one equal
weight, weigh each one differently, or vary the weightings of each forecast
over time.

   Business analysts can combine forecasts to develop the best forecast
possible. The composite forecasts of several methods have been proven
to outperform the individual forecasts of any of those methods used to
generate the composite.

PROMOTION PLANNING   In APO Demand Planning, you can plan promotions or other special events separately from the rest of the forecast.
Use promotion planning to record either one-time events, such as the
millennium, or repeated events, such as quarterly advertising campaigns.
Other examples of promotions are trade fairs, trade discounts, dealer al-
lowances, product displays, coupons, contests, freestanding inserts, as well
as non–sales-related events, such as competitors' activities, market intelligence, upward/downward economic trends, hurricanes, and tornados.

   The effect of a promotion is calculated using causal techniques to measure past promotional impact and is projected into designated periods in
the future. Manual adjustments to a promotion are made in future periods
for planning purposes to reflect new merchandising strategies.

LIFE CYCLE PLANNING   A product's life cycle consists of different phases:
launch, growth, maturity, and discontinuation. In this process, you model

the launch, growth, and discontinuation phases. You can define a phase-in profile or a phase-out profile for a product, or other characteristics. A similar function is "like" modeling, which allows you to use the historical data from one product to forecast the demand of another product.

COLLABORATIVE DEMAND PLANNING   Collaborative demand planning between manufacturers and their distributors allows both partners to streamline their work processes and ultimately benefit from a more accurate forecast, better market transparency, greater stability, reduced inventory, and better communication. Starting from one forecast, all the partners collaborate to produce a final forecast, which becomes the basis for all further planning in the partner companies.

The APO solution implements the Collaborative Planning Forecasting and Replenishment (CPFR) process, which is a cross-company and cross-industry scenario developed by the Voluntary Interindustry Commerce Standards (VICS) association.

CHARACTERISTIC-BASED FORECASTING   In SAP APO Demand Planning, you can create a forecast based on the characteristics of configurable end products; for example, the forecast can be based on the characteristics: color, engine, and air conditioning of the end product—a car. Moreover, you can forecast the demand for a combination of several characteristics, thus taking into account the mutual interdependency of the demand for these characteristics.

SAP's Characteristics-Based Forecasting allows you to forecast many different variants of the same product and react swiftly to changes in market demand. You can also place orders with your suppliers for assemblies and components in a timely fashion.

KIT PLANNING   Besides planning demand for a product, you can also forecast dependent demand at different planning levels by exploding bills of materials.

You can use this method for a kit that consists of several finished products (which can also be sold separately). Planning demand for the kit generates dependent demand, which you can combine with the independent demand for single products. Then you can use the overall demand by product for supply, production, and procurement planning.

Supply Planning

SUPPLY NETWORK PLANNING   SAP APO's Supply Network Planning integrates purchasing, manufacturing, distribution, and transportation, so you can simulate and implement comprehensive tactical planning and sourcing decisions on the basis of a single, global consistent model. Supply Network Planning uses advanced optimization techniques, based on constraints and penalties, to plan product flow along the supply chain. The results are optimal purchasing, production, and distribution decisions; reduced order fulfillment times and inventory levels; and improved customer service.

Starting from a demand plan, Supply Network Planning determines a permissible short- to medium-term plan for fulfilling the estimated sales volumes. This plan covers both the quantities that must be transported between two locations (e.g., distribution center to customer or production plant to distribution center), and the quantities to be produced and procured. When making a recommendation, Supply Network Planning compares all logistical activities to the available capacity.

The Deployment function determines how and when inventory should be deployed to distribution centers, customers, and vendor-managed inventory accounts. It produces optimized distribution plans based on constraints (such as transportation capacities) and business rules (such as minimum cost approach, or replenishment strategies).

The Transport Load Builder (TLB) function maximizes transport capacities by optimizing load building. In addition, the seamless integration with APO Demand Planning supports an efficient SOP process.

In Supply Network Planning, you are provided with standard planning books (and views) for each of the various types of planning available (i.e., interactive SNP, Sales and Operations Planning, Distribution Resource Planning, Transport Load Builder, Vendor Managed Inventory, and Scheduling Agreement Processing). You can, however, create your own planning books, using standard ones as templates.

SAFETY STOCK PLANNING Safety stock is the quantity of additional stock procured and/or held to satisfy unexpectedly high demand. Safety Stock Planning within Supply Network Planning allows you to meet a service level while creating a minimum amount of safety stock throughout your entire supply chain for all intermediate and finished products at their respective locations.

HEURISTIC The heuristic (experience-based learned rules) is a part of a repair-based planning process consisting of the heuristic, capacity leveling, and deployment. The heuristic process considers each planning location sequentially and determines sourcing requirements. It lumps all requirements for a given material in the location into one requirement for the period. The heuristic determines the valid sources and quantity based on predefined percentages for each source (quota arrangements) or procurement priorities for transportation lanes. Requirements are then passed through the supply chain to calculate a plan; however, this plan is not necessarily feasible. The planner must use capacity leveling to formulate a feasible plan. The next process flow is typical:

- Perform a heuristic run.
- Level capacity.
- Run deployment.
- Run TLB.

CAPACITY LEVELING The Supply Network Planning run produces a plan that meets all the demand requirements (e.g., sales orders and dependent demand); however, the resulting plan is not necessarily feasible. Capacity leveling, a function within Interactive Planning, enables you to smooth your production schedule, either manually or using a methods-based approach, based on how the available resource capacity in your supply chain is able to meet demand. With capacity leveling, you have the opportunity to build up inventory or increase capacity to ensure that you can meet demand without overstocking and to avoid periods of resource overload or underuse. You can easily analyze alternatives and replan, even reforecast, before putting the plan into production.

You can adjust the plan by modifying supply or consumption or by changing the production and transportation orders manually. You can modify supply by changing the resource master data. You also can modify consumption by leveling the capacity on the active resource or by using an alternate resource (shifting the order from one resource to another manually). In addition, you can manually edit production and transportation orders.

OPTIMIZATION The Supply Network Planner's (SNP) optimizer offers cost-based planning. This means that it searches through all feasible plans to try to find the most cost-effective one. *Total costs* refer to:

- Production, procurement, storage, and transportation costs
- Costs for increasing the production capacity, storage capacity, transportation capacity, and handling capacity
- Costs for falling below the safety stock level
- Costs for delayed delivery
- Stock out (or shortfall quantity) costs

In the optimizer view, a plan is feasible when it satisfies all the Supply Chain Model constraints that you activated in a special profile called SNP Optimizer Profile. The feasibility of a solution can involve due date constraint violations or safety stock constraint violations. Due dates and safety stocks are soft constraints; in other words, they are constraints to which you assign violation costs. The optimizer proposes a plan that will violate soft constraints only if, according to the costs specified in the system, it is the most cost-effective plan.

As part of optimization-based planning, the optimizer makes sourcing decisions. This means that costs are used as a basis to decide:

- Which products are to be produced, transported, procured, stored, and delivered (product mix) and their quantities
- Which resources and which production process models are to be used (technology mix)
- The dates on which products are to be produced, transported, procured, stored, and delivered
- The locations at which, or to which, products are to be produced, transported, procured, stored, and delivered
- Alternate resources
- Demand violation penalty costs
- Safety stock violation penalty costs
- Procurement costs
- Shelf life
- Cost multipliers
- Location-specific products

DEMAND AND SUPPLY MATCH   This function is based on Capable-to-Match, (CTM), engine which is described later in the chapter but is mentioned here for the sake of completeness.

Distribution Planning

DISTRIBUTION RESOURCE PLANNING   In Supply Network Planning, you are provided with standard planning books (and views) for each of the various types of planning available. The planning books are practically identical with interactive Supply Network Planning; however, here you can also view the distribution receipts and distribution issues. You can create your own planning books, using the standard planning books as templates.

DEPLOYMENT   After production is complete, deployment determines which demand can be fulfilled by the existing supply. If the produced quantities match actual quantities planned in SNP planning, the result of deployment is a confirmation of the supply network plan. If the available quantities are insufficient to fulfill the demand or exceed the demand, the system makes adjustments accordingly, depending on whether you are running the deployment heuristic or the deployment optimization. The deployment run generates deployment stock transfers. The Transport Load Builder then uses these stock transfers to generate transportation plans and build transport loads.

TRANSPORT LOAD BUILDER   The primary purpose of the Transport Load Builder is to use the results of the deployment run (deployment stock transfers) to create multiproduct TLB shipments while ensuring that:

- Means of transport are filled to maximum capacity
- Means of transport are not filled to below minimum capacity

Minimum and maximum values for capacity (cubic volume and weight) and pallets to build a load are defined in a profile called TLB Profile. The system generates as many valid TLB shipments as possible (with regard to the minimum and maximum values). The TLB also checks whether the manually altered TLB shipments respect the minimum and maximum values; if not, it generates alerts.

The TLB combines deployment stock transfers to form feasible transport units. If the deployment stock transfer is for a Vendor Managed Inventory (VMI) customer, the results are processed as sales orders in the transactional system. If not, it processes the results as a company-internal TLB shipment. Additional conditions for VMI customers can be specified.

There is no tracking of resource usage and no consideration of product-specific constraints (e.g., flavor migration) or special transport requirements (e.g., package orientation or refrigeration).

REPLENISHMENT   There are several possible scenarios for replenishment. One of them is VMI. In general, the scenarios differ by industry. Basic components of a replenishment process are deployment and the TLB.

VENDOR MANAGED INVENTORY   Because it is necessary to combine forecasts from sales, or customers or partners with historical information in order to develop inventory targets, VMI is well suited to a collaborative scenario. The classic VMI process, in which vendors plan replenishments for their customers, can be extended to a collaborative replenishment process with more scope for interaction.

COLLABORATIVE SUPPLY AND DISTRIBUTION PLANNING   The starting point of collaborative Supply and Distribution Planning is Safety Stock Planning. It combines the pure demands with the company's strategy to guarantee customer satisfaction. Supply Planning tries to satisfy the demand in an optimal way, spreads production to the resources, explodes the bill of materials, and organizes the procurement of semi-finished goods or raw materials. Distribution Planning considers the available products and satisfies the real demands due to flexible rules. It includes an optimal loading of the transport vehicles.

PRODUCTION PLANNING   Production Planning enables the planner to create feasible production plans across the different production locations (also with subcontractors) to fulfill the customer demand on time and to the standard expected by the customer. For the long- and medium-term time horizon, rough-cut planning is based on time buckets and determines resource requirements (machines, humans, production resource tools) and materials. Solvers, real-time data, and high supply chain visibility (key performance indicators, alerts) support the planner's decision-making process.

DETAILED SCHEDULING   Detailed Scheduling delivers optimized order sequences that can be released for production. Solvers simultaneously take into account constraints and costs to schedule the optimized order sequence. Dynamic alerts and order-pegging structures improve visibility. Due to the seamless integration with the execution and inventory management system, material shortages or critical resource situations can be seen immediately, and the schedules can be manually or automatically adjusted.

Detailed Scheduling fulfills requirements from the process and discrete industries that are takt-based[1] and job scheduling for configurable and non-configurable products in a make-to-stock (MTS) and/or make-to-order (MTO) environment; block planning, campaign planning and push production for process industries

The APO Optimization Extension Workbench (APX) provides a new means of making optimization strategies more flexible. Transactional simulation capability is provided for scenario analysis, and if certain cases are found to be acceptable, they are made executable. The primary purpose of the workbench is to extend the standard planning tools in APO to include user-specific optimization components. These individual optimizers are launched directly from APO. Together with the standard optimizers and heuristics, they form one planning system. This system provides the right degree of flexibility to be adapted to the precise needs of the user.

In addition to the functional integration of the external optimizer in the standard APO component environment, the optimizer is to be incorporated closely so that it can freely use the APO data stock (from the live Cache and the database server). The optimization results can then be returned to the APO data set.

CAPABLE TO MATCH   Capable-to-Match (CTM) Planning uses constraint-based heuristics to conduct multisite checks of production capacities and transportation capabilities based on predefined supply categories and demand priorities. The aim of the CTM Planning run is to propose a feasible solution for fulfilling demands. The CTM Planning run is powered by the CTM engine, which matches the prioritized demands to the available supplies in two stages. First, it builds the CTM application model based on the master data that you have entered. Then it matches supply to demand on a first-come, first-served basis, taking production capacities and transportation capabilities into account.

MATERIALS REQUIREMENTS PLANNING   Materials Requirements Planning (MRP) is part of the production planning process and generates replenishment schedules for all manufactured components, intermediates, purchased parts, and raw materials. MRP sets due dates for production orders and purchase requisitions through lead-time scheduling, depending on buffers, operation times, lot-sizing rules, and so on. The planning run is supported by optimization tools when resource situations can be taken into account simultaneously.

Transportation Planning

COLLABORATIVE SHIPMENT FORECASTING   Based on Internet-enabled planning books, you can exchange and adjust forecast information between your customers (which will be based on product forecast) and your carriers (who will give you data about the expected number of resources or vehicles they will provide in a specified time frame). This function is supported in APO Demand Planning.

LOAD CONSOLIDATION   SCM provides different possibilities to consolidate deliveries and orders to shipments. It is possible to combine orders based on rules and strategies, based on APO optimization logic. You also can do this interactively and manually in R/3 as well as in APO, and through collaboration over the Internet. If you decide to rely on your carrier's abilities to consolidate orders to shipments, you can give the carrier access to deliveries over the Internet, where it can consolidate shipments. During load consolidation, SCM considers multidimensional capacity constraints of the resources. This function is provided by APO.

MODE AND ROUTE OPTIMIZATION   Mode and route optimization is at the heart of Transportation Planning. The goal is to create the lowest cost transportation plan while guaranteeing customer service. The system assigns inbound and outbound orders to modes (truck, ship) and creates the needed shipments. The optimization algorithm used to do these assignments is controlled by cost profiles, delivery dates, and constraints of the ship-to and ship-from sites.

CARRIER SELECTION   After you have created optimized routes (shipments), you must assign carriers to these routes. You can do this manually in the execution system (R/3) or in APO. APO offers four options to do so:

1. **Priority.** Certain carriers have different priorities on certain lanes.
2. **Freight cost.** The least-cost carrier for this shipment will be selected.
3. **Business share.** APO assigns shipments in order to ensure that specified carriers receive a defined volume of business.
4. **Freight exchange.** The shipment data are communicated to a freight exchange that ensures the assignment.

COLLABORATIVE SHIPMENT TENDERING   The assignment of a carrier to a shipment needs to be confirmed by the carrier (tendering). Tendering can be done via Internet dialog or communication via Electronic Data Interchange (EDI) or Extensible Markup Language (XML) files. The carrier can accept the tender, reject it, or accept the tender with modifications. Tendering can be done in R/3 or APO.

Supply Chain Execution

Materials Management

INVENTORY MANAGEMENT   The Inventory Management program manages the stocks of a company in quantities and values. It is integrated with supply chain accounting and is responsible for goods receipts, goods issues, and managing different stock categories (available, blocked stock, in quality assurance, etc.) and special stocks (including consignment stock, project stock, etc.). Inventory Management enables a summarized visibility of stocks in the supply chain.

STOCK MANAGEMENT FOR NETWORKS   Stock Management for Networks is a high-performance engine for the management of stock quantities within logistics processes. For this purpose, it needs to keep near–real-time information: which quantities of a physical inventory are stored, on which handling unit, at which location. It is able to support inventory management functions along the entire supply chain. The management of stock quantities consists of:

- Keeping the stock quantities
- Recording the stock quantity changes resulting from goods movements
- Answering queries about stock quantities and stock movements

BID MANAGEMENT You can start bidding processes periodically. Alternatively, you can trigger them directly from a demand that is not yet assigned to a vendor or that cannot be fulfilled by the assigned vendor. The demands can be requests for quotations, auctions or reverse auctions. Reporting functions are available for the results of the bidding process.

REQUISITION AND PURCHASE ORDER MANAGEMENT Requisition and Purchase Order Management consists of dedicated processes for the purchasing of direct materials, indirect materials, and services (e.g., subcontracting for components, Internet-based employee-centered approach for maintenance repair and overhauls [MROs]). These processes include functions for informing the purchasing department of required materials and services with or without material master, releasing requisitions, assigning the source of supply to requisition, converting the requisitions to purchase orders, and to controlling the follow-on activities. Functions for transportation management and foreign trade are available for the inbound side as well as for the outbound side; and they provide reporting functions for purchasing.

GOODS RECEIPT Goods Receipt is a follow-on activity to purchase order, the basis for updates of the Accounting and Control modules and the basis for Inventory Management. It can trigger warehouse management and quality management processes.

CONTRACT MANAGEMENT Contract Management includes functions important for the negotiation phase, administration, and monitoring of contracts and scheduling agreements. It links to source determination.

CATALOG MANAGEMENT This e-commerce component enables procurement, using vendor catalogs, by generating an enterprise-specific search engine.

GOODS ISSUE The outbound delivery forms the basis of goods issue posting. The data required for goods issue posting are copied from the outbound delivery into the goods issue document, which cannot be changed manually. Any changes must be made in the outbound delivery itself. In this way, you can be sure that the goods issue document is an accurate reflection of the outbound delivery. When you post goods issue for an outbound delivery, these functions are carried out on the basis of the goods issue document:

- Warehouse stock of the material is reduced by the delivery quantity.
- Value changes are posted to the balance sheet account in inventory accounting.
- Requirements are reduced by the delivery quantity.
- The serial number status is updated.
- Goods issue posting is automatically recorded in the document flow.
- Stock determination is executed for the vendor's consignment stock.
- A work list for the proof of delivery is generated.

After the goods issue is posted for an outbound delivery, the scope for changing the delivery document becomes very limited. This prevents any discrepancies between the goods issue document and the outbound delivery.

DETERMINATION OF EXTERNAL DEMANDS External Demand is determined from the data describing a demand for a material that is procured externally. Some of these describing data are the quantity that is required, the release-to-supplier-date of the demand, the goods receipt date for the delivery, and the location where the material has to be shipped.

SOURCE DETERMINATION When a demand has been determined, it is necessary to assign a source of supply to it (e.g., an external supplier). The SAP system provides functions for automated assignment of a source to a demand (e.g., in the case that a single sourcing strategy is in place or quota arrangements between several suppliers are defined) as well as for the manual assignment.

CONFIRMATION In purchasing, a confirmation is information provided by a supplier to a customer with regard to ordered goods (e.g., the confirmed delivery date for a certain quantity of ordered materials). Possible types of confirmation include:

- Order acknowledgments
- Loading or transport confirmations
- Shipping notifications
- Inbound delivery

PURCHASING STATISTICS Purchasing statistics are different standard analyses and reports that monitor purchasing operations (e.g., how many goods for purchase orders for the last month have been received) and facilitate the detailed analysis of the purchasing activities and procurement processes taking place within your enterprise (e.g., ranking your suppliers with regard to purchasing values.

INVENTORY CONTROL   In order to control inventory, different standard analyses and reports display actual stock situation according to quantity-based as to value-based criteria. Other reports are available for monitoring characteristics on a periodic basis.

PHYSICAL INVENTORY MANAGEMENT   Physical Inventory Management manages physical inventory for your company's own stocks or for special stocks in your warehouse. SAP supports these physical inventory procedures:

- Periodic inventory
- Continuous inventory
- Cycle counting
- Inventory sampling

Physical inventories for legal reasons, for balance sheet purposes, or for internal controlling reasons are also supported.

DEAL CAPTURE MANAGEMENT   The Deal Capture Management allows you to handle all kinds of trading contracts within the trading companies. The key instrument is the Trading Contract, which consists of purchasing and sales information integrated in one document. The Trading Contract covers the common back-to-back business as well as one-sided deals. This enables the brokerage company to handle the complete transaction, including the payment of a brokerage commission.

Manufacturing

MAKE TO ORDER   The make-to-order process supports customer order–specific planning and production. The make-to-order process is industry dependent. The solution supports assembly processes for (non)configurable products in a repetitive manufacturing environment or the production of (non)configured products with production orders. For both processes, the visibility of the customer order is key. This visibility is achieved with dynamic alerts and order-pegging structures during planning and execution.

REPETITIVE MANUFACTURING   Repetitive manufacturing is a rate-based lean production control system. Based on production and assembly lines, the takt times are used for scheduling. Optimizers and heuristics are available for model-mix planning and line balancing. Continuous input and output is considered during scheduling. The production runs without any orders for run schedule quantities and production versions. Back flush of labor and material at reporting points supports the lean execution process.

FLOW MANUFACTURING   In a flow manufacturing environment, the customer demand from Customer Relationship Management (CRM) will be pulled through the production process. The key elements of the solution are line design and line balancing, demand management, line sequencing/model-mix planning, lean execution, back flush, and kanban management.

SHOP-FLOOR MANUFACTURING   In shop-floor manufacturing, production orders track and control the production. The real-time integration among CRM, production planning, and execution improves quality and speed of processes. The confirmation of labor and material issues takes place at operation level. Milestones, back flushing, and automatic goods receipts can reduce the number of business transactions. Multilevel production processes can be controlled. The seamless integration to quality management enables quality inspections during production. Other characteristics are control of rework, batch tracking, and serial number management.

LEAN MANUFACTURING   In a flow manufacturing environment, the customer demand from CRM will be pulled through the production process. The key elements of the solution are line design and line balancing, demand management, line sequencing/model-mix planning, lean execution, back flush, and kanban (visible record, signboard, etc.) management.

PROCESS MANUFACTURING   Process manufacturing supports the plant as a multiprocess facility. Resource and recipe management are the basis for planning and sequencing of batches or production lots. The Solver schedules the process order sequence to avoid such costs as cleanout or changeover. The Solvers utilize production campaigns, block planning, or detailed scheduling focusing on critical resources. Process orders are used for scheduling, execution, and costing. Process management coordinates the data exchange between the SAP execution and connected process control systems. These processes can be documented and evaluated. The seamless integration with the quality management ensures process control and stability.

Batch Management fulfills the requirements of the pharmaceutical and chemical industry for managing and tracking batches or production lots during the whole production process.

PRODUCTION PLANNING Production planning enables the planner to create feasible production plans across the different production locations (and with subcontractors) to fulfill customer demand in time and to the standard expected. For long- and medium-term time horizons, rough-cut planning is based on time buckets and determines requirements of resources (machines, humans, production resource tools) and materials. Solvers, real-time data, and high supply chain visibility (KPIs, alerts) support the planner's decision-making process.

DETAILED SCHEDULING Detailed scheduling delivers optimized order sequences that can be released for production. Solvers simultaneously take into account constraints and costs to schedule the optimized order sequence. Dynamic alerts and order-pegging structures improve visibility. Due to the seamless integration with the execution and inventory management system, material shortages or critical resource situations can be seen immediately, and schedules can be adjusted accordingly, manually or automatically.

Detailed scheduling fulfills requirements from the process and discrete industries (takt-based and job scheduling for configurable and non-configurable products in an MTS and/or MTO environment: block planning, campaign planning, and push production for process industries).

The SAP APO Optimization Extension Workbench (APX) provides a new means of making optimization strategies more flexible. The primary purpose of the workbench is to extend the standard planning tools in SAP APO to include user-specific optimization components. These individual optimizers are launched directly from SAP APO. Together with the standard optimizers and heuristics, they form one planning system. This system provides the right degree of flexibility to be adapted to the precise needs of the user.

In addition to the functional integration of the external optimizer in the standard SAP APO component environment, the optimizer is incorporated closely so that it can freely use the SAP APO data stock (from the live Cache and the database server). The optimization results can then be returned to the SAP APO data set.

BATCH MANAGEMENT In various industry sectors, particularly the process industry, you have to work with homogeneous partial quantities of a material or product throughout the entire quantity and value chain. In many systems, a batch is the quantity or partial quantity of a particular material or product that is manufactured according to the same recipe.

- Following are the various reasons for knowing the relationship of batch number to the recipe number with which it was made: Legal requirements (e.g., guidelines on Good Manufacturing Practice [GMP]) or regulations on hazardous materials

- Defect tracing, recall activities, recourse requirements
- The requirement for differentiated quantity-based and value-based inventory management (e.g., through heterogeneous yield/result quantities or unequal constituents in production)
- Usability differences and the monitoring thereof in materials planning, sales and distribution, and production
- Production or technical requirements (e.g., material quantity calculation on the basis of different batch specifications)
- Department of defense (DOD) requirement on its suppliers for diagnostic and investigative purposes in cases of failures or to study the performance of new technologies

Order Promising and Delivery

GLOBAL ATP   Global ATP (Available to Promise) can be used in heterogeneous system landscapes to provide necessary information as quickly as possible. Global ATP is one of the central methods of SAP APO that utilizes live Cache, a technology in which data is stored in the form of time series. Flexible rules ensure either product substitution or location substitution in case of a shortcoming of materials and components. Global ATP is also able to consider capacity information that can be either checked directly or modeled in the product allocation.

DISTRIBUTION   Distribution provides controlled release of sales requirements to alternative locations. The delivery might be shipped to the customer directly from the fulfilling locations (more than one delivery) or by consolidation to one location and one complete shipment to the end customer.

REALLOCATION OF SUPPLY AND DEMAND   SAP Reallocation allows you to select a range of products or documents (in the background or synchronously) while considering the supply network environment. Reallocation selects variants of materials, customers, orders, items, deliveries, delivery items, and so on, that represent listings of orders/items partially confirmed, unconfirmed, confirmed with requested dates, and confirmed with dates other than requested dates to consider the latest availability and capacity situations.

PROOF OF DELIVERY   Proof of Delivery (POD) is an instrument involved in business processes in which an invoice is issued only after the customer has confirmed the delivery's arrival. In addition to the proof of delivery itself, you can record the POD date, POD time, the actual quantity that arrived, and the reason for possible differences in quantities. This information is especially important for deliveries in which the delivery quantity varies because of the nature of the goods or for which the exact delivery quantity is unknown from the start. You are now in a position to issue an accurate invoice based on the customer's confirmation of goods received. It is no longer necessary to create credit memos after the fact. The reasons for deviation that occur most often in real-world scenarios—stock shrinkage, theft, certain characteristics of goods (e.g., volatility), and transportation damage—are recorded and analyzed in the system. This analysis is especially valuable when you are negotiating with forwarding agents, vendors, or customers, since all deviations can be shown.

ADVANCED SHIPPING NOTIFICATION   The Advanced Shipping Notification is a document from the vendor listing the exact materials, the quantities, and the delivery date with reference to a purchase order.

Warehouse Management

INVENTORY MANAGEMENT   SAP Inventory Management manages the stocks of a company in quantities and values. It is integrated with supply chain accounting and is responsible for goods receipts, goods issues, and managing different stock categories (available, blocked stock, in quality assurance, etc.) and special stocks (including consignment stock, project stock, etc.). By using SAP Inventory Management, you can view a summary of stocks in the supply chain.

INBOUND/OUTBOUND

Strategies   SAP Warehouse Management allows you to manage your material flow, using advanced put-away and picking strategies. In the standard system, strategies for put away include random put away (next empty bin), bulk storage, fixed bin, or addition to stock. The picking strategies include standard strategies first-in, first-out (FIFO), last-in, first-out (LIFO), picking by shelf life expiration date (SLED), or partial quantities first. For customer-specific strategies, solutions can be self-defined in user exits.

Goods Receipt/Goods Issue   With the Warehouse Management System, you can control the goods receipt and goods issue processes at a physical level. Goods receipts are possible from purchase order, inbound deliveries (advance shipping notice), stock transport orders, or production. Goods receipt starts the put-away process, which is supported by different strategies. The goods issue process in the SAP Warehouse Management system includes all physical activities for fulfilling an outbound delivery or shipment. It includes rough workload estimates in advance of the actual process, picking waves to group the activities efficiently, and pick and put on the ramp pack functions.

Value-Added Services   SAP Warehouse Management supports value-added services, such as customer-specific packing or labeling.

Production Supply   SAP Warehouse Management can handle the material supply of storage bins in production. Picking for work orders is supported by advanced strategies and combined with Handling Unit Management. You can also pack for a specific work order.

TASK AND RESOURCE MANAGEMENT   Task and Resource Management controls the tasks in the warehouse and optimizes the sequence in which the tasks are executed. It ensures that in the warehouse, the right task is processed by the right resource at the right time. Task and Resource Management helps to minimize the routes in the warehouse. This easy-to-use system seamlessly integrates into the SAP Logistics Execution System.

RADIO FREQUENCY/BAR CODING   SAP provides direct radio frequency (RF), allowing the use of mobile RF terminals and handhelds with scanning devices. This enables immediate and error-free data transfer, setting a high standard of quality for warehouse transactions. The character-based or graphical terminals and handholds receive data directly from the SAP system without using a middleware product and transfer results immediately to wherever they are needed. Configurable barcode setup allows you to use bar code standards (e.g., EAN128 or SSCC) as well as any defined bar code systems you define yourself.

PROCESS INTEGRATION

Handling Unit Management   You can use Handling Unit Management (HUM) to reflect packing-based logistics structures in SAP R/3. In SAP Warehouse Management, you can use handling units to process warehouse movements, such as put away, picking, and stock transfers. Furthermore, handling units can be created in the warehouse, labeled, and picked for existing deliveries. HUM allows you to uniquely identify packages—for example, pallets—in the warehouse and throughout the supply chain. It includes EAN 128 and SSCC18 labeling. The handling units can be nested and packed with different materials or batches.

Serial Numbers   Serial numbers are known in the warehouse through Handling Unit Management.

Batch Management   Batch management is integrated into all SAP Warehouse Management processes. It includes handling of batches and batch determination for delivery picking and production supply and in internal warehouse processes. Also, active ingredient processing is integrated into the batch determination process in Warehouse Management.

Quality Management   SAP Warehouse Management is integrated with Quality Management. This allows warehouse administrators to manage and track inspection lots that are stored in the warehouse.

Hazardous Materials   Although many materials that are classified as dangerous can be placed into storage along with other goods, some require special handling and placement into specially designed storage facilities. Some examples of these materials include explosives, petroleum fuels and oil, poisons, corrosive liquids, and radioactive materials. SAP Warehouse Management is designed to manage the handling and storage of hazardous materials.

VISIBILITY

Warehouse Activity Monitor   The Warehouse Activity Monitor helps a manager to oversee, plan, and optimize work processes in the warehouse. It provides a tool to notify those responsible if there are delays or errors in the overall system. The monitor also helps to identify and correct warehousing problems or critical processes soon after they occur.

Radio Frequency Monitor   The monitor for RF activities lets you display the current workload and resource capacity in the entire warehouse. It is a graphical tool that gives an overview of the current workload status in the groups that workers are assigned to. Using the RF Monitor, a warehouse manager can easily access and influence the work process by redistributing tasks between different work groups and prioritizing the tasks within a group.

Task Monitor (available with TRM)   The Task Monitor allows you to manage and control the resources and tasks in a site. It enables a manager to influence allocation of tasks to different resources and to perform various operations (e.g., tasks, resources). Compared to the RF Monitor, the Task Monitor drills down to a more detailed view of tasks (e.g., picking, packing, and weighing), which can be generated from different R/3 Enterprise documents.

SAP Business Information Warehouse To analyze warehouse activities, information is extracted from the SAP Logistic Execution System (SAP LES) module of the Warehouse Management system and is transferred to the SAP Business Information Warehouse (SAP BW), where it evaluates and reduces the extensive information from Warehouse Management to a few essential performance measurements. Key performance indicators for Warehouse Management support the analysis of the physical flow of quantities and workload in the warehouse.

Delivery Monitor The Delivery Monitor provides an overview of deliveries in working processes. On one hand, it gives an overview of the workload in different areas: for example, shipping, transportation and invoicing. On the other hand, it provides the possibility of processing documents that have the same selection criteria collectively. Using this tool, specialists in different execution areas of the company can get a quick overview of their workload, drill down to single documents, and trigger follow-up activities.

DECENTRALIZED WAREHOUSE Customers can decide to use SAP Warehouse Management as a stand-alone system, connected with a central ERP system. This interface is also available as a standard interface for the connection of certified partner WM systems. The system distributes master data and inbound/outbound deliveries automatically. All quantity-related processes, physical movements, and picking/packing operations are handled in the decentralized WMS. All financial-based functions (such as valuation, credit limit check, and ATP) are handled in the central system.

An enhancement of the system communication covers the changeability of deliveries triggered centrally.

CROSS-DOCKING Cross-docking speeds up the fulfillment process by shipping pallets that are in goods receipt without putting them away. The Warehouse Management System supports the planning process from fulfillment coordination, by instructing warehouse workers with cross-dock transfer orders.

Cross-docking also is supported as a spontaneous function for missing parts. This is done by the WM system when it decides to fill orders from receiving rather than from stored stocks.

YARD MANAGEMENT Yard Management gives the warehouse an overview of stocks on trailers, trucks, or railcars in the yard. Sequencing functions decide which stock has to be received into the warehouse and at what point in time.

VALUE-ADDED SERVICES   Value-adding activities in the warehouses have to be priced and invoiced. Support for service activities on warehouse operations enable a company to decide on the type of activities, retrieve the value of a group of activities around a warehouse process, and invoice these activities to the warehouse customers, both internal and external.

SLOTTING   Slotting enables the warehouse to store incoming goods based on (cube) volume, weight, and future sales demand. Rearrangement of existing stock based on demand data is also supported. This functionality interacts closely with SAP APO Demand Planning.

AUTOMATED WORKLOAD RELEASE   Automated workload scheduling and release supports the control and timing of activities in the warehouse based on progress control and the time it takes to pick, pack, and move the required goods to the outbound area. Activities of several picking groups can be monitored through the physical goods movement processes.

Transportation Execution

EXPRESS SHIP INTERFACE   The Express Shipment Interface (XSI) offers a generic customizable online interface to express carriers. XSI supplies three basic functions:

1. Assign unique, carrier-specific parcel IDs to outbound parcel shipments.
2. Print parcel labels.
3. Retrieve tracking information.

The tracking information is displayed in the standard SAP R/3 screen. It mirrors the complete itinerary of the parcel and is pulled on demand out of the carrier's system.

SHIPPING   SCM provides different options for consolidating deliveries and orders as shipments. It can combine orders based on rules and strategies, based on optimization logic in SAP APO, or interactively and manually in SAP R/3 and SAP APO. It also allows you to combine orders using collaboration over the Internet. If you decide to rely on your carrier's abilities to consolidate your orders into shipments, you can give it access to your deliveries through the Internet, where it can consolidate your shipments.

Different types of shipment documents have been defined to enable you to reflect in the system the various forms of transportation used. You can use shipment documents to:

- Specify shipment stages, legs, border crossing points, and load transfer points
- Assign service agents and means of transport
- Define the packaging for goods (Handling Unit Management)
- Specify planned transportation deadlines
- Record actual transportation deadlines and statuses
- Specify output required for transportation (such as shipping papers, XML and EDI messages)
- Define transport-relevant texts
- Separate document types deal with inbound and outbound shipments

COLLABORATIVE SHIPMENT TENDERING   In collaborative tendering, based on your actual shipment plans and orders, you can tender your offers to your carriers over the Internet or through XML or EDI, directly into your carrier's or forwarder's system. This collaborative process enables you to integrate your business partners into your business processes and keep control of your plans. This process is described in more detail below.

Freight Exchange   SAP has partnerships with several freight exchanges. mySAP SCM enables you to automatically transfer your shipments into the systems of those freight exchanges, to seamlessly integrate their service provider community into your network. This function is supported in SAP R/3 LES and SAP APO.

FREIGHT COSTING AND INVOICING

Freight Cost Calculation   An accurate and detailed freight cost calculation is essential for the verification of invoices sent from the carrier or to self-bill carriers. Shipment costs are calculated using the standard condition technique for pricing.

Freight Conditions   Freight rates are the basis for the shipment costs calculation. The totals of the different freight rates that are used for a particular transaction give the shipment costs. Freight rates are stored in the system in the form of condition rates that can be created at a very detailed level.

Freight Cost Settlement   After shipment cost calculation has been completed, the settlement process is initiated with the relevant service agents. Within the settlement process, SAP is able to carry out settlement for multiple carriers that may have taken part in a shipment. Both costs and accruals are posted. The users then decide if they would like to settle the costs with the carrier through classic invoice verification or through an automated self-billing function. With self-billing, the evaluated receipt settlement feature is used in purchasing to pay the service agents automatically, based on the calculated shipment costs. If required, aspects of the shipment costs can be billed to the customer directly.

DISTANCE DETERMINATION SERVICE   The Distance Determination Service retrieves distances from third-party providers. It is an add-on for transportation.

FREIGHT COSTING EXTENSION   The Freight Costing Extension extends the ability to charge a customer an amount that differs from that paid to a carrier for transportation services and includes tariff reference data, routing guide, customer freight invoicing, and intercompany settlement of freight costs.

The Customer Freight Invoicing engine allows companies to simultaneously manage buying and selling tariffs with consideration to competitive freight discounts, equalization, and out-of-territory moves.

The Freight Costing Extension is an add-on for transportation.

Foreign Trade/Legal Services

LEGAL CONTROL   This Foreign Control module covers the foreign control laws from the United States, European countries, Japan, and Australia. The generic design lets you use them for other countries too. You can simulate planned business transactions to analyze whether there may be any difficulties during export (such as embargoes or a boycott), and you can create a file for the authorities.

DOCUMENTARY PAYMENTS   The Documentary Payments function provides single-screen access to transactions related to this area, such as guarantees of payment, documents against payment, letters of credit, and certain insurance guarantees. The key benefit of this function is that it can be combined with Credit Management.

Monitoring and alert reporting allow you to control the documentary payment flow.

PREFERENCE   The Preference function can have cost-saving effects for trading with countries that are members of the European Preference (European Union, Middle East and Asian Countries, North Africa, South Africa,

Mercursor, Mexico) and of the North American Free Trade Agreement (NAFTA) Preference (United States, Canada, Mexico).

The Preference processing tasks allow you to determine whether products qualify as being produced according to the rules stipulated by the trade area from which the export takes place. Preference handling is divided into logical steps that build on one another.

One function is Vendor Declaration, which enables you to request necessary vendor declarations or to run a report with all the expiring vendor declarations. An additional function allows you to determine preferences, for individual materials or collectively.

PERIODIC DECLARATIONS   Declarations to several authorities from the European Union, NAFTA, European Free Trade Association (EFTA), and Japan can be handled. This module currently supports 18 countries. It includes the maintenance of individual customs data for goods coming from different regions of the world). The medium used is paper, CD or DVD, EDI, or e-mail, depending on the individual national laws.

COMMUNICATION/PRINTING   A very important part of foreign trade is the capability to print or send the foreign trade/customs data in the official format. More and more countries offer the option of transferring the customs data via EDI.

CUSTOMS/FOREIGN TRADE DATA SERVICE   SAP helps you access services that provide customs and foreign trade data that is continuously updated according to current regulation. The SAP interface allows you to load these complex data into the operating system. The medium can be a file, a CD or DVD, or the Internet.

Supply Chain Coordination

Supply Chain Event Management

PROCUREMENT VISIBILITY   For procurement, the Supply Chain Event Management (SCEM) process begins with the creation of purchase orders. During inbound delivery from the supplier to the customer, all parties involved, including logistics providers, ensure the flow of information by sending messages to SCEM, reporting both timely delivery and any unplanned events. If, for example, a delay is reported, rescheduling can start automatically for subsequent processes, such as production or order fulfillment. Following the goods receipt at the site, a quality check takes place, and the goods can be put away in the warehouse. By offering communication channels,

SCEM makes the entire procurement process transparent at every stage, both for customers and for partners. Both parties can monitor when events are planned to take place and when they actually occur.

MANUFACTURING VISIBILITY SCEM for manufacturing manages events throughout the production process from planning to the end of production. During production, process steps can be reported back, ensuring a transparent manufacturing process. In most cases, companies want this kind of transparency only for internal purposes, since these data are not meant for external publication. However, it is also possible to provide information on events to external parties, such as customers, subcontractors, or sold-to parties, using various channels to provide the information quickly and to ensure transparency of planned and actual events.

FULFILLMENT VISIBILITY SCEM for fulfillment starts with the creation of the sales order. After receiving order confirmation, the customer can monitor the process status through the Internet. After picking, packing, and loading activities are complete, outbound delivery begins. During internal activities and outbound delivery to the customer, all parties concerned, including logistics providers and forwarding agents, ensure the flow of information by sending messages to inform SCEM of both timely delivery and any unplanned events.

By offering monitoring and visibility tools, SCEM makes the entire fulfillment process transparent at every stage, both for customers and for partners. Both parties can monitor when events are planned to take place and when they actually occur.

ASSET LIFE CYCLE TRACKING In the case of assets, SCEM deals mainly with high-value movable assets used for containing and transporting goods. Examples of these assets are containers, intermediate bulk containers, and vehicles.

On one hand, asset life cycle, including ownership, condition, and location, must be managed. On the other hand, assets contain and transport goods, and every single run is a process in itself: from the customer order to packing or loading into the asset, transportation to the customer, emptying the asset, sending it back, and cleaning it. This process is completed when the customer is invoiced and preparation begins for the next transportation process.

LOGISTICS SERVICE PROVIDER SCEM provides logistics service providers (LSPs) with visibility into the flow of materials and information. The third- or fourth-party service provider can view the current state of the materials under way within the supply network and get alerted on time if an exception occurs. This broadens the service offerings of LSPs to customers. SCEM provides decision support with a high resolution to monitor service levels and allows the control of complex supply networks. In addition, SCEM can record the collaboration performance of all partners. The documentation of the actual actions and activities during the fulfillment process helps to solve contractual issues.

RAIL FLEET MANAGEMENT EXTENSION   Extensive query and operational transactions are integrated into SCEM to manage current status, estimated times of arrival, product contents, last container contents, and sighting/claims log management (CLM) history. The sighting/CLM history includes railcar tracking, fleet management tools, plant maintenance, mileage credit reporting, detention billing, and lease/sublease reporting.

The Rail Car Management engine allows companies to scan for adverse conditions, such as rail cars that are delayed, off-route, or overdue, or for a freight car that has been loaded improperly, is mechanically defective, or has safety violations. The engine continuously monitors rail cars and alerts the Transportation Management System to the change in conditions. By accessing route information, including segments, transit times, and distances between rail junctions and passing points, transportation planners can more accurately manage their product and equipment.

ON-SITE EVENT MANAGEMENT EXTENSION   The On-Site Event Management extension provides functions for managing the status and location of rail equipment while at a plant, rail yard, or other facility.

Supply Chain Performance Management

KEY PERFORMANCE INDICATORS   Key performance indicators (KPIs) provide a means of judging the performance of business processes internally by time period, collaboratively with others within your supply chain, and externally by benchmarking against similar companies. SCM supports the metrics in the Supply Chain Operations Reference (SCOR) model created by the Supply Chain Council, and includes more than 300 preconfigured supply chain KPIs, such as delivery performance, forecast accuracy, and return on assets. These measures can be used as they are, or modified and enhanced to fit your specific situation, although in my own practice I use a subset of them at only ninety six.

STRATEGIC PERFORMANCE MANAGEMENT   On a strategic level, SCPM gives you the feedback needed for true closed-loop supply chain management, which is key to driving continuous improvement, delivering superior performance over time, and ensuring that your supply chain continues to be efficient and competitive. The two areas of concentration include:

1. **Balanced Score Card SEM-CPM** (Corporate Performance Monitor) supports the definition, analysis, visualization, and interpretation of key performance indicators and Balanced Scorecards and thus increases the effectiveness of managerial strategy finding and implementation. Elements of SEM-CPM are value driver trees, measure catalogs, and management cockpit scenarios. SAP SEM with its component SEM-CPM offers innovative concepts for the interpretation and visualization of KPIs. The concept of the Balanced Scorecard, for example, includes nonfinancial measures in the enterprise performance management and thus goes beyond the scope of regular management reporting.
2. **Sales and Operations Planning in SAP APO** allows monitoring of various plans from sales, marketing, and manufacturing to keep in line with the overall business plan.

OPERATIVE PERFORMANCE MANAGEMENT On a day-to-day operational level, the solution provides constant surveillance of key performance measurements and automatically generates an alert when there is a deviation from plan, so that you can keep processes working at maximum efficiency.

The Supply Chain Cockpit in SAP APO allows constant surveillance of the entire supply chain. The Alert Monitor and Broadcasting functions draw attention to bottlenecks and allow you to inform users of potential problems in their area.

SUPPLY CHAIN ANALYTICS Analytical applications provide the basis for measuring and optimizing across the entire supply chain. These applications are more than just reporting; they are closed-loop scenarios that feed information back into the transactional systems. They include the collection of data from various operational systems (including non-SAP) to create the basis for analytical applications. Data from Dunn and Bradstreet and Nielsen can be collected as well as data from the Web. Analytical applications also include alerts, workflows, and what-if analyses.

COLLABORATION PERFORMANCE INDICATOR In an increasingly collaborative environment, it is important to measure the performance of the interactions of every partner involved in the supply chain. This is exactly what collaboration performance indicators (CPIs) do.

A CPI is the measure of performance associated with the responsiveness of all organizations involved in a process with cross-organizational interdependencies. The information provided by a CPI can be used to determine how an organization's cooperation compares with an agreed-on standard.

Therefore, CPIs are key components for an organization's move toward best practice.

Fulfillment Coordination

DISTRIBUTED ORDER MANAGEMENT   Fulfillment coordination controls the actual fulfillment of a sales order. It sets the touch point of customer order management in CRM and order fulfillment within Supply Chain Management.

Fulfillment coordination controls follow-up activities in the logistics execution that result from the customer order and determines the partners involved. It forwards the workload for warehousing and transportation or further logistics services to the partners involved.

The delivery of a sales order can be executed by different internal or external partners in the fulfillment process. When stocks are distributed over different physical locations—a process that can be handled by internal or external partners—it is necessary to determine which partners to use and provide the information important to do the actual work on time. Possible partners in the outbound fulfillment process are different profit centers within the enterprise, such as warehousing departments, or external business partners, such as logistics service providers.

Fulfillment coordination enables the split of a sales order into work packages for the actual fulfillment at the site where materials are stored. The warehouses and transportation management are informed about the materials and quantities that have to be picked, packed, and shipped.

With fulfillment coordination, shipments can be consolidated for execution to achieve a better overall efficiency in the fulfillment process. The confirmation of fulfilled services by transportation management or site management is reported back to fulfillment coordination, where it is forwarded to billing and inventory management.

INBOUND FULFILLMENT   Fulfillment coordination coordinates the process of receiving materials from procurement. It provides information about the locations where materials are received and put away in the procurement process. It also controls the inbound fulfillment process and determines partners who will be involved in the actual execution.

During the receiving process, activities such as packing, repacking, or other value-added services may be necessary. These activities have to be determined, and the workload for the actual fulfillment has to be passed to the appropriate business partner. In fulfillment coordination, the process flow is dependent on whether the involved parties are internal or external business partners. When stocks are distributed over different physical locations (which can be handled by internal or external partners), it is necessary to determine the partners and provide them with the necessary information to do the actual work on time.

Fulfillment coordination enables shipment consolidation in order to reduce freight costs. It can also split the original purchase order into separate packages for logistics handling. These packages contain information about the processes that have to be executed, such as cross-docking, assembly, or storage in the warehouse.

After all physical processing is done, the actual inbound received quantities and items are reported back to inventory management, where the purchase order can be updated and forwarded to invoice verification. The stocks are updated in inventory management.

STOCK TRANSFER Fulfillment coordination facilitates the handling of stock transfers between locations of the supply chain. It determines the fulfillment partners involved and assigns the actual requests for fulfillment services to the delivering and receiving sites and to transportation management. For stock transfer requests, fulfillment coordination creates follow-up requests for value-added services and cross-docking in transshipment points or warehouses, and handles the necessary confirmations and notifications. Stock transfers can be consolidated with other movements, such as inbound orders from suppliers or outbound orders for customers.

After confirmation that the services are fulfilled, the goods movement postings are reported to inventory management and billing.

CROSS-DOCKING In the process of cross-docking materials, materials are processed directly from the goods receipt area to the point of use or goods issue area without first being put away in the warehouse. Fulfillment coordination enables a cross-location supply chain-oriented processing of cross-docking. Cross-docking enables a quick distribution of materials without processing many steps or even put-away in the distribution centers.

Therefore, fulfillment coordination has to provide timely information for the distribution centers or other locations involved in the process. The inbound shipments have to be identified, and processes concerning the contained packages or handling units have to be prepared in order to avoid time-consuming repackaging.

Fulfillment coordination controls the communication between the central distribution centers and creates the order that specifies which handling units have to be handled and how. The actual execution is fulfilled by site or warehouse management. Cross-docking also includes handling of packages at transshipment points or terminal hubs without warehouse management functions.

Finally, the confirmation of services executed is reported back to fulfillment coordination and forwarded to billing and inventory management.

Supply Chain Collaboration

Supply Chain Portal

ENTERPRISE PORTAL Information is the lifeblood of the supply chain. But too often, people are overwhelmed by the maze of data, which means they cannot take the necessary actions to increase productivity and keep the supply chain competitive.

Supply Chain Management cuts through the maze with the Enterprise Portal, which lets employees collaborate with coworkers down the hall or across the globe. They can even reach across enterprise boundaries, enabling people to forge closer relationships with suppliers, partners, and customers. In addition, the Enterprise Portal enables business partners to participate in each other's supply chain activities. The result is seamless collaboration across the entire supply chain network.

The Enterprise Portal gives all participants a single point of access to the information, applications, and services they need, everything from mySAP.com solutions to other enterprise systems and online exchanges. In this way, users can respond to customer demands, quickly adapt to changes, and consistently deliver a high level of service. The Enterprise Portal is based on the specific role of each individual, both within the organization and at partner and customer sites. And it can be personalized to meet each individual's needs so people can easily tap into relevant content. It also works with Web browsers and is designed for mobile computing, enabling users to access information anytime, anywhere, and on any device.

Inside the portal, employees as well as business partners can run the whole range of SCM solutions, including the SCM Alert Monitor, a standalone component of SAP APO that enables you to have a unified approach to monitor the planning situations. It notifies you of any critical situation occurring in one of the SAP APO applications, such as Demand and Supply Planning, Production Planning and Detailed Scheduling, or Transportation Planning and Vehicle Scheduling. Planners can define the rules and conditions under which the Alert Monitor should inform them of a violation. Based on this monitoring process, the plan can be readjusted whenever necessary.

Collaboration Processes

COLLABORATIVE PLANNING, FORECASTING, AND REPLENISHMENT Collaborative Demand Planning between manufacturers and their distributors allows partners to streamline their work processes and ultimately benefit from a more accurate forecast, better market transparency, greater stability, reduced inventory, and better communication. Starting from one forecast, all partners collaborate to produce a final forecast, which becomes the basis for all further planning in the partner companies.

Collaborative Planning, Forecasting, and Replenishment (CPFR) has the potential to deliver increased sales, organizational streamlining and alignment, administrative and operational efficiency, improved cash flow, and improved return-on-assets performance. The CPFR process model has been developed by the Voluntary Industry Commerce Services (VICS) Association in cooperation with leading retailers, consumer packaged goods manufacturers, as well as consulting and software providers. The CPFR process model represents voluntary guidelines aimed at structuring and guiding supply chain partners in setting up their relationship and processes.

VENDOR MANAGED INVENTORY Through the Vendor Managed Inventory (VMI) program, the seller can provide value-added services by performing replenishment planning tasks for buyers. By increasing visibility into actual consumer demands and inventory consumption as well as seller's stock level, VMI programs allow sellers to make better decisions on how to deploy goods across various sellers, which leads to better customer service levels, reduced inventory levels and stock-out situations, and lower sales cost. Both buyer and seller parties benefit from reduced cycle time and lower overhead, since the process can be highly automated.

SUPPLIER MANAGED INVENTORY Through the Supplier Managed Inventory (SMI) program, the seller can estimate future demands better and provide value-added services by receiving demand forecasts from buyers and performing replenishment planning tasks for buyers. By increasing visibility into MRP results as well as the seller's stock level, SMI programs allow sellers to make better decisions on how to deploy goods across various sellers, which leads to better customer service levels, reduced inventory levels and stock-out situations, and lower sales cost. Both buyer and seller parties benefit from reduced cycle time and lower overhead, since the process can be highly automated.

SUPPLIER CAPACITY COLLABORATION The objective of Supplier Capacity Collaboration is to collaborate with subcontractors to balance outsourced workloads with a close supply network. The original equipment manufacturer (OEM) provides outsourced tasks/requirements to its subcontractors and evaluates their commitments. The coordination service, together with supply chain analytics, supports the decision making to adjust OEM's product schedule by considering subcontractors' commitments as constraints and propagates them up and down the supply network.

Supply Chain Integration

CORE INTERFACE Out-of-the-box integration between SAP application components is guaranteed via the SAP Plug-In Strategy. Core Interface (CIF) is an SAP R/3 enhancement and is part of the SAP R/3 Plug-In, enabling the seamless integration of SAP R/3 systems with the SAP APO.

The underlying technology for component integration is RFC (Request for Comment, qRFC [queue RFC], sRFC [synchronous RFC], etc.). Supply Chain Management is tightly integrated into SAP's solution landscape, enabling seamless, comprehensive business processes. Via open Business Application Programming Interfaces (BAPIs), integration of SCM components with non-SAP components is also supported.

EXCHANGE INFRASTRUCTURE By offering an exchange-based infrastructure, Supply Chain Management enables modeling of transactions and processes across companies and across systems, offering them on a robust platform. Based on a native Web infrastructure that leverages open standards, the exchange infrastructure (EI) makes it possible to manage the broad diversity of highly heterogeneous components from a multitude of vendors running in various technology environments. The integration capabilities capture shared business semantics and act as a mediator between the services and their technical realizations. These integration capabilities include technical functions, such as Web service discovery, queuing, mapping, and routing. They also establish an infrastructure for business process management and high-performance execution within and across organizational boundaries.

Through system-specific adapters, Supply Chain Management connects to most major third-party systems and automates Supply Chain Management process steps to create and activate plans, orders, event messages, and various other documents.

The SAP Exchange Infrastructure is also a solution for industry standards support. SAP is actively participating in a range of horizontal and vertical e-business standardization organizations and efforts, such as Organization for the Advancement of Structured Information Standards (OASIS), Rosetta Net, XML, XML Common Business Library (xCBL), Human Resources XML (HR-XML), Extensible Business Reporting Language (XBRL), and the Interactive Financial Exchange (IFX) Forum, which help businesses to collaborate in a more seamless and reliable manner by significantly reducing total integration costs. The relevant e-business standards are then reflected in the Integration Repository and the Integration Directory by providing interfaces and implemented Web services following these standards. Evolving e-business technology standards are making an impact and are reflected in the new infrastructure, which can capture all existing and upcoming XML standards.

MOBILE SUPPLY CHAIN MANAGEMENT   Mobile technologies promise to revolutionize the supply chain. Anytime, anywhere, access to information means supply chain participants can reach new levels of visibility and productivity— and increased profits. With support for mobile business, Supply Chain Management puts companies on the cutting edge. From supplier to sales force, from shop floor to shipper, from warehouse to customer—all supply chain participants have instant access to the information they need.

Support for mobile business means visibility is increased as information flows seamlessly from bar code to palmtop to enterprise system. Automated data capture replaces error-prone manual input. And decision makers are empowered wherever they happen to be. So suppliers, manufacturers, distributors, and retailers can collaborate, execute, satisfy customers, and meet business goals.

Value Chains

The following figures present the detailed value chains. The figures are self-explanatory for those interested in knowing the mechanics of KPIs and their effect on dependent variables of the enterprise.

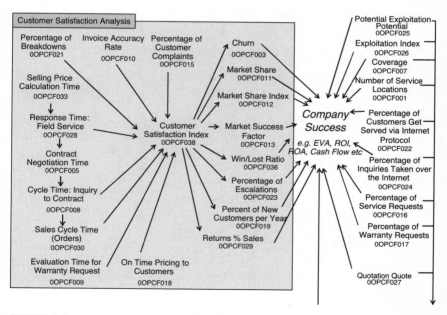

FIGURE 3.9 Customer and Market Focus (Part I)

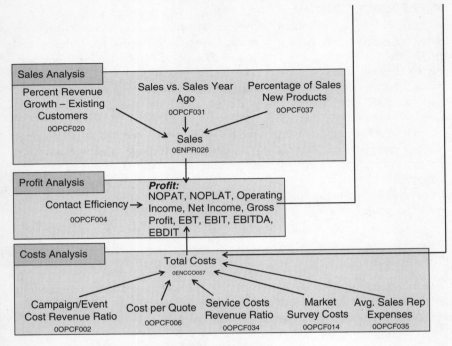

FIGURE 3.10 Customer and Market Focus (Part II)

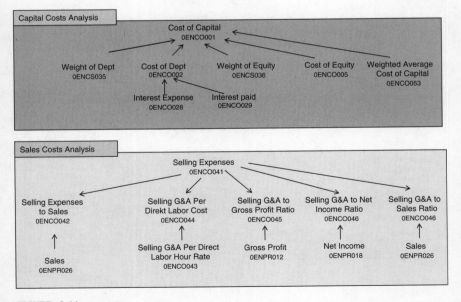

FIGURE 3.11 Costs I

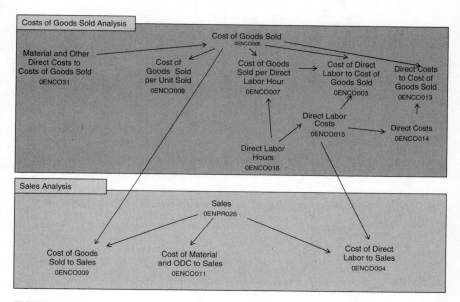

FIGURE 3.12 Costs II

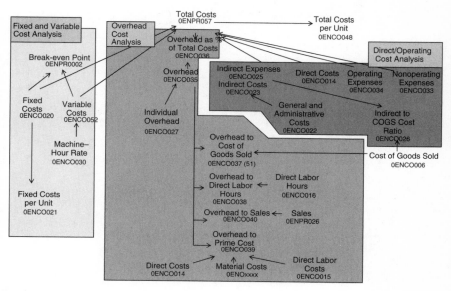

FIGURE 3.13 Costs III

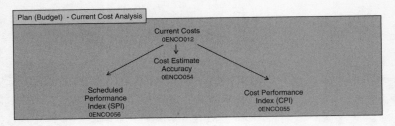

FIGURE 3.14 Costs IV

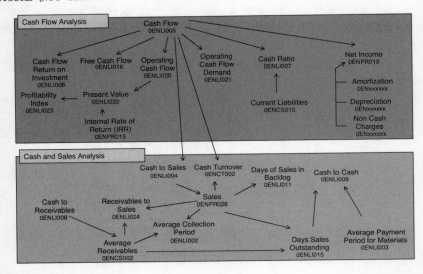

FIGURE 3.15 Profitability I

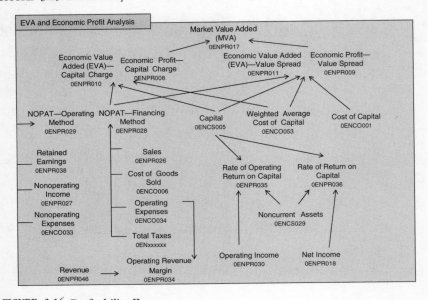

FIGURE 3.16 Profitability II

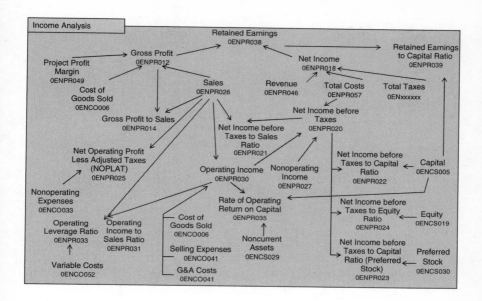

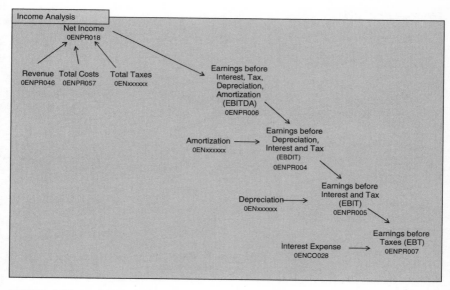

FIGURE 3.17 Profitability III

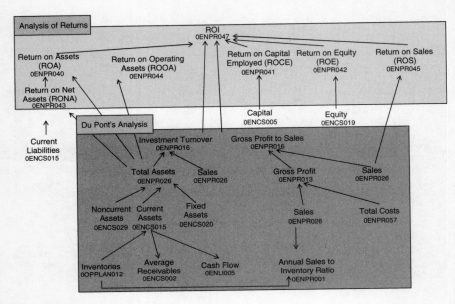

FIGURE 3.18 Profitability IV

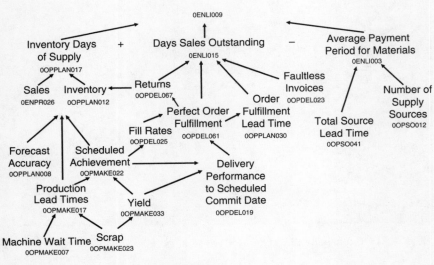

FIGURE 3.19 Cash-to-Cash Cycle Time

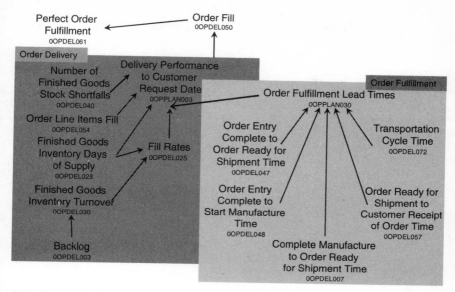

FIGURE 3.20 Order Fill

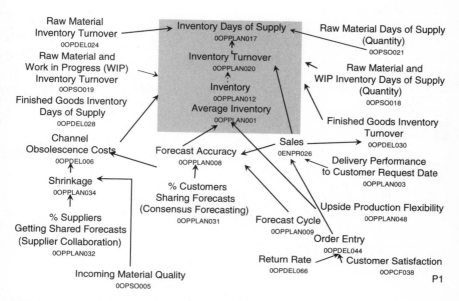

FIGURE 3.21 Inventory Days of Supply

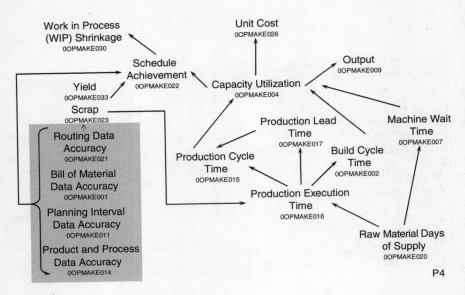

FIGURE 3.22 Capacity Utilization

Raw Material Inventory Turnover

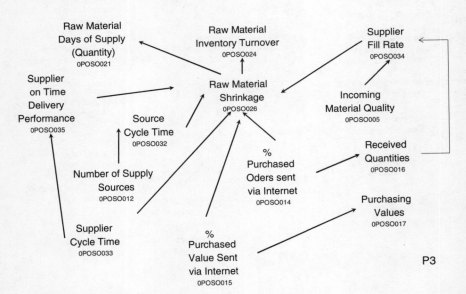

FIGURE 3.23 Raw Material Inventory Turnover

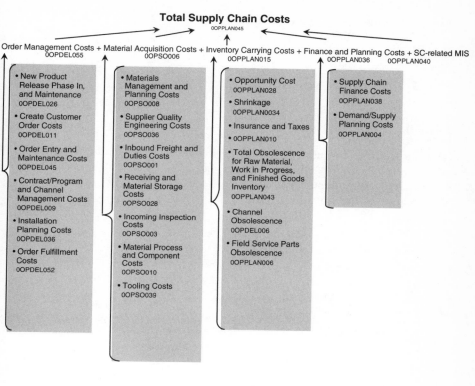

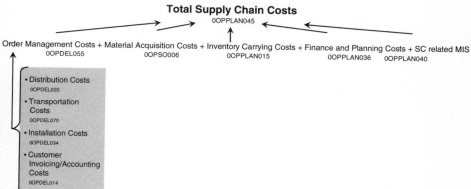

FIGURE 3.24 Total Supply Chain Costs

Key Performance Indicators

Figure 3.25 shows the key performance indicators of the Supply Chain Management domain.

Benefits

The first column in Figure 3.26 shows the independent variables (causal, represented by a KPI) that can result in a favorable effect on another variable (a dependent variable, an effect variable, represented by a KPI) listed in the second column. Thus, this figure forms a table of causes and effects which can be used to modulate the supply chain performance.

KPI	KPI Explanation
Total supply chain costs(0)	Total supply chain costs are the sum of supply chain–related miscellaneous (MIS), finance and planning, inventory carrying, material acquisition, and order management costs.
	Supply chain–related MIS + supply chain finance and planning costs + inventory carrying costs + material acquisition costs + order management costs
Order management costs(1)	Order management costs are the aggregation of these cost elements: create customer order costs, order entry and maintenance costs, contract/program and channel management costs, installation planning costs, order fulfillment costs, distribution costs, transportation costs, installation costs, customer invoicing/accounting costs.
Material acquisition costs(2)	Material acquisition costs include costs incurred for production materials: sum of materials management and planning, supplier quality engineering, inbound freight and duties, receiving and material storage, incoming inspection, material process engineer.
Inventory carrying costs(3)	Inventory carrying costs include the costs of carrying inventory of finished goods, raw materials, and work in progress (WIP). They also include the opportunity cost; shrinkage of inventory at each stage; insurance and taxes; total obsolescence of raw materials, WIP, and finished goods inventory; channel obsolescence and field service parts obsolescence costs.
Supply chain finance and planning costs(4)	These include all costs associated with taking possession of material.

FIGURE 3.25 Key Performance Indicators

Supply chain–related MIS costs(5)	Supply chain–related miscellaneous costs are costs incurred in the operation of a business that cannot be directly related to the individual products or services produced. These costs, such as light, heat, supervision, and maintenance, are grouped in this category
Order management costs(1)	Order management costs include the aggregation of these cost elements: create customer order costs, order entry and maintenance costs, contract/program and channel management costs, installation planning costs, order fulfillment costs, distribution costs, transportation costs, installation costs, and customer invoicing/accounting costs.
	Create customer order costs + order entry and maintenance costs + contract, program and channel management costs + installation planning costs + order fulfillment costs + distribution costs + transportation costs + installation costs + customer invoicing, accounting costs
New product release phase-in and maintenance costs	These costs include releasing new products to the field; maintaining released products; assigning product IDs; defining configurations and packaging; publishing availability schedules and release letters and updates; and maintaining product databases.
	Releasing new products to the field costs + maintaining released products costs + assigning product ID costs+ defining configurations and packaging costs + publishing availability schedules costs + release letters and updates costs + maintaining product databases costs
Create customer order costs	This area includes costs for creating and pricing configurations to order and preparing order documents.
	Creating and pricing configurations to order costs + preparing order documents costs
Order entry and maintenance costs	This area includes costs for maintaining the customer database, credit check, accepting new orders and adding them to the order system as well as later order modifications.
	Costs for maintaining the customer database + credit check costs + accepting new orders and adding them to the order system costs + later order modifications costs
Contract, program, and channel management costs	This area includes all costs for activities related to contract negotiation, monitoring progress, and reporting against the customer's contract, including administration of performance or warranty-related issues.
	Activities related to contract negotiation costs + monitoring progress costs + reporting against the customer's contract costs
Installation planning costs	Installation planning costs include costs for installation engineering, scheduling and modification, handling cancellations, and planning the installation.
	Installation engineering costs + scheduling and modification costs + handling cancellations costs + planning the installation costs

FIGURE 3.25 (*Continued*)

Order fulfillment costs	Order fulfillment costs include costs for processing the order, allocating inventory, ordering from the internal or external supplier, scheduling the shipment, reporting order status, and initiating shipment.
	Order processing costs + costs for allocating inventory + costs for ordering from the internal or external supplier + costs for scheduling the shipment + reporting order status costs + initiating shipment costs
Distribution costs	This area includes costs for warehouse space and management, finished goods receiving and stocking, processing shipments, picking and consolidating, selecting carrier, and staging products/systems.
	Warehouse space and management costs + finished goods receiving and stocking costs + processing shipments costs + picking and consolidating costs + selecting carrier costs + staging products, systems costs
Transportation costs	Transportation costs include all company-paid freight and duties from point of manufacture to end customer or channel.
Installation costs	This area includes costs for verifying site preparation, installing, certifying, and authorizing billing.
	Verifying site preparation costs + installing costs + certifying costs + authorizing billing costs
Customer invoicing, accounting costs	This area includes costs for invoicing, processing customer payments, and verifying customer satisfaction.
	Invoicing costs + processing customer payments costs + verifying customer satisfaction costs
Material acquisition costs(2)	Material acquisition costs include costs incurred for production materials: sum of materials management and planning, supplier quality engineering, inbound freight and duties, receiving and material storage, incoming inspection, and material process engineering.
	Materials management and planning costs + supplier quality engineering costs + inbound freight and duties costs + receiving and material storage costs + incoming inspection costs + material process engineering and tooling costs
Material management and planning costs	Included here are all costs associated with supplier sourcing, contract negotiation and qualification, and the preparation, placement, and tracking of a purchase order. This category includes all costs related to buyer/planner's direct and indirect expenses.
	All costs associated with supplier sourcing + contract negotiation and qualification costs + preparation, placement, and tracking of a purchase order.
Supplier quality engineering costs	This area includes the costs associated with the determination, development/certification, and monitoring of suppliers' capabilities to fully satisfy the applicable quality and regulatory requirements.

FIGURE 3.25 (*Continued*)

Inbound freight and duties	This area includes freight costs associated with the movement of material from a vendor to the buyer and the associated administrative tasks. Duties are those fees and taxes levied by government for moving purchased material across international borders and the customs brokers' fee.
	Freight costs + duties + customs brokers fees
Receiving and material storage costs	This area includes all costs associated with taking possession of and storing material. It includes warehouse space and management, material receiving and stocking, processing work orders, pricing, and internal material movement.
	Warehouse space and management costs + material receiving and stocking costs + processing work orders costs + pricing costs + internal material movement costs
Incoming inspection costs	This area includes all costs associated with the inspection and testing of received materials to verify compliance with specifications.
	Inspection + testing costs
Material process engineering costs	Material process engineering costs are associated with tasks required to document and communicate material specifications as well as reviews to improve the manufacturability of the purchased item.
	Document and communicate material specification costs + reviews costs
Tooling costs	Tooling costs are those associated with the design, development, and depreciation of the tooling required to produce a purchased item.
	Tool design costs + tool development and depreciation costs
Inventory carrying costs(3)	This area includes costs of carrying inventory of finished goods, raw materials, & WIP. It also includes the opportunity cost; shrinkage of inventory at each stage; insurance and taxes; total obsolescence of raw materials, WIP, and finished goods inventory; channel obsolescence and field service parts obsolescence costs.
Opportunity costs	This area includes the opportunity cost of holding inventory.
	Cost of capital × average net value of inventory
	Average net value of inventory= (Days of supply of raw material + WIP + finished good) × cost of the same
Shrinkage	Shrinkage equals the costs associated with breakage, pilferage, and deterioration of inventories.
	Breakage costs + pilferage costs+ deterioration of inventories costs
Work in process (WIP) shrinkage	WIP shrinkage consists of the costs associated with breakage, pilferage, and deterioration of WIP inventories.
	WIP breakage + WIP pilferage + deterioration of WIP inventories
Finished goods shrinkage	This area includes the costs associated with breakage, pilferage, and deterioration of finished goods inventories.
	Finished goods breakage + finished goods pilferage + deterioration of finished goods inventories

FIGURE 3.25 (*Continued*)

Insurance and taxes	This area includes the cost of insuring inventories and taxes associated with the holding of inventories.
	Insurance costs + inventory tax costs
Total obsolescence for raw material, WIP, and finished goods inventory	This area includes inventory reserves taken due to obsolescence and scrap
	Obsolescence inventory + scrap inventory
Channel obsolescence costs	This area includes aging allowances paid to channel partners and provisions for buy-back agreements.
	All costs related to channel obsolescence
Field service parts obsolescence	This area includes field service parts reserves taken due to obsolescence and scrap.
	Obsolescence inventory + scrap inventory
Supply chain finance and planning costs(4)	These costs include all those associated with taking possession of material.
	Costs associated with supply chain finance and planning
	Supply chain finance costs + demand, supply planning costs
Supply chain finance costs	This area includes costs associated with paying invoices, auditing physical counts, performing inventory accounting, and collecting accounts receivable (does not include customer invoicing/accounting costs)
	Paying invoices costs + auditing physical counts costs + performing inventory accounting costs + collecting accounts receivable costs
Demand, supply planning costs	This area includes costs associated with forecasting, developing finished goods or end item inventory plans, and coordinating the demand/supply process across entire supply chain, including all channels (not including miscellaneous associated costs).
	Forecasting costs + developing finished goods or end item inventory plans costs + costs for coordinating demand, supply process

FIGURE 3.25 (*Continued*)

CAUSE	EFFECT
Supply Chain Planning	
Reduce late orders	Improve customer service
Improve customer retention and loyalty	Increase revenue
Optimize capital equipment and asset utilization	Manage fixed assets
Reduce administration, improve business processes	Reduce operating costs
Lower logistics costs	
Supply Chain Design	
Reduce late orders	Improve customer service
Improve customer retention and loyalty	Increase revenue
Optimize capital equipment and asset utilization	Manage fixed assets
Reduce administration, improve business processes	Reduce operating costs
Lower logistics costs	
Demand Planning	
Improve forecast accuracy	Improve customer service
Reduce order lead-time	
Collaborate with business partners	
Efficient promotion planning and trade spending	Lower working capital
Improve capacity utilization	
Reduce inventory levels	Reduce operating costs
Supply Planning	
Improve forecast accuracy	Improve customer service
Visibility to vendor/supplier inventory	Lower working capital
Reduce inventory levels	Reduce operating costs
Lower logistics costs	
Distribution Planning	
Reduce late orders	Improve customer service
Improve order fill rate	Increase revenue
Optimize capital equipment and asset utilization	Manage fixed assets
Improve inventory visibility	Reduce operating costs
Production Planning	
Improve product/service quality	Improve customer service
Improve forecast accuracy	
Lower work-in-process inventory	Lower working capital
Reduce material and component obsolescence	
Shorten order-to-cash cycle	
Reduce inventory levels	Reduce operating costs
Transportation Planning	
Reduce late orders	Improve customer service
Better service levels	
Improve order fill rate	Increase revenue
Improve capacity utilization	Lower working capital
Lower logistics costs	Reduce operating costs
SUPPLY CHAIN EXECUTION	
Materials Management	
Reduce material and component obsolescence	Lower working capital
Lower cost procured goods and services	
Reduce inventory levels	Reduce operating costs

FIGURE 3.26 Benefits—Causes and Effects

Improve procurement processes	
Improve inventory visibility	
Manufacturing	
Improve forecast accuracy	Improve customer service
Improve order fill rate	Increase revenue
Reduce inventory carrying costs	Lower working capital
Improve capacity utilization	
Order Promising and Delivery	
Reduce late orders	Improve customer service
Better service levels	
Improve order fill rate	Increase revenue
Reduce order processing costs	Reduce operating costs
Improve inventory visibility	
Transportation Execution	
Reduce late orders	Improve customer service
Better service levels	
Optimize capital equipment and asset utilization	Manage fixed assets
Lower logistics costs	Reduce operating costs
Foreign Trade/Legal Services	
Better service levels	Improve customer service
Reduce transaction costs	Reduce operating costs
Reduce administration, improve business processes	
SUPPLY CHAIN COORDINATION	
Supply Chain Event Management	
Better service levels	Improve customer service
Improve customer retention and loyalty	Increase revenue
Gain market share	
Reduce time-to-market and volume	
Improve return-on-investment (ROI) of fixed assets	Manage fixed assets
Supply Chain Performance Management	
Better service levels	Improve customer service
Collaborate with business partners	
Improve customer retention and loyalty	Increase revenue
Shorten order-to-cash cycle	Lower working capital
Fulfillment Coordination	
Collaborate with business partners	Improve customer service
Improve order fill rate	Increase revenue
Reduce time to market and volume	
Visibility to vendor/supplier inventory	Lower working capital
Reduce administration, improve business processes	Reduce operating costs
SUPPLY CHAIN COLLABORATION	
Supply Chain Portal	
Collaborate with business partners	Improve customer service
Personalized customer interaction	
Visibility to vendor/supplier inventory	Lower working capital
Reduce administration, improve business processes	Reduce operating costs
Improve inventory visibility	

FIGURE 3.26 (*Continued*)

Collaboration Processes	
Collaborate with business partners	Improve customer service
Improve order fill rate	Increase revenue
Reduce time to market and volume	
Visibility to vendor/supplier inventory	Lower working capital
Reduce administration, improve business processes	Reduce operating costs
Supply Chain Integration	
Collaborate with business partners	Improve customer service
Improve return on investment of fixed assets	Manage fixed assets
Reduce administration, improve business processes	Reduce operating costs

FIGURE 3.26 (*Continued*)

Case Example

This chapter described key performance indicators and their relationships with the organization's independent and dependent variables. Independent variables were described as the action items that would impact related dependent variables. This relationship was graphically illustrated by the value chains. Since value chains may be difficult to understand, Figure 3.26 was provided to show the causes (independent variables or action variables) and effects (dependent variables or benefits). I used the steps described in the text: I considered what action variables I wanted to modulate to achieve my hoped-for result (benefit) and what technology would act as an enabler.

This case study illustrates how I used the value chain principle in practice. I was hired by the Tech Center of Company A, which was among the top Fortune 100 companies. My base was the Tech Center, and I was expected to impact its core manufacturing technology with the novel computer-integrated manufacturing (CIM) technologies. On my first day, the boss wanted me to visit the head of the Systems Division and offer my assistance. He and the top boss asked me, "Sam, how soon can you build a CIM showcase so that all of our worldwide divisions, which have spent more than $56 million studying how to do it rather than doing it, can stop tinkering with methodologies and get on with it?" In the course of these conversations, I soon had gotten two promises from them: They would let me build a new business if circumstances warranted it, and they would let me cherry-pick the components of CIM technologies. Cherry-picking would save me substantial amounts of time. Establishing a new business was important.

(*Continued*)

(Continued)

All the existing businesses of this manufacturing behemoth had established legacy systems and practices that would fight change and establish barriers that would consume my time. After achieving these two concessions, I was looking forward to finishing a proof-of-concept demonstration in one to two years.

I also attended Company A's new business meetings. Early in my tenure there, I attended a meeting with four entrepreneurs from California. Their business plan was for a new business to manufacture multilayer cofired ceramic packages that were used as chip carriers. Intel and others were the end users. Eventually I was asked why I was at the meeting and what I could do. I replied that I could CIM the factory so that the manufacturing cost would be 50% less than what it would be without the new technologies. They asked how. I quickly showed them the CIM architecture (Figure 3A), which I had been developing for several months.

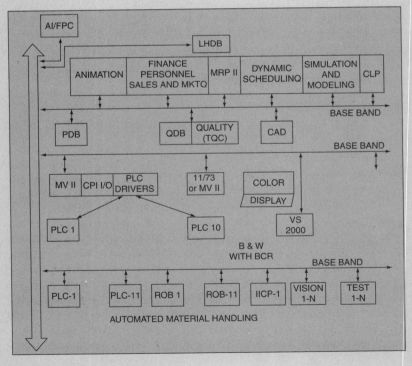

FIGURE 3A CIM Architecture

This generic architecture must be tailored to the business to which it is applied. Then each technology has to be customized to suit the practice of the subject business. When I walked the entrepreneurs through the components of my technology, I showed them specifically the:

- **Functionality.** What it would do.
- **Benefits** (key performance indicators [KPIs]). What it would achieve. These were just ballpark figures because I did not have as-is conditions with me, so to-be could not be firmed up until later.
- **Actions** (KPIs). What and how you have to use it to achieve the benefits.

Their response was a resounding yes to my technology. They said that they had known that it was achievable but did not know how to accomplish it.

The rest is history. I went to my bosses, and we bought into the Californians' business plan. When the return on investment debates were taking place, the healthy contribution from CIM technologies whetted Company's appetite so much that instead of investing the $37 million the Californians had asked for, we invested orders of magnitude more. Betting was on the great performance results we were expecting.

This case study would be perfect if I was writing it for a full-service enterprise software, because Supply Chain Management concentrates only on plan, source, make, and distribute aspects of an enterprise. In my architecture, we have an additional emphasis on make (manufacturing) and CAD (PLM).

I formed the interdivisional team and moved them to California, far away from the daily pressures of their home organizations on the East Coast. We started work at a rented location. Way before the factory was built, I had all the equipment delivered without a purchase order. This was possible because DEC, our principal vendor, had full faith in me and the company that it would not suffer any financial loss.

As I began to lay down the planning for customizing my concepts to fit the new business, I met with our new partners. I extracted all the practice parameters by asking what the parameters were at the last place they worked. This helped us to create the as-is models. Then came the issues of soft practices: the workflow models and related practices. They reminded me that *I* was authorized to pick the technology that would produce 50% less cost to manufacture. So I could create the soft practices that the chosen technology required. That confirmation was

(Continued)

(Continued)

great for my team. By now I had hired the external consultants who would develop the workflow policies and procedures for the entire suite of ERP and SCM systems.

To get ready for the first demonstration, we needed a forecast to feed into MRP. The only thing we got from the entrepreneurs was the monthly forecast from the director of marketing. The rest of the numbers were driven from it and the practices and constraints of the business and equipment.

We finished the CIM showcase at the end of one year, and we cut the company's first purchase order using my CIM systems after one and half years of the team moving to California. Thus the SCM journey for this company began from the scratch. The approach to building this technology base was Big Bang: Plan at once and implement all technologies in parallel. It was based on the principles of knowing the action variables (KPIs), benefit variables (KPIs), and functionality of technologies that act as the enablers.

Chapters 5, 6, and 7 detail the stepwise usage of the principles described in the case study along with further case examples regarding how a functional architecture can be developed driven by the value drivers and benefits achieved with key performance indicators.

Bibliography

Bansal, Sam. "Supply Chain Management," Speech presented at the SAP Sales Boot Camp, Singapore, August 1999.

Bansal, Sam. "Technologies for Extended Supply Chains," Speech presented at the Eye for SCM, Singapore, January 2000.

Bansal, Sam. "SAP Solutions in Manufacturing," Speech presented at the Rockwell conference, Singapore, March 2000.

Bansal, Sam. "SAP Solutions in High-Tech Manufacturing," Speech presented at Summit Malaysia, Kuala Lumpur, Malaysia, April 2000.

Bansal, Sam. "Experiences in Automotive Supply Chain Optimization," Paper presented at the Eye for Auto conference, Singapore, February 2001.

Bansal, Sam. "KPIs of the Supply Chain Domain of Auto Sector," Paper presented at the Industry Workshop at the Eye for Auto conference, Singapore, February 2001.

Bansal, Sam. "Performance Improvement via Outsourcing," Keynote speech at the Global IT/Software Outsourcing conference, Atlanta, Georgia, March 2002.

Bansal, Sam. "Trends and Methodologies in Business Consulting: KPI-Based Performance Improvement," Paper presented at the International Federation of Automatic Controls, Barcelona, Spain, July 2002.

Bansal, Sam. "Experiences in Problems and Solutions of Supply Chain Systems," Paper presented at the Winter Simulation Conference, San Diego, Winter 2002.

Bansal, Sam. "Theory and Practice of Advanced Planner and Optimizer," Paper presented at the Winter Simulation Conference, New Orleans, Winter 2003.

Shapiro, Jeremy F. *Modeling the Supply Chain.* Pacific Grove, CA: Duxbury Press, 2001.

CHAPTER 4

Product Life Cycle Management

Introduction

Product Life Cycle Management (PLM) is said to be an imperative for innovation, a new business strategy, a new gizmo for being competitive. It has been heralded as the single tool that will reduce time to market, improve both the top and the bottom lines, changing the silo culture of an organization to a unified life cycle data management system. Whatever the claims of the proponents—sellers or champions of this technology—the truth is, even I believe in these claims, as I demonstrate later. When I was involved in launching and supporting SAP's Supply Chain Management (SCM) technology in the Asia Pacific region, I often used to wonder about the impact of SCM on an organization. However, PLM would be the single tool that would transform and take off from where computer-integrated manufacturing (CIM) had left the industrial scene. To support this cryptic message, let us review the chain of progress: First, a long time ago, there was computer aided design (CAD), and then came computer aided manufacturing (CAM), followed by CIM, then concurrent engineering (CE), and, finally, PLM began to emerge. Functionality began to increase and so did the benefits. While vendors have been plentiful, market researchers believe that eventually, three top-tier vendors will be the only healthy survivors.

Theoretically speaking, even in the mid-1980s the need was felt to have a single database that would contain all the design, process, and quality data of component lots and, eventually, that of a product lot. Then came the need to have a single database that could create, capture, validate, populate, and manage the data throughout the different stages in the product's life. If this could be done, why not integrate it with project/program management tasks and then provide tools for analysis, reporting, and decision making? Then, if this was possible in real time and in collaboration with partners, would it not expedite time to market? These thoughts led to the creation of today's PLM. If this tool could change the culture from multiple databases to a single repository of the entire enterprise's data, it would eliminate the silo culture, a huge impediment to cost, discovery, and time to market. While building the new semiconductor fabrications, chief financial officers often encountered the problem of how to capture the life cycle of the assets, starting when they had only a hole in the ground. Likewise, Department of Defense personnel wanted to track a program that eventually would become a physical something: a plane, a missile, or a ship. Answers to all these challenges can be found in the PLM suite of tools and technologies.

This chapter is based on the Author's practice at SAP and other clients and employers and SAP Solution Maps. Hence there are heavy references of SAP PLM functionality. All products are SAP's and where applicable the trademarks of SAP are owned by them all over the world.

This chapter covers PLM architecture, its fundamental building blocks, detailed component descriptions, key performance indicators, the five-day cycle with PLM scenario, mapping of design to release tasks with various PLM component technologies, a summary of how to establish a business case, and significant issues of PLM implementation if undertaken as an innovation or performance improvement initiative. Champions and business case development are discussed later in this book. However, conceptual thoughts on these two areas also are discussed here.

Architecture of a PLM System

As Figure 4.1 shows, the PLM system manages the product design and change process. It encompasses the life cycle of a product from design to manufacturing, service, and even obsolescence planning. Because it is centered around data, its chief function is to capture and manage the data for the entire life cycle of a product. But because all the data are in a single repository, more and more tools and analytics can be added. Since visualization and simulation can expedite time to market, they—as well as Web-enabled networking and collaborative tools—can be added to the PLM suite of functionality.

Figure 4.2 presents the fundamental components of an effective PLM system: product and process design, change and configuration management, preventive and predictive management, program and project management, Web-based life cycle collaboration and analytics, quality management, environment health and safety, and authoring tools and visualization and simulation. The diagram shows how they fit in with each other.

Detailed Component Descriptions

This section gives the details of a good product life cycle management system.

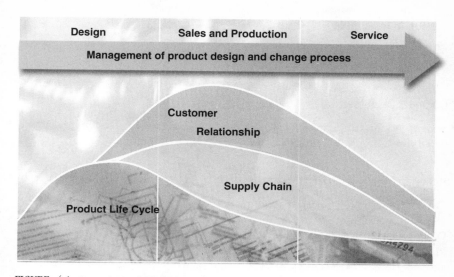

FIGURE 4.1 Overview of PLM System
Source: © Copyright (2009). SAP AG. All rights reserved.

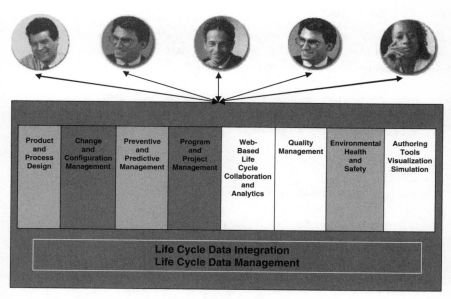

FIGURE 4.2 Fundamental Components of a PLM System
Source: © Copyright (2009). SAP AG. All rights reserved.

Version Management

Automatic or manual document versions are used to represent different change or delivery statuses of a document.

Document Vaulting

Secure storage and retrieval of documents is available. Document search capabilities are based on metadata and content of documents.

Integrated Viewing

The integrated viewer can display most two-dimensional (2D) pixel, vector, and some text formats, as well as three-dimensional (3D) model formats. Digital mockup viewing enables the display of the new or changed product in the development phase, as a graphical 3D model. Redlining functions support digital processing and the change process for original files. Remarks can be made on the original files available to all partners of the business process.

Document Distribution

Document distribution includes automatic or manual routing and transmission of documents to internal and external partners and transfer of documents to caching servers or external systems.

Status Management

The processing cycle of a document can be presented in a status network.

Document Conversion

Automatic or manual conversion of a CAD drawing into a read-only 2D or 3D viewing format is available.

Integration

Integration tools include:

- **CAD Integration.** Additional integrations are available via the complementary software program. CAD integration enables the designers to access data in the production system and use this information in their CAD applications. Alternatively, designers can create data in the production system directly from CAD data. Since data can be transferred between the CAD system and the SAP system in both directions, inconsistency of the data in the two systems is avoided. CATIA V4, Pro/ENGINEER, AutoCAD, Solid Works, Solid Edge, IDEAS, Inventor, and Unigraphics are supported by CAD integration.

- **Office Integration.** In document management, you can use document templates and save user-defined application toolbars, macros, key combinations, formatting, and AutoText entries for Microsoft Word documents. For Microsoft Excel documents, you can use add-in programs that enhance the Microsoft Office application by means of user-defined commands and special functions.

- **PDM Integration.** Open interfaces are available to exchange product data with third-party product data management (PDM) applications. For a list of certified PDM interfaces, see the complementary software program.

- **GIS Integration.** This interface enables linking of a geographical information system (GIS), and the document management system to an R/3 object, such as a functional location object in asset life cycle management, for the purpose of locating the asset.

- **SCADA Integration.** A supervisory control and data acquisition system (SCADA) recognizes events that have been predefined in asset life cycle management. This type of interface passes filtered data to a document that is linked to an asset.

- **DMF Integration.** The integrated digital manufacturing (DMF) system is intended to enhance collaboration and sharing of information across product design, production planning, engineering, and execution. Engineers are enabled to work concurrently on the product definition, design, and manufacturing process planning, reducing the total planning cycle and speeding ramp-up to production.

- **Data Replication.** Data replication allows you to distribute a product from a central PLM system to operational PLM systems. The product data are collected in consistent data packages and then transferred to target systems using Application Link Enabler (ALE) or internet protocols XML/HTTP technology. It incorporates replication of products instead of single objects, clustering of all relevant data in consistent packages, initial load of a product into a new system, periodic update of operational systems with new product versions, simultaneous distribution to multiple target systems, and notification of interested persons.

- **Integration with CRM.** Knowledge bases defined with variant configuration can be exported to the sales configuration engine of customer relation management (CRM Mobile Sales). Knowledge bases contain all information about the classes, characteristics, characteristic values, and dependencies belonging to a configurable product.

- **Integration with SCM.** Routings, product structures, and recipe data can be released to production and supply chain planning. Integrated engineering change management and order change management ensure a closed-loop process to introduce and plan product or sales order changes in production orders. Configurable products, including structures based on the Integrated Product and Process Engineering (IPPE) model, can either be passed directly to the advanced planner and optimizer to support repetitive manufacturing processes or converted into bill-of-material (BOM) structures.

- **Easy DMS Interface.** Easy document management system (DMS) Interface displays the hierarchical structure of files and folders in a document management system. With the Easy DMS Interface, you can, for example, manage personal and group document structures and documents, check in documents from Microsoft Explorer using Drag and Drop, check documents in and out directly from Microsoft Office applications, search for documents and add them to a work list, maintain classification data, and create object links.

- **Integration with SRM.** The integration with SRM (sourcing relations management) enables engineers and purchasers to create a bid invitation within SRM and to link it to collaboration within PLM folders in order to support the collaboration processes in engineered goods sourcing scenarios. This integration helps companies better to optimize product costs at the early design stage by bringing engineering and sourcing closely together, thereby increasing process efficiency and a shorter time to market through better communication between engineering and purchasing teams.

- **Primavera Integration.** PLM Asset Life Cycle Management offers an interface to Primavera P3 software to support customers using Primavera for their project-oriented maintenance (POM) procedures to plan production outage events. POM supports these key processes: work identification and selection, planning/budgeting optimization/simulation, and execution and support for unplanned work.

Product and Process Design

Product and process design elements are discussed next.

- **Product Structure Management.** This element offers a range of structures (e.g., feature and requirement structure, functional structure, and product structure) to optimize engineering processes right from the very start of product development. The basis of this application is IPPE.

- **Material Management.** This element manages the master data for all materials that a company procures, produces, stores, or sells.
- **BOM Management.** In the bill of material, you manage all the assemblies and components of the product and their technical data. By defining separate BOMs for the different areas within the company, such as engineering or production, each area has its own view of the product with the specific data it requires.
- **Routing Management.** In a routing, you plan the operations (work steps) to be carried out during production, the activities to be used in the operations as a basis for determining dates, capacity requirements and costs, the use of materials during production, the use of work centers, and the quality checks to be carried out during production.
- **Variant Configuration.** With the Variant Configurator, you can describe and easily manage all the possible variants of a product. In the ordering process, the customer is able to configure a product to exactly match his or her requirements.
- **Document Structure Management.** Document structures can be used to maintain complex sets of documents with or without engineering change, control, and revision.
- **Classification System.** The Classification System allows you to use characteristics (e.g., color or size) to describe all types of objects (e.g., materials, documents, or equipment) and to group similar objects in classes. Using the characteristics as search criteria ensures that you can find objects with similar or identical characteristics as quickly as possible.
- **Product Formulation and Recipe Development.** The recipe management system supports the development of product definitions, the product formulation process, and the creation of recipes for manufacturing products. The developer can drive product development forward using structured product and raw material specifications in the form of non–machine-specific and cross-plant formulas and recipes, independent of existing material masters. Functions for determining product properties can calculate the properties of products from the properties of raw materials (e.g., compositions, nutritional values, and product prices). Detailed search functions allow you to find previous definitions and approaches so that you can build on these results by making sure that failed attempts are not repeated. In this way you can reduce costs and development time and speed up the development process. Functions such as workflow, project management, status management, and change management also help to control and monitor product development processes.
- **Basic Data and Tools.** The joint implementation of specification management, reporting, and the functions of the information system for

both Recipe Management and Environmental Health and Safety (EH&S) means that information can be closely linked together. In this way, you guarantee that product development information provides an up-to-date and consistent base for subsequently determining product safety and dangerous goods classifications. It also informs responsible departments early on about product changes that must be dealt with, which can then be included in the change process.

- **Multilevel Recipe Management/Scale-Up.** As a rule, the development of new products takes place on an enterprise-wide basis and is then adjusted, for example, according to country-specific conditions and legal requirements and in the next stage, realized at machine level. The multilevel functions of Recipe Management support this process. Enterprise-wide general recipes, area-specific site recipes, and machine-related master recipes are available. Functions support the transition processes and enable you to easily recognize and manage the relationships between them. This allows production to be linked to the conversion of laboratory standards to production standards early on, thus speeding up the conversion and, with it, the time to market.
- **Trial Management.** Trial Management brings together the different functions of PLM in a workbench. You can use the workbench to initiate and manage the steps involved in product definition and development as well as the creation of samples and their quality inspections.

Change and Configuration Management

Elements of change and configuration management are presented next.

- **Change Management/Claim Management.** A claim is a notification type that is used to trigger a corrective action.
- **Engineering Change Management.** Engineering Change Management can be used to change various aspects of production master data (e.g., BOMs, task lists, materials, documents, and some early engineering objects) with history (with date validity) or depending on specific conditions (with parameter affectivity). Changes take effect under precisely defined conditions (precise date or specific effectivity parameter value). The changed object is saved twice: in its state before and after the changes. A change master record or Engineering Change Request/Engineering Change Order (ECR/ECO) controls and documents the changes. Materials and documents can be assigned a revision level as well.
- **Order Change Management.** Order Change Management (Change Management for production orders) identifies existing procurement

elements (production orders, planned orders, or purchase orders) that are affected by either an engineering change or a change to a sales order for a configurable product.

- **Configuration Management.** With Configuration Management, you identify the objects that describe a product in a particular life cycle phase and collect them in a configuration folder. With different configuration folders in various life cycle phases, you manage the configuration of products and projects across those different phases.

Asset Life Cycle Management

Asset Life Cycle Management tracks assets for the entire life cycle, until they are retired. It is the most important feature for situations such as when a new fabrication plant is being built or the Department of Defense is funding a new war plane.

Technical Asset Management

Technical asset management elements include:

- **Structuring Technical Assessment.** Asset Life Cycle Management offers a far-reaching structuring solution for the technical objects in a company. The display of objects can be object-based, function-based, structured by type or individual object, single level or multilevel.
- **Serial Number Management.** When you have many similar objects in your company that you want to maintain and manage as stock items, you can label them as individual items using serial numbers. Serial number management allows you to integrate individualized material with maintenance processes.
- **Change Management.** Asset Life Cycle Management allows changes to complex technical asset structures. Change documents and application log files allow you to keep track of any changes made to technical assets and operative instruments, such as maintenance plans and orders.
- **BOM Management.** In Asset Life Cycle Management, BOMs are predominantly used for spare parts management.
- **Document Management.** Asset Life Cycle Management is perfectly integrated with the Document Management System, allowing you to view all important documents related to a technical object or operation in the order.

- **Approvals.** You can tailor maintenance execution processes (e.g., notification handling) to needs and add further control mechanisms to processes by making them subject to approval (e.g., cost approvals).
- **Warranty Management.** Control maintenance costs with the help of Warranty Management.
- **Management of Production Resource Tools.** Users can plan precisely and ensure accurate order processing by assigning production resource tools to specific maintenance operations.
- **Counter and Measurement Readings.** You can apply performance and condition-based maintenance by using counter and measurement readings.
- **Interfacing Industry-Specific Systems.** From engineering and design in a CAD system, you can branch directly to the maintenance of master data in Asset Life Cycle Management, where you can display the engineering and design documentation. You can link a geographical information system (GIS) that offers information about the geographical position of objects and create malfunction reports. Furthermore, you can transfer data from process control systems or SCADA, which describe the condition or use of an object, directly to Asset Life Cycle Management.
- **Connecting Commercial and Technical Assets.** An open interface to asset accounting enables you to settle activities that must be capitalized directly to relevant assets and also create new assets under construction. You can also display both the financial and the maintenance-specific views of assets.
- **Fleet-Management.** This solution helps to keep the fleet running at peak efficiency. It supports users in resource planning for vehicles and employees, procurement, refueling, and maintenance.
- **IT Asset Management.** Asset Life Cycle Management offers a solution with which you can manage the complete life cycle of an asset. It applies not only to maintenance-intensive production assets but also to movable assets, such as information technology equipment.

Preventive and Predictive Maintenance

Every vertical needs preventive and predictive maintenance (PPM) capabilities, whether they are fabrication plants, oil refineries, or textile plants. PPM components are discussed next.

- **Time- and/or Performance-Based Preventive Maintenance.** This solution provides an automatic determination for preventive maintenance work. By scheduling maintenance plans, Asset Life Cycle

Management automatically generates orders and notifications for the work due.

- **Condition-Based Maintenance (SCADA Integration).** Optimal asset condition is vital for a trouble-free production process. When interfacing a process control system SCADA, critical data are monitored and, if required, immediately transferred to PLM Asset Life Cycle Management so that appropriate measures can be taken in time.
- **Condition-Based Maintenance (Calibration Inspection).** Calibration Inspection is a systematic examination used to determine whether a piece of equipment meets previously specified requirements. If not, appropriate steps can be taken immediately.
- **Task Lists for Maintenance Planning.** To avoid redundancy and save time and effort, you can define work that consists of a series of standardized steps in a task list. Then you can include the task list in the maintenance plans whenever required. You can define time and resources, such as work groups, utilities, or materials required to execute the work in the task list.

Maintenance Execution

The next tools support the execution of maintenance work orders.

- **Notification-Based Problem Handling.** For malfunction-based maintenance, Notification-Based Problem Handling is an efficient way to document problems and streamline follow-up measures. You can use the notification for dispatching problems straight to the responsible contact person or for solving them by yourself, based on information provided by the solution database. Notification-Based Problem Handling also includes employee self-service tools, such as the Internet Service Request (ISR).
- **Notification and Order Processing.** Asset Life Cycle Management ensures an effective maintenance process, from the reporting of a malfunction and release of a rush order to the correction of the problem and the completion of the order.
- **Mobile Asset Management.** Mobile Asset Management comprises a broad range of business applications to be processed online or offline on a mobile device (e.g., recording counter readings, processing notifications and orders).
- **Web-Based Processing.** Asset Life Cycle Management offers versatile solutions for Web-based maintenance execution, from notification processing to online recording of counter and measurement readings.
- **Printing Shop Papers.** Shop papers carry key information for maintenance execution. Asset Life Cycle Management allows the printing of

orders with all relevant documents, such as drawings, maintenance task lists, and material withdrawal slips.

- **Catalog Management.** Catalog Management helps you enter structured information (e.g., damage codes, cause codes, etc.) in completing maintenance orders or notifications. This makes confirmations easy and enables you to run systematic evaluations on the asset condition.

- **Capacity and Requirements Planning.** Capacity and Requirements Planning is crucial for successful order planning. Capacity data are derived from the responsible maintenance work center. Requirements planning is used to specify the estimated time needed to complete operations for a maintenance order.

- **Spare Parts Management.** Spare Parts Management integrates with materials management, including identification of stock/nonstock material, material availability checks, and procurement processes. Asset Life Cycle Management offers options for spare parts handling, including BOM management and a hit list of materials where they are used in the order.

- **Catalog Integration and E-Procurement of Maintenance, Repair and Overhaul (MRO) Parts.** E-procurement of MRO parts offers a selection of the correct spare parts. It reduces time, cost, and administrative effort for ordering. It allows e-procurement of parts and services, helps shorten the complete replacement process, and saves additional costs by allowing quality comparisons.

- **Scheduling.** Scheduling allows you to streamline maintenance planning and processing. In maintenance planning, you set a start date for the order, and all operations are scheduled accordingly to obtain optimum processing performance.

- **Management of Internal and External Resources.** Asset Life Cycle Management allows you to integrate external parties in the maintenance process. Either you include external parties for processing certain operations or you put external service providers in charge of complete maintenance processes.

- **Workflow Management.** The Business Workflow system can be used to automate and streamline internal communication processes in maintenance, for example, in notification processing.

- **Maintenance Budgeting.** To keep maintenance costs at bay, you must monitor them precisely. You can use the cost estimate in the order as a control mechanism and receive a warning when costs reach or exceed the budgeted limit.

- **Project-Oriented Maintenance/Revisions.** A shutdown or turnaround is always a critical production outage event that has to be planned thoroughly. Asset Life Cycle Management helps you achieve a safe shutdown process in the shortest possible time at minimum cost.

Work Clearance Management

Work clearance management elements include:

- **Work Clearance Management Objects.** These objects are used to control and monitor safety measures. Work approval, application, and work clearance documents are available.
- **Work Approvals.** Work approvals are key to ensuring safe working conditions. Work Clearance Management controls and regulates critical processes with clever approvals of management.
- **Lockout/Tag Out.** In Lockout/Tag Out, technical objects are isolated electrically or separated mechanically from other parts of the technical system. Afterward it is safe to perform maintenance work or tests. The operational processing of Lockout/Tag Out is described, using the operational cycle. You can use checks and simulations to ensure that lockout/tag out can be processed safely and free of conflict.
- **Integration with Maintenance Order Processing.** Aspects of safety in the workplace must be considered when executing maintenance work in order to ensure a safe working environment. These safety measures can include issuing permits for radiation protection, fire protection, or lockout/tag out.
- **Work Clearance Document Library.** This library covers the complete logic on how lockout/tag out processes for security-relevant areas or objects have to be handled.

Program and Project Management

Program and Project Management is of the most important features of today's PLMs.

Project Planning
- **Project Structure.** In order to carry out a project in its entirety, project goals must be precisely described and the project activities to be carried out must be structured. The central structures in PLM Program and Project Management are work breakdown structures (WBS) and networks, with their attendant activities and milestones.
- **Project Builder and Project Planning Board.** The Project Builder is the central tool used for setting up and monitoring projects. It integrates all the application-specific functions that are required in a user-friendly working environment. The Project Planning Board is a graphical tool that simplifies project planning, combining tabular and graphical data to provide a global overview.

- **Resource Planning/Work Force Planning.** Resource Planning and Workforce Planning help plan the resources required for the work that is carried out internally in a project. It includes defining a project team by assigning a project organization, capacity planning for activities via work centers, and planning the workforce on an individual level.
- **Documents.** Project management is fully integrated into the document management system of PLM Life Cycle Data Management. Assigning documents is supported by all DMS functions (i.e., versioning and vaulting). You can view the originals of assigned document masters and maintain them directly in the Project Builder. You can search for project documents using various search engines and publish them for external access on the Internet.
- **Costs.** Costs can be planned using Easy Cost Planning, a configurable HTML-based user interface in an end user–focused, easy-to-use environment. Making use of network calculation of internal and external work, services and procurement planned in activities are automatically calculated. Other planning possibilities include costing using assigned orders and structural cost planning.
- **Revenues.** The billing plan is either automatically updated by the sales order or planned manually in the project. It includes dates on which payment requests or invoices affecting sales are sent to customers. Dates and milestone progress can be used to trigger the billing procedure. You can also benefit from resource-related sales pricing/billing.
- **Budget.** The budget differs from project cost planning in its binding nature. Budget availability controls all expenditures during the execution phase. Additionally, the original budget can be broken down into smaller packages of released budget to allow an even more accurate availability control. All budgets can be planned by year or as overall values.
- **Scheduling Functions.** Scheduling is carried out forward and backward according to the relationships between activities. Constraints are taken into account, earliest and latest dates are calculated, and floats are determined. Based on this, you can analyze the critical path within the network. In addition, actual and forecast dates influence the schedule during execution.

Project Execution

- **Confirmation.** Using confirmation, you can confirm actual time and costs for the project. Computer Aided Time Sheets (CATS) offers an ergonomic time entry interface and allows you to confirm time for many objects, including Work Breakdown Structures, elements, and activities.

The times entered become the actual times and costs for the project. Full change and cancellation handling are also provided.

- **Project-Oriented Procurement/Production.** Using the assignment of material components to network activities, you can determine the assemblies and raw materials that must be reserved or ordered for a project and trigger procurement using MRP or purchasing. Bills of material can be assigned using the bill of material (BOM) in project structures (PS) interface.

- **Claims Management.** Claims Management processes any project-relevant information, such as variances or claims from third parties. In order to trigger the process, the persons responsible are identified and informed via workflow. Necessary activities can be planned and tracked together with the claim status. By using the claim information system, you can track the progress of claims.

- **Payments.** During execution, payment of relevant postings—through integration of other solutions—feeds project cash management and provides the most accurate information possible on incoming and outgoing payments. Payment information can be used to run various analyses as well as interest calculations.

- **Project Progress.** Progress analysis/earned value analysis is the tool to determine planned and actual project progress values. It obtains information on the state of projects and how they are developing. Another tool, milestone trend analysis, displays the dates of the relevant milestones in a project at different report dates, both in graphical and tabular form. Progress tracking/expediting allows you to monitor the progress of projects based on events.

- **Progress Tracking.** Progress Tracking enables you to closely monitor the progress of network components in the Project System and purchase orders in materials management. By tracking events that you have defined in Customizing for Progress Tracking or in the Progress Tracking function itself, you gain improved control over the progress of network components or purchase orders.

- **ProMan.** ProMan consolidates procurement process information from a variety of applications in a structured and individual overview, which can be configured by the user. Data can be accessed from the Project System, purchasing, material requirements planning, production, and inventory management. All objects and documents in the Project System are taken into account: both planned and unplanned objects, and documents created manually.

- **Project Information System.** The Project Information System is a flexible, comprehensive information system that can be used to monitor and control project data. It can be used to evaluate individual, partial, or multiple projects. The system includes overview reports and reports offering various degrees of detail. The system is designed to meet the needs of both project management and project personnel. Predefined structures should be available to link with the data warehouse system.

Interfaces

- **Open Project System.** Open Project System (Open PS) is a suite for modern communication between the Project System and other project management systems and personal organizers. In the first stage of this development, you are able to exchange data with Microsoft Project® and Palm Pilot®.
- **Collaborative Project Management (CPM).** CPM enables the realization of innovative ideas in development projects, simplifies internal processes, and supports methodologies such as QS9000 and Stage Gate. In CPM, object links are used to link existing project management objects to project elements. Using object links, it is possible to display the data of project management objects (e.g., costs, budget, dates, WBS element master data, activities) in the CPM application as well as include these data in CPM evaluations.
- **Balanced Scorecard.** When it comes to strategic management, instruments like the Balanced Scorecard (a tool within Strategic Enterprise Management) often are used to visualize the situation of a company. With the integration of project enterprise data with the balanced scorecard, you can create projects or WBS elements directly in the Balanced Scorecard and link them to strategic initiatives set up to change the company's situation. Dates as well as financial key figures can be monitored directly within the Balanced Scorecard.

Program Management

- **Portfolio Management.** Making decisions about the current product portfolio is the key to ensuring the future success of a company. One instrument for comparing products and deriving strategic decisions is Portfolio Analysis. By displaying products three-dimensionally (x and y axis + size of bubble), you can quickly grasp the situation at hand. Popular dimensions for Portfolio Analysis are, for example, market growth, market share, sales volume or technology attractiveness, economic success probability, and sales volume.
- **Evaluating Strategic Product Developments.** Strategic program management provides a comprehensive planning scenario that allows you to evaluate existing product portfolio and make crucial decisions, regarding, for example, whether to discontinue a product, implement a new product, or intensify production.
- **Scenario Simulation.** When decision-relevant factors from outside the company (market, prices, etc.) or inside the company (costs, capacities,

etc.) change, the products mix may have to be rearranged (e.g., intensified or removed). To react quickly to these trends, managers need the information available at any given time and any place.

- **Life Cycle Planning.** Life cycle cost and revenue planning allows for planning the product life cycle in a series of steps that can also be integrated into existing planning applications. The planning scenario is built within Strategic Enterprise Management.
- **Life Cycle Costing Actuals.** Point of sales data (profitability analysis as the main source of data) delivers product-specific sales and costing data. These data are combined with data from product-specific investment (assets) and development (projects). Reporting can take place in Data Warehouse. The resulting report shows the product cash flow and contains all necessary data to depict the complete product life cycle.

Life Cycle Collaboration and Analytics

This section outlines the elements of life cycle collaboration and analytics.

Design Collaboration

- **Hierarchical Structuring.** You can collect and structure product and project information in a logical collaboration-based framework. You also can organize and locate information quickly and easily with the ability to create folders in any desired hierarchical sequence.
- **Document Versions.** A wide variety of objects/documents can be assigned to any folder, including Office documents or CAD drawings. The version control mechanism ensures that all collaboration partners can track the change history of a document.
- **Back-End Integration.** Documents, materials, and BOMs can be exchanged between Collaboration Folders (cFolders) and the back-end system. External users can maintain or create material BOMs. For this, only a browser is required.
- **Notification.** The Notification function can be used to warn of any changes that may be made to documents or subfolders within collaboration. Additionally, other team members can be actively notified of any tasks they have to work on, either by e-mail or by notifications within cFolders.
- **Meetings/WebEx Integration.** When sharing information synchronously is relevant, PLM offers the integration of WebEx Inc's real time communications platform to help customers work on collaboration projects in real time over the Web. Users can access the meeting functions from the cFolder interface and organize or track these meetings within their cFolder meeting inbox.

- **Redlining/Markup.** The integrated ECL viewing capabilities allow the markup/redlining of 2D and 3D drawings.
- **Datasheet Handling.** Specifications often require that quantifiable characteristics related to products are provided. Data sheets simplify this process by allowing the import classification system to structure the characteristic values you want to provide in a bidding process. Comparison of data sheets between vendors is simplified by presenting an overview of all data in Excel.
- **Work Areas/Competitive Scenarios.** Separate supplier work areas can be created with individual authorization settings for managing information exchange during the competitive bidding procurement process. Integration with the SRM Bidding Engine will be based on the cFolder competitive scenario.
- **Status Management.** Status Management allows project managers to set up an easy-to-handle process control on the fly. A status profile consists of freely definable statuses and the transitions between them. A status profile can be assigned to documents, data sheets, materials, BOMs, folders, areas, and collaborations.
- **Distributed Content Server Management.** The use of distributed content servers is supported. Users can choose the closest content server to decrease network traffic and improve speed of access.
- **Large File Handling.** FTP-connectivity is supported for users with low-bandwidth Internet connections.

Collaborative Project Management

- **Templates.** Templates can be created for a project with all objects and for checklists, to simplify and standardize the creation of an operational project.
- **Team.** A project team consists of several project participants who play different roles in the development process. A project participant can be an internal employee or an external business partner.
- **Phases.** A phase is a clearly defined period in a project used for structuring the project. A phase begins with the release and ends with an approval. Checklist items are assigned and tasks are assigned to a phase.
- **Quality Gates/Milestones.** Quality Gates are planned to achieve a controlled transition between phases and are represented in the application as approvals. To complete a phase, a team of decision makers must approve it. During the approval, the decision makers confirm that the goals in a phase, which are needed in the following phase(s), have been achieved. Milestones can be modeled using checklist items or tasks.
- **Tasks.** Tasks are used to plan and schedule required processing steps and assign them to the person responsible. The processing state of

a task is documented by a processing status and by reporting actual values. Tasks belong to phases in a project and can be linked to a checklist item. A task can be relevant to the approval of a phase; that is, the task must be confirmed before the phase can be approved.

- **Scheduling.** The system calculates the earliest and latest start and end dates of project elements (for checklist items, only end dates). Earliest dates are calculated forward based on the start date of the project definition. Latest dates are calculated backward based on the end date of the project definition. Relationships are the basis of scheduling.
- **Interactive Bar Chart.** The system displays tasks and checklist items as bars or points in time in a calendar diagram, corresponding to their duration and their position in time. Depending on the status of the project, they can be changed in an interactive bar chart.
- **Checklists.** Checklists serve as control lists and contain checklist items confirmed by a project participant. Checklist items represent important requirements that have to be met in order to reach the project goal. Checklist items are relevant to the approval of a phase (i.e., a checklist item must be completed before the phase can be approved).
- **Documents.** Documents play an important role in development projects and can be the input or output of a phase. Templates serve as a reference for the creation of new documents. Documents consist of metadata (e.g., a short text, the person responsible, and the status) and the document itself (content). Documents can be added to all elements of a development project, except the team. For clarity, documents can be structured within folders.
- **Object Links.** Object Links are used to link an existing business object (e.g., customer inquiry, specification, bill of material, work breakdown structure, inspection plan, etc.) to a project element. Those objects document the development process and grant access to information about product development. The interface for Object Links makes it possible to link business objects of different origin to a project and to display data of these objects in the application or include it in project evaluations. These objects can be located in different systems. In addition to the system on which CPM runs, these systems can be other systems or even Office-based solutions (e.g.,a Microsoft Access database).
- **Confirmation.** Confirmations are used to document a completed task. Before a checklist item can be marked as completed, all related tasks must be confirmed. Dependencies between the phase and the tasks exist and can take different forms. For example, a phase can be approved only if all tasks relevant to the approval of that phase have been completed. After a phase has been approved, the Confirmation of the tasks relevant to the approval of this phase can no longer be changed.

- **Approval and Digital Signature.** An approval is a part of a phase in a development project. During an approval, decision makers document that the goals in a phase, which are needed in the following phase(s), have been achieved. An approval is like a mutual contract and refers to a clearly defined processing state. The system takes the mutual contract into account by creating an approval document (PDF file) and by protecting ("freezing") the phase from subsequent modifications. The approval document the system creates is accepted as an official document and contains all information relevant to the approval. All decision makers involved in the approval sign this document with a digital signature. By doing so, they grant or deny their individual approval. A phase can be approved only if the signatures of all assigned decision makers have been given.
- **Control Plan.** The Control Plan can be maintained according to the Advanced Product Quality Planning (APQP) methodology.

Quality Collaboration

- **Quality Certificate for Delivery.** This function enables customers to obtain a quality certificate over the Internet for goods delivered. Customers can either retrieve a certificate that is created instantly or access one that is stored using Archive Link.
- **Recording Inspection Results on the Web.** With an Internet transaction server, customers can provide the vendor with an HTML entry screen on the Internet. The vendor then records and saves the inspection results on the Web. The results are transferred directly to the corporate system.
- **Exchange Quality Certificate Data.** This function offers easy access to the quality data in certificates. You can send the certificate to the target system in electronic form. If the quality certificate relates to a delivery to a customer, the inspection results on the certificate can be automatically transferred to a goods receipt inspection lot or manually to another inspection lot type. A quality certificate can be processed flexibly in the recipient's system. It can be sent in reference to a customer delivery, to a particular inspection lot, or to a batch.
- **Request to Deviate from Specification.** You can contact a business partner to request permission to deviate from the specification. For example, if a vendor part does not meet specifications, you can document this fact as a defect in a quality notification. During the notification processing, you can request permission from an internal or external notification partner to use the same vendor part in production.

Analytics

- **Product Design Optimization.** Product Design Optimization with the Concurrent Costing tool provides product cost information in the early product development stages. Based on the target costing approach, this enables design-to-cost engineering and early cost optimization. The possibility of calculating product characteristics as well as design alternatives provides valuable information for the product design team

- **Project Information System.** The Project Information System is a flexible, comprehensive information system that can be used to monitor and control project data. You can evaluate individual projects, partial projects, or multiple projects. The system includes overview reports and reports offering various degrees of detail. The Project Information System is designed to meet the needs of both project management and ordinary project personnel. Predefined information cubes are available for the Business Information Warehouse (BW).

- **Quality Information System.** The Quality Information System is used to condense and evaluate inspection data and problems related to inspections using various standards and reports. It uses predefined business content in the Business Information Warehouse.

- **Reporting and Asset Information System.** Asset Life Cycle Management offers a broad range of reporting features for technical objects and operative instruments, such as orders and notifications. The information system also provides strategic evaluations for a company, including mean time to repair/mean time between repairs (MTTR/MTBR) analysis.

- **Asset Business Content.** Asset Life Cycle Management also offers Business Content in the BW. Notification- and order-based information cubes and queries provide important information on asset availability, performance, and costs.

- **Web Reporting Using Data Warehouse.** This tool offers accurate and up-to-date information in the right context. Through its architecture, it fits seamlessly into the varied IT landscapes of software systems, thereby allowing data to be retrieved from a variety of sources.

- **Environmental, Health and Safety**
  - *Waste Management: Life Cycle Analysis.* Listing of the total amount of waste that must appear in a waste life cycle analysis according to the waste code and point of generation. The analysis also contains the description of the waste, the justification for the necessity for waste disposal, and the final destination of the waste (disposal facility).
  - *Industrial Hygiene and Safety:* 1000-Employee Quota. The 1,000-employee quota is used to evaluate the total number of accidents and determine how frequently accidents occur per 1,000 full-time employees.

Enterprise Portal Content
- **Business Package for Assets.** This package provides a complete e-business solution to manage, track, and control all asset-related information across the complete product and asset life cycle, throughout the extended supply chain. It offers easy access to asset-related data for all types of users.
- **Business Package for Products.** This e-business solution enables you to efficiently manage product data in a quality-oriented way. Without losing time, you can make important product information available for all logistic processes across the entire business. This business package offers internal and external users current product information regarding materials, bills of material, and document data.
- **Business Package for Projects.** Project-related data are stored at different places within the PLM Program and Project Management solution. This business package helps to depict these data in an easy-to-use way. Access to project-related data, assigned documents, and milestones is part of this package.
- **Integration of Enterprise Portal Knowledge Management.** Documents stored using the Document Management System of PLM Life Cycle Data Management can be accessed via the Knowledge Management platform of the Enterprise Portal. The content and the attributes of a document, as well as links to other objects, can be accessed. The federated search allows documents to be found across repository borders, using complex search strategies. The Knowledge Management platform provides access to the organization's documents stored in different repositories, such as file servers, Web servers, and different document management systems. A repository manager provides the integration with PLM Life Cycle Data Management.

Quality Management

This section outlines the elements of quality management.

Audit Management
- **Supplier Audits.** Audit management allows you to plan, process, and evaluate all kinds of supplier audits.
- **Product Audits.** Audit management allows you to plan, process, and evaluate all kinds of product audits.
- **Process Audits.** Audit management allows you to plan, process, and evaluate all kinds of process audits.
- **Environment Audits.** Audit management allows you to plan, process, and evaluate environmental audits.

- **System Audits.** Audit management allows you to plan, process, and evaluate all kinds of system audits.
- **Assessments.** Audit management allows you to plan, process, and evaluate all kinds of assessments.

Quality Control

- **Stability Studies.** Stability or shelf-life studies provide a means of testing and evaluating products during various stages of the product life cycle. By conducting stability studies, you can determine how products will hold up under controlled environmental conditions over predefined periods of time.
- **Engineering Workbench (EWB).** This planning tool optimizes all quality planning tasks. The EWB allows you to process several task lists simultaneously and easily retrieve and collate data from different plans.
- **Product Structure Browser.** This browser allows the hierarchical display of related objects in a product structure. During inspection planning, for example, you can check whether task lists exist for a particular product. By expanding a product structure further, you can also display additional information, such as assigned inspection characteristics, documents, and so on.
- **Specifications.** Specifications and inspection plans are the basis for quality controls at all stages of the product life cycle. PLM Quality Management provides the tools for defining and managing such specifications and inspection plans.
- **Sampling Plans.** These plans can be defined to control sample drawings for goods receipts and in-process and post-process inspections.
- **Standard Operating Procedure Management.** Standard operating procedures (SOPs) are instructions used during inspections. Change management can be used to alter SOPs. Using the Document Management System, you can create, release, and maintain SOPs as instructions for inspection operations. Inspection methods can also be used as SOPs.
- **Mobile Inspection Using PDAs.** This tool allows the recording of inspection results using personal digital assistants (PDAs) when you are away from your desk. Field inspections, inspection tours, and inspections of heavy or difficult-to-reach objects are some of the possible applications.
- **Sample Management.** This tool allows you to plan and automatically generate samples (physical samples, pooled samples, and/or reserve samples) at goods receipt or in production. You can create individual sample master records for all kinds of sample types (e.g., goods receipt samples, environmental samples, and competitor samples).

- **Laboratory Integration.** This tool provides a link between classical LIMS (Laboratory Information Management System) functions, such as Sample Management and Results Recording, and logistical processes, such as Purchase Order Processing or Vendor Evaluation. To manage a laboratory effectively, you need to have access to up-to-date and relevant data from the supply chain. This integration can be ensured by using PLM Quality Management.
- **Usage Decision and Release.** Inspections can be triggered and carried out for all kinds of samples (e.g., for samples from incoming goods inspections, from production, and from goods issues).
- **Certificate of Analysis.** You can create a certificate of analysis (COA) for batches, inspection lots, or deliveries.
- **Statistical Process Control (SPC).** You can use this tool to evaluate inspection results with the aid of control charts for evaluations or trend analyses. The inspection data can also be exported using the QM-STI (Statistical Data Interface) interface, if required.
- **Problem Management.** This tool serves to record problems, to notify the person responsible for processing (partner), and to determine, execute, and monitor tasks and actions. Problem Management is directly integrated with the results recording process.
- **Calibration of Test Equipment.** You can use this function to automatically generate calibration orders on a regular basis and to execute equipment inspections with calibration instructions. It allows inspections of technical objects, such as functional locations or equipments, and the release of test equipment and follow-up activities.
- **Quality Information System.** This system is used to condense and evaluate inspection data and problems related to inspections using various standards and reports. It uses predefined business content in the Business Information Warehouse.

Quality Improvement

- **Advanced Product Quality Planning (APQP).** APQP is supported by the Web application Collaborative Project Management under Life Cycle Collaboration and Analytics. APQP supports the development of high-quality products that will satisfy the customer on time, at the lowest possible cost. This application improves the development process by focusing on planning and failure prevention at an early stage, to reduce subsequent nonconformity costs.
- **Notification.** Notifications are a flexible tool for recording, processing, and managing unplanned events or problems in a company. The problems may be the result of planned or unexpected events, and may deal with company-internal or external processes.

- **Internet Service Request.** This tool is the intranet medium for finding a goal-oriented solution quickly. Information can be recorded quickly and easily, then searched directly for suitable solutions, to create and dispatch notifications, and to track the processing status of requests at any time.
- **Quality Manual.** The Quality Manual in the Knowledge Warehouse simplifies the creation and administration of the company's quality manual based on the requirements of ISO 9000 & GMP (good manufacturing practice)
- **Web Reporting Using Data Warehouse.** The tool offers accurate and up-to-date information in the right context. Through its architecture, it fits seamlessly into the varied IT landscapes of software systems, thereby allowing data to be retrieved from a variety of sources.

Environmental Health and Safety

This section outlines the elements of environmental health and safety (EH&S).

Basic Data and Tools

- **Specification Management.** This highly flexible database tool manages the property data of various EH&S-related data objects, such as substances, agents, dangerous goods classifications, waste catalogs, and packaging material specifications. The standard properties can be enhanced as required by the user with no limitations. Specification Management is also used with Recipe Management.
- **Phrase Management.** This tool provides library-based text management for any textual information used in EH&S. It has a standard interface to phrase library content providers.
- **EH&S Expert and EH&S Easy Expert.** These are rule-based expert systems to calculate secondary data, such as risk classification, risk and safety phrase determination from substance properties, and composition of a product
- **Report Generation and Report Management.** By using this tool, any EH&S-related document—for example, material safety data sheets (MSDS), standard operating procedures, tremcards (hazardous substance labels), and waste manifests—can be created and stored in the document database.
- **EH&S Web Interface.** This interface provides Internet access to the company's EH&S document database containing MSDS, labels, and tremcards.

- **Global Label Management.** This tool manages different types of labels, which are EH&S-related or related to other business processes.
- **Specification Information System.** This system provides search capabilities using simple or complex criteria for each specification object. The results are displayed in an online list view or can be downloaded to Microsoft Excel.

Product Safety

- **Specification Management.** Specification Management is a highly flexible database tool for managing the property data of various EH&S-related data objects such as products, substances, agents, dangerous goods classifications, and packaging material specifications. The standard properties can be enhanced as required by the user with no limitations. Specification Management is also used with Recipe Management.
- **Automatic Product Composition Calculation.** The product composition of substance ingredients is calculated automatically from the bill of material in production planning.
- **Rule Based MSDS Authoring.** This is a rule-based expert system to calculate secondary data, such as risk classification, risk and safety phrase determination from substance properties, and composition of a product.
- **Automatic MSDS Generation.** Material safety data sheets can be created automatically and stored in the document database for the product.
- **Global Label Management.** This tool manages different types of labels, which are EH&S-related or related to other business processes. The labels can be printed from the business processes, for example, from outbound delivery.
- **Material Safety Data Sheet Shipping.** MSDS documents are shipped to customers using integration in sales and distribution. After relevant changes, the current version subsequently is shipped to any recent recipient. Manual shipping is also supported.
- **EH&S Web Interface.** This tool provides Internet access to the company's EH&S document database containing MSDS, labels, and tremcards.

Hazardous Substance Management

- **Substance Management.** Substance Management is a highly flexible database tool for managing the property data of substances and agents. The standard properties can be enhanced as required by the user with no limitations. Substance Management is also used with Recipe Management
- **MSDS Import.** Manages the process of importing vendor MSDSs, delivered either as paper documents or electronically, into the EH&S document database and linking them to the purchased substance.

- **Rule Based Classification.** This is a rule-based expert system to calculate secondary data, such as risk classification, risk and safety phrase determination from substance properties, and composition of a product.
- **Hazardous Substance Related Document.** Any EH&S-related document—for example, material safety data sheets, standard operating procedures, transport emergency cards, or hazardous substance label—can be created and stored in the document database.
- **Release Hazardous Materials for Purchasing.** Material to be purchased can be blocked or released for purchasing based on its hazard properties.
- **Hazardous Substance Inventory.** This tool reports the actual stock level of hazardous substances.
- **Substance Information System.** This tool provides search capabilities for substances using simple and complex criteria. The results are displayed in an online list view or can be downloaded to Microsoft Excel.
- **Substance Tracking.** This tool manages the process of tracking and controlling material distribution based on substance composition and characteristics related to regulatory or company policy requirements. From purchasing through product distribution, material purchases, movements, storage, use, and distribution can be identified and controlled (approved, held, etc.) based on substance levels and quantities. Inventory reports can also be produced.
- **Life Cycle Balance Ecosystem.** This tool assesses EH&S risks and costs throughout a product's entire life cycle, from the initial raw material through production, customer use, recycling, and final disposal.

Dangerous Goods Management

- **Dangerous Goods Regulatory Data.** This tool enters and updates regulatory data in the specification database or imports regulatory data from content providers using a Web-based interface.
- **Dangerous Goods Classification.** This tool groups the classification of a product together for each regulation and links this classification to any material that is classified identically.
- **Dangerous Goods Checks.** This tool integrates with sales, distribution, and transportation, checking against regulations depending on mode of transport and route (e.g., transportation approval, packing requirements, mixed loading, and limited quantities).
- **Dangerous Goods Documents.** This tool creates and prints dangerous goods data on delivery notes and packing lists. It also creates and prints transport emergency cards for road and inland waterway transportation.

Waste Management

- **Waste Basic Data Management.** This tool manages waste generators within the site organization. It manages waste transporters, disposal companies, and authorities as business partners and also manages the disposal channels.
- **Hazardous Waste Permit.** This tool defines and monitors hazardous waste permits issued and approved by authorities.
- **Waste Disposal.** This tool covers the processing of on-site and off-site disposal and transportation of hazardous waste as dangerous goods. It also manages disposal documents in accordance with the regulations integrated into the Supply Chain Management solution.
- **Waste Inventory Management.** This tool tracks waste generation, movements, and inventory by quantities.
- **Waste Costing.** This tool manages disposal costs and disposal settlement.

Industrial Hygiene and Safety

- **Work Area Data Management.** The work area is the central object in industrial hygiene and safety (IHS) in EH&S. It is the point of reference for numerous processes, including risks assessments, checklists, safety measures, and documents. Using the work area, IHS professionals can map exactly the organization and structure of an enterprise from the point of view of industrial hygiene and safety. Integration in other solutions allows you to create references to existing structures in application lifecycle management (ALM) (functional location), Supply Chain Management (storage location, work center), or Human Resources (organizational management objects).
- **Work Area Pattern.** Patterns are special work areas without a reference to a location or organizational level. They can be used to create standardized exposure profiles and risk assessments. The pattern function works according to the principle of multiplication.
- **Work Area Integration.** The work area object in IHS can refer to the functional location (ALM), storage location, work center, and several organizational management objects.
- **Risk Assessment.** This is the major process to determine, analyze, and prevent all risks and exposures in the employees' working environment. Standard analysis methods, such as the measured value-reference value comparison, the evaluation of questionnaires, or comparison with standardized criteria, are available to calculate the specific rating, severity, and probability of a risk or exposure.
- **Measurement Management.** This tool processes and manages measurement data, including all operations and tasks in defining, executing,

evaluating, and documenting measurements. The object of a measurement can be a hazardous substance or a physical agent, for example.

- **Document Assignment.** Documents in the Document Management System such as pictures or maps can be assigned directly to work areas or incident/accident log entries.
- **Incident Accident Management.** This tool includes the recording and managing of accident data, generating and managing accident reports, and the creation and management of accident statistics and accident analyses.
- **Standard Operating Procedures.** These are IHS documents created on the basis of work area data and substance information.
- **HIS Information System.** This is a central information source for IHS professionals that offers several standard IHS reports, such as hazardous substance register, accident statistics, and risk assessment overview.
- **Safety Measures.** With Safety Measures, an IHS professional can trigger and track various measures (technical, organizational, and person-related) to prevent risks and exposures.
- **Health and Safety Briefings.** These briefings are intended to inform employees about the accident and health risks they encounter at work, the safety measures required to avoid such risks, and the current industrial hygiene and safety and accident prevention regulations. EH&S IHS uses Human Resource Training and Event Management to cover this functionality.
- **Questionnaire.** This generic tool is used for creating specific questionnaires, such as site inspections or risk assessment checklists, on the basis of a multilingual question catalog. The questionnaire can be filled out directly in the system or printed out and scanned back into the system afterward.
- **Site Inspection.** Site Inspections are part of a systematic and preventive company safety policy. They are intended to determine to what extent company-wide health protection and safety standards have been put into action.

Occupational Health

- **Medical Service.** This tool is the technical object for recording all relevant health surveillance protocol data, such as examinations, medical test results, diagnoses, restrictions, consultations, medications, and follow-up appointments.
- **Proposal List.** A report determines the relevant health surveillance protocols for a person based on the exposures he or she is subject to and the trigger values for a health surveillance protocol, and displays them in a proposal list.

- **Scheduling.** This tool lists the medical services for a person, with access to phone numbers and details of absences in Human Resources. It includes the option of sending invitations and questionnaires to the person with scheduled appointment dates.
- **Inquiry/Illness Log.** The detailed recording of injury-specific information is a legal requirement in many countries. Using integration with EH&S industrial hygiene and safety, the data from the injury/illness log can be transferred to incident/accident management. This enables first aid centers and accident administration to work together more effectively.
- **Brief Consultation.** This tool is a quick and easy documentation function for routine medical tasks, such as providing medication or advice (in person, by phone, or by e-mail). The tool makes it possible to enter, document, and evaluate necessary information even within the course of day-to-day activities.
- **Vaccination.** All medically relevant information (such as batch numbers) is easy to enter, and follow-up appointments can be generated automatically. Vaccinations performed by third parties can also be documented to keep a full record of a person's vaccination history.
- **Questionnaire.** This generic tool enables you to create specific questionnaires, such as a health surveillance protocol questionnaire, on the basis of a multilingual question catalog. The questionnaire can be filled out directly in the system or printed out and scanned back into the system afterward.

PLM: Why It Is So Important, What It Can Do, and How It Does It

In response to changing capital market demands, "want it now" customer demand, and fast-moving competition, companies are under unprecedented pressure to generate profitable products at high speed.

This relentless pressure leaves little, if any, room for error. Customers are conditioned to expect the rapid availability of an alternative product, most likely from a competitor, if one company's new product has problems or is delayed. That means products need to be right the first time, on time and defect free. On a related front: Capital markets place the majority of a company's valuation on expectations that forward earnings will be driven by successful innovation at a highly predictable rate.

It may all seem overwhelming, but it is believed that these demands on product development have met their match with new processes, organizational adaptations, and technologies. Enabled by a new class of Product Life Cycle Management applications, companies today can reduce development cycle times by half and accelerate new product market success by factors of 2 or more.

Why the dramatic impact? To put the importance of Product Life Cycle Management in perspective: Product Life Cycle Management is to product information what enterprise resource planning is to enterprise resource information or customer relationship management (CRM) is to customer information. It represents a new way to plan, organize, manage, measure, and deliver new products or services.

Improving Endemic Supply Chain Problems

A fresh look at Product Life Cycle Management shows how it can provide what for many companies has been the missing product development link: the capability to truly integrate existing enterprise resource management (ERM) and CRM capabilities with integrated and real-time product information. By doing so, it brings the informed input of every relevant constituent into a product's planning, definition, design, development, manufacture, sale, movement, support, and even retirement.

Equally important, this kind of rigorous Product Life Cycle Management means companies are better able to rationalize the design, development, and overall management of their product portfolios.

Field experience working with clients points to the next areas in which Product Life Cycle Management can help resolve long-standing hurdles to innovation, productivity, and profitability:

- **Knowing Which Product to Pursue.** Without tracking, analysis, and planning of product features and customer requirements, companies often expend resources on dead-end ideas before they get the right product completed. By aggregating key insights and capturing known facts, dramatic new approaches to what to do and when to do it are possible.
- **Long Product Cycle Times.** Margin erosion, excessive discounting, and erratic materials management and inventory profiles are common signs that product delivery performance is too far behind a market window. The only answer is to do it right the first time and get it done faster. Doing this requires an unprecedented degree of enterprise-wide synchronization, concurrent development, work management, and data configuration control.
- **High Product Development and Launch Costs.** High recurring and nonrecurring product costs often indicate an overreliance on internal solutions, squandering of resources on developmental dead ends, and not managing evolving insights in a way that allows the true enterprise costs of certain decisions to be determined. Appropriate responses include

earlier and more effective collaboration with third parties, integration with enterprise resource information, and the enhanced integration of product engineering tools. Product Life Cycle Management provides a foundation for building these vital links.

- **Substandard Product Quality.** Excessive failure rates often point to a breakdown in requirements definition at the front end and weak engineering change-order mechanisms after the problem has surfaced. Product Life Cycle Management provides access to key insights early, facilitates bringing the right parties to the table at the right time, and accelerates by factors of 10 the ability to process a change when it is required.
- **Faster Introductions, Better Products.** Product Life Cycle Management fundamentally changes the nature of product development. All parties work collaboratively, particularly while the product's design is can be influenced. Product Life Cycle Management helps companies achieve better products faster to the markets.
- **Repeatability.** This function is attained by leveraging intellectual property assets and enforcing standardized, repeatable, and dependable work methods.
- **Lower and Steeper Learning Curves.** These benefits are achieved through access to the right information for a multitude of enterprise-wide participants, not just engineering.
- **Concurrent Work Efforts on Different Product Components.** Work can be done on different components concurrently by synchronizing development around object configurations and ongoing changes and updates, something that is impossible to do at any scale without technology enablement.

Abilities with Deep and Widespread Impact

Product Life Cycle Management works in three ways in an enterprise:

1. It provides a single, virtual workspace in which product content, process information, and program status information are fully integrated and under configuration and version control.
2. It enables the precise status of a product at any stage of its life to be accessed and modified through appropriate security protocols, both within and external to the company.
3. It integrates resource information with content creation processes through the connection of workflow and cost information with the product's developmental state.

Product Life Cycle Management is ultimately about getting better products to market faster. It also can deliver cost-management and revenue-generating benefits.

Not Business as Usual

In companies that use Product Life Cycle Management, the method and speed with which information is shared and accessed is fundamentally altered. Employees view and interact with relevant information sooner and more clearly, thus giving them the opportunity to provide input and feedback in a manageable way.

This greater access to information and improved ability to collaborate enables companies to utilize concurrent engineering teams. These teams can share a controlled workspace and leverage their content contributions in a highly parallel and synergistic manner. Doing so changes the serial mess often associated when marketing gives requirements to engineering and engineering, in turn, releases impossible-to-build designs to manufacturing, resulting in late-shipping products that cannot be supported effectively without major changes.

Perhaps the most profound change from a design standpoint is a marked reduction in the number of engineering change orders. Because product design and development are sequenced virtually and the information is managed concurrently, collaborations among design, engineering, and production can be accomplished significantly earlier and at near–real-time speed, thus eliminating the causes of most change orders. Change orders that do need to be processed benefit from increased data integrity and linkages to other enterprises and applications.

In addition to greater speed and more data integrity, companies can apply Product Life Cycle Management in a number of innovative ways, so Customer Relationship Management can result in new insights into what products or product configurations the company should be selling and at what cost. Similarly, building on insights from prior products, platform-based product families, and reusable objects further yields dramatic reductions in spending on wrong product solutions or needless reinvention.

PLM Features and Benefits in Details

Table 4.1 presents the details of PLM support and the resulting benefits that accrue. For many items, if a tangible benefit does not accrue, the corresponding cell is left blank. In other words, only tangible benefits are listed in the table. In brief, the 20 PLM features listed in the left column

TABLE 4.1   PLM Features and Benefits

PLM Supports	Benefit
Life Cycle Data Management	
24 × 7 customer self-service	Improve customer service
Reduce time to market and volume	Increase revenue
Improve RFQ/RFP processes	
Offer multiple points of access	
Improve sales lead generation and process	
Improve capacity utilization	Lower working capital
Visibility to vendor/supplier inventory	
Improve procurement processes	Reduce operating costs
Reduce product returns	
Improve delivery of training and education	
Product Structure Management	
Improve product/service quality	Improve customer service
Improve forecast accuracy	
Reduce time to market and volume	Increase revenue
Improve RFQ/RFP processes	
Improve customer retention and loyalty	
Integrated service/repair scheduling	Lower working capital
Visibility to vendor/supplier inventory	
Reduce inventory levels	Reduce operating costs
Reduce order processing costs	
Improve procurement processes	
Lower logistics costs	
Reduce product returns	
Recipe Management	
Offer multiple points of access	Improve customer service
Improve product/service quality	
Improved quality and accuracy	
Shorten proposal/quotation cycle	
Complaint management and tracking	
Reduce time to market and volume	Increase revenue
Enable cross-sell/up-sell capability	
Offer multiple points of access	
Fewer returns, more efficient process	Lower working capital
Reduce administration, improve business processes	Reduce operating costs
Reduce inventory levels	
Re-deploy labor to higher value-added	
Reduce transaction costs	
Reduce product returns	
Lower communications expenses	

TABLE 4.1   *(Continued)*

PLM Supports	Benefit
Integration	
Improve product/service quality	Improve customer service
Improve forecast accuracy	
Reduce time to market and volume	Increase revenue
Integrated service/repair scheduling	Lower working capital
Visibility to vendor/supplier inventory	
Reduce inventory levels	Reduce operating costs
Improve procurement processes	
Lower logistics costs	
Reduce product returns	
Change and Configuration Management	
24 × 7 customer self-service	Improve customer service
Improve customer retention and loyalty	Increase revenue
Visibility to vendor/supplier inventory	Lower working capital
Improve capacity utilization	
Increase inventory turns	
Integrated service/repair scheduling	
Reduce inventory levels	Reduce operating costs
Improve procurement processes	
Lower logistics costs	
Reduce product returns	
Project Execution	
Reduce late orders	Improve customer service
Improve product/service quality	
Improve forecast accuracy	
Develop new markets	Increase revenue
Develop service offerings	
Reduce time to market and volume	
Gain market share	
Extend market share	
Minimize investment in operating facilities	Manage fixed assets
Reduce administration, improve business processes	Reduce operating costs
Improve procurement processes	
Lower logistics costs	
Interfaces	
Reduce late orders	Improve customer service
Improve product/service quality	
Improve forecast accuracy	
Develop new markets	Increase revenue
Develop service offerings	

(Continued)

TABLE 4.1   (*Continued*)

PLM Supports	Benefit
Reduce time to market and volume	
Gain market share	
Extend market share	
Minimize investment in operating facilities	Manage fixed assets
Reduce administration, improve business processes	Reduce operating costs
Improve procurement processes	
Lower logistics costs	
Design Collaboration	
Improve product/service quality	Improve customer service
Collaborate with business partners	
Improved quality and accuracy	
Shorten proposal/quotation cycle	
Develop new markets	Increase revenue
Develop service offerings	
Reduce time to market and volume	
Improve RFQ/RFP processes	
Lower cost of procured goods and services	Lower working capital
Improve procurement processes	Reduce operating costs
Lower communications expenses	
Improve asset and maintenance management	
Reduce travel related expense	
Collaborative Project Management	
Improve product/service quality	Improve customer service
Collaborate with business partners	
Improved quality and accuracy	
Reduce time to market and volume	Increase revenue
Efficient campaign planning and management	
Reduce product returns	Reduce operating costs
Improve recruiting, hiring, and HR processes	
Quality Collaboration	
Offer multiple points of access	Improve customer service
Improve product/service quality	
24 × 7 customer self-service	
Collaborate with business partners	
Improved quality and accuracy	
Develop service offerings	Increase revenue
Maximize profitability by customer	
Offer multiple points of access	
Improve customer retention and loyalty	
Outsource excess capacity	

TABLE 4.1   *(Continued)*

PLM Supports	Benefit
Lower cost procured goods and services	Lower working capital
Reduce administration, improve business processes	Reduce operating costs
Reduce order processing costs	
Improve procurement processes	
Reduce transaction costs	
Lower communications expenses	
Reduce travel-related expense	
Analytics	
Improve forecast accuracy	Improve customer service
24 × 7 customer self-service	
Provide a single face to the customer	
Complaint management and tracking	
Develop new markets	Increase revenue
Reduce time to market and volume	
Improve customer retention and loyalty	
Gain market share	
Efficient campaign planning and management	
Reduce inventory carrying costs	Lower working capital
Audit Management	
Offer multiple points of access	Improve customer service
Improve product/service quality	
Collaborate with business partners	
Strengthen partnerships and account management	
Improved quality and accuracy	
Complaint management and tracking	
Maximize profitability by customer	Increase revenue
Improve RFQ/RFP processes	
Offer multiple points of access	
Improve customer retention and loyalty	
Fewer returns, more efficient process	Lower working capital
Lower-cost procured goods and services	
Reduce administration, improve business processes	Reduce operating costs
Improve procurement processes	
Reduce product returns	
Lower communications expenses	
Reduce travel-related expense	
Quality Control	
Offer multiple points of access	Improve customer service
Improve product/service quality	
Improved quality and accuracy	
Maximize profitability by customer	Increase revenue

(Continued)

TABLE 4.1   (*Continued*)

PLM Supports	Benefit
Offer multiple points of access	
Reduce administration, improve business processes	Reduce operating costs
Improve procurement processes	
Reduce transaction costs	
Lower communications expenses	
Improve delivery of training and education	

Quality Improvement

Offer multiple points of access	Improve customer service
Improve product/service quality	
Improved quality and accuracy	
Complaint management and tracking	
Develop service offerings	Increase revenue
Maximize profitability by customer	
Offer multiple points of access	
Improve customer retention and loyalty	
Fewer returns, more efficient process	Lower working capital
Lower-cost procured goods and services	
Reduce administration, improve business processes	Reduce operating costs
Reduce order processing costs	
Improve procurement processes	
Reduce product returns	
Lower communications expenses	

Product Safety

Reduce late orders	Improve customer service
Reduce order lead time	
Improve product/service quality	
Collaborate with business partners	
Improved quality and accuracy	
Complaint management and tracking	
Reduce administration, improve business processes	Reduce operating costs

Hazardous Substance Management

Collaborate with business partners	Improve customer service
Reduce administration, improve business processes	Reduce operating costs
Reduce order processing costs	
Improve procurement processes	
Lower logistics costs	

Dangerous Goods Management

Reduce late orders	Improve customer service
Improved quality and accuracy	
Reduce administration, improve business processes	Reduce operating costs

TABLE 4.1 *(Continued)*

PLM Supports	Benefit
Waste Management	
Reduce administration, improve business processes	Reduce operating costs
Lower logistics costs	
Industrial Hygiene and Safety	
Complaint management and tracking	Improve customer service
Reduce administration, improve business processes	Reduce operating costs
Improve recruiting, hiring, and HR processes	
Lower logistics costs	
Occupational Health	
Complaint management and tracking	Improve customer service
Reduce administration, improve business processes	Reduce operating costs
Improve recruiting, hiring, and HR processes	

create 5 tangible benefits: improving customer service, increasing revenue, lowering working capital, reducing operating costs, and managing fixed assets.

PLM Key Performance Indicators

Table 4.2 presents what I believe are the most important KPIs. There is no absolute rule as to which KPI must be applied. Furthermore, each KPI must be treated as a vector and its up or down direction determined by the goal of the project. For example, the number of engineering change orders generally should go down. Then there is competition between SCM and PLM. Which area do you credit for reducing the total SCM costs, SCM or PLM? The case can be made that since PLM is a life cycle system that helps every application, it must be given at least some credit. This argument can be extended to CRM, finance, and so on. Other initiatives may also claim credit for certain improvements. Suffice it to say that KPIs are given for the knowledge but the credit taken for the corresponding improvement should be done with due deliberation and thoughtfulness. The reader may want to contact this author for further clarification or to discuss how to do a business case with KPIs.

TABLE 4.2   KPIs and Their Explanations

Key Performance Indicator	Explanation/Definition
% of escalations	The number of escalations expressed as a % of total installations.
Response time: field service	The time a customer has to wait after sending a service request.
Service costs revenue ratio	Revenue created from service work versus costs.
Build-to-ship cycle time	Average time from when a unit/product is deemed shippable by manufacturing until the unit/product actually ships to a customer. (Sum of time difference between "ready to ship" — "date of shipment")/total number of shipments)
Average development cost per new product	Average development cost divided by the number of new products.
Concept approval cycle time	Time required to approve the concepts of a new product and start the development process.
Detailed schedule creation time	Number of hours required to create a detailed project schedule.
Engineer change order (ECO) costs	Costs incurred through revisions to a blueprint or design released by engineering to modify or correct a part. The request for the change can be from a customer or from production quality control or another department.
Engineer change order (ECO) costs as a % of research and development (R&D) costs	Expressed as a % of R&D costs.
Engineering change order time	Number of days between receipt of ECO and delivery of final redesigned design drawings.
Installation planning costs	Includes costs for installation engineering, scheduling and modification, handling cancellations, and planning the installation.
Installation planning costs as a % of order management costs	Expressed as a % of order management costs.
Lead times: product development	Time from concept to product launch.
New product release phase-in and maintenance costs	Includes releasing new products to the field; maintaining released products; assigning product ID; defining configurations and packaging; publishing availability schedules, release letters, and updates; and maintaining product databases.

TABLE 4.2   *(Continued)*

Key Performance Indicator	Explanation/Definition
	Releasing new products to the field costs + maintaining released products costs + assigning product ID costs + defining configurations and packaging costs + publishing availability schedules costs + release letters and updates costs + maintaining product databases costs.
Number of engineering change orders	Total number of revisions to a blueprint or design released by engineering to modify or correct a part, ECOs. The request for the change can be from a customer or from production quality control or another department.
Number of prototypes built	Number of prototypes built before approval.
% of external project initiations	The % of new projects initiated by a customer versus internally.
% of new components	"New components" (never used before and not present in any company database) versus all components used in a design.
Project setup time	Average time spent on doing the project setup, creating the project plan and budget.
R&D costs as a % of revenue	R&D costs expressed as a % of revenue.
R&D costs as a % of total costs	R&D costs expressed as a % of total costs.
R&D costs	All costs involved in the R&D process.
Annual sales-to-inventory ratio	By comparing inventory to sales, this ratio indicates whether there is too little or too much inventory to support the given level of sales. The objective is to have the smallest level of inventory while still meeting sales requirements efficiently. Note: Cost of goods sold is generally used for this estimate (see *Inventory Turnover*), but sales may substitute for it. The sales-to-inventory-ratio has to be annualized, because sales accumulate over the year and Inventory balances remain more or less constant from quarter to quarter.
Average project revenue	Total revenue of projects per total projects contracted.
Average working capital	Computed by adding the working capital values at the beginning and the end of an accounting period and dividing by 2.

(Continued)

TABLE 4.2   *(Continued)*

Key Performance Indicator	Explanation/Definition
Cash-to-cash cycle time	Represents the time from when a company spends a dollar on purchased material to when it realizes a dollar received in revenue and has a direct impact on the company's cash flow. Effective supply chain planning reduces the inventory conversion period by manufacturing, processing, and selling goods more quickly. This in turn reduces the cash-to-cash cycle.
Channel inventory	Finished goods inventory that is allocated to a particular distribution channel (i.e., original equipment manufacturing OEM goods, retail). Finished goods inventory allocated to a particular distribution channel/Finished goods inventory × 100
Customer invoicing, accounting costs	Includes costs for invoicing, processing customer payments, and verifying customer satisfaction.
Customer invoicing, accounting costs as a % of order management costs	Includes costs for invoicing, processing customer payments, and verifying customer satisfaction. Expressed as a % of order management costs. (Invoicing costs + processing customer payments costs + verifying customer satisfaction costs)/order management costs × 100.
Customer receipt of order to installation complete	Includes product installation, acceptance and product up-and-running time, in calendar days. (Sum of time difference from "customer receipt of order" − "installation complete")/total number of installations
General and administrative expenses	All expenses incurred in connection with performing general and administrative activities. Examples are executives' salaries and legal expenses.
Indirect cost of goods sold to cost ratio	Overhead expenses are not directly related to the manufacturing of the company product. Note: Direct costs + indirect costs are equivalent to cost of goods sold. Comparing indirect with direct costs is one way of monitoring the outflow of funds because of rising overhead.
Operating income	Equal to sales less all related expenses applying to the normal business activities (cost of goods sold, general and administrative expenses, selling expenses).
% of planned maintenance work	Expressed as a % of total maintenance work.

TABLE 4.2   (*Continued*)

Key Performance Indicator	Explanation/Definition
Bill of material data accuracy	Indicates the quality of the bill of materials (BOMs) that is used for the planning process. Only corrections of errors should be counted.
Build cycle time	The average cycle time for build-to-stock products.
Machine wait time	Queue time for a specific machine; queue time and wait time for an operation.
Managerial and professional headcount full-time equivalents	Managers and professionals in full-time equivalents (FTEs) not doing operational work but responsible for planning, controlling, budgeting, administration.
Product and process data accuracy	Indicates the quality of the data that are used for the planning process (bills of material, routings, planning interval data). Only corrections of errors should be counted.
Production lead time	Average time it takes for an order or product to go through the shop floor.
Incoming inspection costs	All costs associated with the inspection and testing of received materials to verify compliance with specifications.
Incoming material quality	Number of received parts fail inspection divided by the total number of parts received. Very similar to parts per million.
Time to market	The time between the start of a project, development, or new product to the time it appears in the market.
Validation time for product configuration	Time spent validating configuration of products per order.
Number of supply sources	Total number of internal and external direct production material suppliers used.
Average sales representative expenses	The average expenses incurred by sales representatives in a period.
Churn	Loss of customers per year as a % of total customers.
Company growth versus market growth	Company growth, based on the annual increase of revenue, compared to the growth of the competitors.
Cost estimate accuracy	% difference in original cost estimate versus final actual (taking into account that the same scope is evaluated). % difference of cost estimate to final cost.
Cost per quote	Total cost to generate a quote.

(*Continued*)

TABLE 4.2   *(Continued)*

Key Performance Indicator	Explanation/Definition
Customer satisfaction index	An abstract measure of how well the company serves the customers. It cannot be predefined, because the company has to find out what customers want and then look at how well it fulfills customers' needs. Usually it is an index.
Cycle time: inquiry to contract	How long it takes, on average, to get an inquiry to a contract.
Invoice accuracy rate	The % of faultless invoices.
On-time pricing to customers	The customer requests a pricing at a specific date. On-time means before or on the specific date.
% of customer complaints	Number of customer complaints expressed as a % of total customers in a period. The average number of customers is the number at the end of the period plus the number at the beginning divided by 2.
Sales cycle time (orders)	The average time from initial inquiry to final billing.
Capacity utilization	A measure of how intensively a resource is being used to produce goods or a service. Some factors that should be considered are internal manufacturing capacity, constraining processes, direct labor availability and key components/materials availability.
Channel obsolescence costs	Aging allowances paid to channel partners, provisions for buy-back agreements.
Contract, program and channel management costs as a % of order management costs	Includes all costs for activities related to contract negotiation, monitoring progress, and reporting against the customer's contract, including administration of performance or warranty related issues. Expressed as a % of order management costs. (Activities related to contract negotiation costs + monitoring progress costs + reporting against the customer's contract costs)/order management costs × 100.
Delivery date accuracy	Difference between planned delivery date and actual delivery date.
Delivery performance to scheduled commit date	% of orders that are fulfilled on or before the original scheduled or committed date.

TABLE 4.2 *(Continued)*

Key Performance Indicator	Explanation/Definition
Demand, supply planning costs	Costs associated with forecasting, developing finished goods or end item inventory plans, and coordinating the demand/supply process across entire supply chain, including all channels (not including management information systems, associated costs).
Demand, supply planning costs as a % of supply chain finance and planning costs	Costs associated with forecasting, developing finished goods or end item inventory plans, and coordinating demand/supply process across entire supply chain, including all channels (not including management information systems associated costs). Expressed as a % of supply chain finance and planning costs. (Forecasting costs + developing finished goods or end item inventory plans costs + costs for coordinating demand, supply process)/supply chain finance and planning costs × 100.
Distribution costs	Includes costs for warehouse space and management, finished goods receiving and stocking, processing shipments, picking and consolidating, selecting carrier, and staging products/systems.
Distribution costs as a % of order management costs	Includes costs for warehouse space and management, finished goods receiving and stocking, processing shipments, picking and consolidating, selecting carrier, and staging products/systems. Expressed as a % of order management costs.
Faultless invoices	The number of invoices issued without error. Examples of potential invoice defects are: change from customer purchase order without proper customer involvement, wrong customer Information (e.g., name, address, and telephone number), wrong product information (e.g., part number, product description), wrong price (e.g., discounts not applied), wrong quantity or wrong terms or wrong date. Expressed as a % of total number of invoices.

(Continued)

TABLE 4.2 *(Continued)*

Key Performance Indicator	Explanation/Definition
Fill rates	The % of ship from stock orders shipped within 24 hours of order receipt.
Finished goods inventory carrying costs	Sum of all costs associated with finished goods inventory: opportunity cost, shrinkage, insurance and taxes, total obsolescence, channel obsolescence, and field sample obsolescence.
Finished goods inventory carrying costs as a % of inventory carrying costs	Sum of all costs associated with finished goods inventory: opportunity cost, shrinkage, insurance and taxes, total obsolescence, channel obsolescence, and field sample obsolescence. Expressed as a % of inventory carrying costs. (Finished goods opportunity cost + finished goods shrinkage + finished goods insurance and taxes + finished goods total obsolescence + finished goods channel obsolescence + finished goods field sample obsolescence)/inventory carrying costs × 100.
Finished goods inventory days of supply	Indicates how many days the inventory can satisfy the demand of finished goods based on value.
Forecast accuracy	Calculated at the shippable end product level for each distribution channel and for both units and dollars. Forecast accuracy = forecast sum − sum of variance/forecast sum. Forecast sum = Sum of the units or dollars forecasted to be shipped in each month based on the forecast generated three months prior. Sum of variances = Sum of the absolute values, at the forecasted line item level, of the differences between each month's forecast as defined and actual demand for the same month.
Material process engineering costs	Costs associated with tasks required to document and communicate material specification, as well as reviews to improve the manufacturability of the purchased item. Document and communicate material specification costs + reviews costs.

TABLE 4.2 *(Continued)*

Key Performance Indicator	Explanation/Definition
Order entry and maintenance costs	Includes costs for maintaining the customer database, credit check, accepting new orders and adding them to the order system, as well as later order modifications.
% of customers sharing forecasts (consensus forecasting)	Sharing forecast with the most important customer leads to better planning (consensus forecasting); therefore, it is not the number of customers that is important but the sales.
% of orders scheduled to customer request	% of orders whose delivery is scheduled to within an agreed time frame as per the customer's requested delivery date. Orders scheduled to the customer's requested delivery date/Total orders scheduled × 100.
% of suppliers getting shared forecasts (supplier collaboration)	Sharing forecast with the most important supplier leads to better planning (supplier collaboration); therefore it is not the number of suppliers that is important but their purchasing value.
Scrap	Actual scrap based on quantity. It makes sense to measure this for every intermediate product.
Scrap expense	Expenses incurred if product does not meet specifications and has characteristics that make rework impractical. Costs of rework + scrap expenses.
Shrinkage	Costs associated with breakage, pilferage, and deterioration of inventories.
Source cycle time	Cumulative lead time—a total average of combined in-plant planning, supplier lead time (either internal or external), receipts, handling, etc., from demand identification at the factory until the materials are available in the production facility—that is required to source 95% of the dollar value of materials from internal and external suppliers.
Supplier fill rate	Quantity of deliveries (of the supplier) divided by the quantity ordered.
Supplier quality engineering costs	Costs associated with the determination, development/certification, and monitoring of suppliers' capabilities to fully satisfy the applicable quality and regulatory requirements.
Total source lead time	Cumulative lead time required to source 95% of the dollar value of materials from internal and external suppliers.

(Continued)

TABLE 4.2 *(Continued)*

Key Performance Indicator	Explanation/Definition
Total supply chain costs	Sum of supply chain–related management information systems, finance and planning, inventory carrying, material acquisition, and order management costs. (Supply chain–related management information systems + supply chain finance and planning costs + inventory carrying costs + material acquisition costs + order management costs)/revenue × 100.
Transportation costs	Includes all company-paid freight and duties from point of manufacture to end customer or channel.
Transportation costs as a % of order management costs	Includes all company-paid freight and duties from point of manufacture to end customer or channel. Expressed as a % of order management costs. All company-paid freight and duties/order management costs × 100.
Transportation cycle time	Time spend for transportation (includes packaging).

Five-Day Cycle with PLM Scenario

A hypothetical five-day cycle time for manufacturing a widget from design to release to manufacturing is presented next. This sample case does not use all the functionality of the subject PLM system. However, it does illustrate the point of cycle time reduction of design to manufacturing. A comparison of the time it takes in a traditional shop to what a PLM shop takes well illustrates the point. The example does not use all support modules of the subject PLM systems. The full suite of the modules is listed in Table 4.1. Note that the subject functionality is generic, spanning many verticals. The functionality may be redundant for a given vertical.

Day 1: Request
- Customer faxes request to widget manufacturing company dealer.
- Dealer faxes request to regional representative, who scans it and sends over the Internet to the product support group.
- The product group team leader:
  - Uses pager, e-mail, and/or voicemail to alert the global team for a late-afternoon electronic conference.

- Starts electronic folder, accessible to all team members, that will include all project information.
- At meeting, team members—engineering, manufacturing, accounting, and suppliers—review information, assign research responsibilities, and set up the workflow plan.
- The team leader:
  - Schedules an electronic conference for the following day.
  - E-mails the dealer with an overview of the action plan.

Day 2: Search

- Team members meet electronically after reviewing the situation.
- Team members make decisions about how to help resolve the request.
- The team leader makes duty assignments and updates the workflow plan.
- Team members work independently to explore possible alternatives.
- At the end of the day, team members:
  - Confer electronically and decide to design a new component that can be built into widgets.
  - Assess design alternatives. Note that instead of this simple part, if it was a heavy assembly they would be using Product Structure, Process Engineering, DFM (design for manufacturing), and possibly Maintenance modules.
  - Review cost and scheduling implications.
- The team leader incorporates information into the project folder.

Day 3: Engineering

- The component supplier, who conferred overnight with staff about its ability to modify the component, gives the team details about the research.
- The team members refine design alternatives, using e-mail and desktop video conferences and information from the component supplier.
- The team meets electronically to:
  - Compare design analysis results in addition to desktop analysis; other methods used are visualization for form fit and simulation.
  - Decide which options to pursue for the needed component.
- The team leader updates the project folder and electronic workflow plan.

Day 4: Answer

- Product team members work concurrently via electronic channels to finalize the change. General workflow, visualization, and simulation continue to be used in collaboration mode.
- The team leader:

- Oversees the release of the work plan.
- Checks with the supplier on the casting of the needed part.
- Updates the project folder and workflow plan.

Day 5: Shipment
- Supplier delivers casting to widget manufacturing company for final machining and shipment to dealer for installation on the customer's tractor.
- Information generated by the project is captured on a customer and product database for future reference.

Mapping of PLM Feature (to Support High-Volume Parts Manufacturing from Concept to Release)

In a high-volume parts manufacturing situation, the listed modules will be used. Here, all the steps that take place in the above examples will take place, but in this case, manufacturing and distribution take on a lot of importance. Several features of the subject PLM will not be used.

- Life Cycle Data Management
- Product Structure Management
- Recipe Management
- Integration
- Change and Configuration Management
- Project Execution
- Interfaces
- Design Collaboration
- Collaborative Project Management
- Quality Collaboration
- Analytics
- Audit Management
- Quality Control
- Quality Improvement

The scenario without the administrative- and communication-oriented task is:

An idea to make something. It may be a customer query or a designer or engineer brainstorm. Using the group technology function you find out if anything like it has been made in the past. If so, the whole PLM is available to cut and paste and be ready for the next steps. Now, the designer assembles the team and assigns the respective tasks. The team does product design, creates the bill of material and moves on to the routings and the rest of the manufacturing engineering. They are continually collaborating and communicating with their subcontractors and raw materials suppliers. While doing all this, 2D and 3D images of the design are transferred back and forth and the visualization for the form fit using simulation technology is done. Finally, and concurrently, the design and manufacturing are settled, including the raw materials and the subcontractors. When finally the release is made to manufacturing, the high data volume capture and the rest follow. During this phase, capture of data as per the data model becomes very important, As are the analytics and reports on SCM and CRM functions. In a high volume plant, maintenance is another add on, and an important, massive task that can be supported. And if the facility is a semiconductor wafer fab or pharmaceutical company, Quality, Audit, EH&S take inordinate importance.

Today's PLMs have more functionality than they require. The situation may change tomorrow, but in my opinion, it is unlikely to happen in the near future.

Significant Issues in PLM Implementation

Issues of a practical nature in implementing PLM that I have encountered include:

- Champion
- Executive sponsor
- Team leader
- Team
- Communication
- Strategic alignment
- Business case
- Skunk works
- Program plan
- Training plan
- Change management
- Risk management
- Quality plan

These topics are covered later in the book. Note that these issues are over and above the feature, functionality, and benefits of PLM.

Future Outlook

The next excerpt describes the future outlook for Product Life Cycle Management:

> *Product lifecycle management will gain in importance against the current economic trend. PLM could enable organizations to improve operational efficiencies associated with the entire life cycle of a product. The approach of covering applications and business processes across enterprise boundaries is not just a temporary vision; it is a common necessity for the next five years. This comprehensive approach has always to focus on human factors as the most important knowledge capital. Therefore, one vision of PLM is to have the ability of managing intellectual property in an engineering network. Capturing engineering knowledge and re-applying intellectual capital will be the most important competitive factor in the next years.[1]*

Case Example

Prior to working for an electronic packaging company in California, I was chief information officer at a top company in Boston. That company also was a cradle of new inventions. Based on the zero-defect manufacturing philosophy, I had developed tools to gather process and quality data and display them, so that the process engineers could determine the process conditions giving rise to quality problems.

In the architecture that I was developing for the electronic packaging company, I had envisioned process and quality databases. They would provide the correlations of quality parameters with the process parameters. The CAD systems would contain the rest of the manufacturing (make) parameters, such as drawings, bill of materials, routing sheets, travelers, and so on.

However, during the proof-of-concept demonstrations, the customer community felt that the only thing lacking was a lot history database (LHDB). My team and I implemented it in a hurry. It was easy to develop as we had all the essential ingredients in place: CAD systems had all the premake data, such as bill of materials, routings, travelers, drawings, and so on; Dynamic Scheduling had all the schedules; the process database had all the processing conditions; and the quality database had all the quality parameters. We kept records of lots and pointers to other databases that had the other pertinent information.

And these databases had lot numbers and other information. Thus, given the lot number, the LHDB could retrieve any of this information for a given lot:

- When was it made
- Which machines was it made on
- Routing and traveler
- Processing conditions for machine in the routing
- Quality results at each step
- Number of input pieces and number of acceptable quality pieces
- Bill of material
- Material sourced from which vendor
- And so on

All this information was made available to everyone in the company. No hierarchical access was implemented. Everybody could look at everything.

In subsequent years, the vendor community has incorporated more functions, such as environmental health and safety, asset management functionality, and others. But the guts of the PLM system remain as described.

Contrast our experience with that of other very large companies using their legacy systems. They had tremendous integration problems that we did not have. Why? The only reason I can offer is that they had human problems of resistance, and no one central person was tasked to push the change through. I had to work hard with the corporate experts so that they do not create barriers and instead approved the design and guided us so we do not make obvious mistakes. Without this assistance, the corporate bureaucracy would have slowed us to crawl speed.

The scope of Product Life Cycle systems keeps on expanding and encroaching on the domains of other systems. That is very natural.

As far action and benefit KPIs and their relationships to functionality and principles of determining them are the same as described earlier in the SCM chapter.

It seems that CAD, CAPE, CAE, and DFM are coalescing with interfaces into PLM systems. That is good, but PLMs as offered by the enterprise software companies mostly provide interfaces with CAD, CAE, CAPE, DFM, and DFA capabilities, although some are beginning to offer CAE and CAPE capabilities.

Bibliography

Bansal, Sam. "Managing Innovations in CIM Environments: Justification and Implementation Paradigms," Agstino Villa & Mauracio Bielli, University of Torino, Italy, 1995.

Gardner, Christopher. *The Valuation of Information Technology: A Guide to Strategy Development, Valuation & Financial Planning.* Hoboken, NJ: John Wiley & Sons, 2005.

PART III

Scorecard Methodology to Align IT Investments with Business Performance (Deliver on Promise)

When I type the words "deliver on promise" into Google, the search engine comes up with "SOA: Delivering on the Promise of Business-Driven IT Article." This sort of claim by vendors is misleading. It implies that you just have to pick the technology and it will deliver the rest—a situation that is far from true.

The truth, which most of us with some experience in the field know, is that a lot of hard work and sweat is required before any technology delivers on its promises. But it is 100% true that if you do not have the appropriate technology foundation, no promise can be delivered. Part II of this book provided detailed functional and cost benefit knowledge of several technologies and some successful case examples.

However, I recognize that it is necessary to describe in detail how scorecard methodology can be applied and how it is derived to align information technology investments with business performance. The chapters in this part provided detailed discussions of questions clients ask before they undertake any large-scale implementation.

CHAPTER 5

Strategy

To develop a scorecard for an organization, it is of the utmost importance to develop a sound strategy. Business goals and objectives are established in light of the strengths, weaknesses, opportunities, and threats (SWOT) analysis, which is further quantified by benchmarking. Information provided in Part II can help you develop the scorecard by identifying the value drivers/independent key performance indicators (KPIs) that will deliver the benefits/dependent KPIs. Knowledge of technology functionality can be put side by side with the quantifiable and achievable value drivers and benefits. I consider this process to be the domain of information technology (IT) investment alignment with business performance. Now you have a scorecard that can be used to drive business performance. Chapter 5 covers these topics; the remaining chapters describe considerations that are part and parcel of realizing the business value.

Enterprise Strategy

Introduction

Both IT and management literature are awash with strategic alignment of systems with enterprise goals. Horror stories and failures have occurred when strategic alignment does not take place or systems and enterprise goals were in misalignment.

This chapter is about developing an IT strategy that is responsive to the business strategy. The IT strategy formulation, or its synchronization with the enterprise strategy, is based on business goals and SWOT analysis. This chapter is the driver for KPI, benchmarking and scorecarding, as-is and to-be modeling, and business blueprinting. It drives planning for all the activities in the realization phase, such as solution architecting, gap analysis, roll-out planning and configuring, planning for change, quality, risk, test management, training, performance measurement, and performance tracking. The next list outlines the relationship of these activities to the various phases of the project.

- Strategy Phase
  - Enterprise strategy
  - KPIs
  - Benchmarking
  - Value estimating
  - Business process reengineering/blueprinting
- Realization Phase
  - Detailed solution architecting
  - Gap analysis
  - Roll-out planning
  - Configuring
- Human Factors
  - Project management
  - Champions
  - Business case: issues in justifying the justified
- Umbrella Items
  - Change management
  - Risk management
  - Quality management
  - Communications management
  - Test plan and test procedures
  - Training
- Performance measurement and performance tracking

Figure 5.1 describes the approach I developed and have been using widely in developing the enterprise strategy. It covers the strategy phase completely and some parts of the realization phase. Human factors, umbrella items, and performance management, while part of the entire exploitation are covered in Part III but not shown on this diagram.

Most corporations I have worked with have not had the patience to cooperate with the IT strategy developers. Hence, you may need to modify/shorten the material presented here to suit the customer mood. The discussion will be of most value in those few situations when business experts are willing to cooperate fully.

Business Goals and Strategies

Items of utmost importance to the strategy developer are:

- Understanding the organization's goals and objectives: understanding the requirements (what needs to be promised)

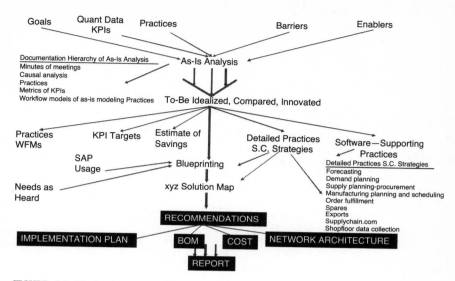

FIGURE 5.1 Methodology (Road Map)

- Linking the goals and objectives with what can be delivered by the systems/IT: delivering to promise
- Understanding the relation to business goals
- Recognizing direct or indirect business benefits
- Discovering the TCO (total cost of operations) effect: what will be achieved by cost reduction from planning, implementation, and operations
- Discovering the direct or indirect continuous business improvement effect

Figure 5.2 illustrates the relationship between the business goal to the business solution via business strategies and business KPIs.

In order to realize any objective, you have to take into account the alternative methods by which it may be achieved. For instance, to enter a new product market, the company may acquire the product or develop it within the organization. It is the customer's decision as to which route to take. The KPIs will reflect the decision made. Also, the systems solution must reflect the business strategy that is chosen.

Questions on the company goals and objectives should be prepared by the developer or the internal/external consultant from which to develop the strategies. Some client teams may not want to answer detailed questions. In this case, it is up to the strategy developing team leader to influence the client team or devise alternative methods to obtain the answers. If answers are not obtained, the project will be at an impasse.

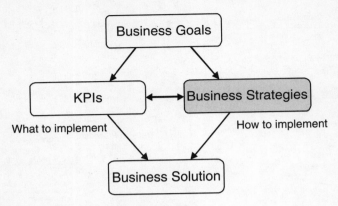

FIGURE 5.2 Business Goals to Business Solutions

Note, however, that any corporation will feel that the following factors could be the opportunities that will drive the corporate strategy and hence impact the systems strategy:

- Prospect of higher profits and returns
- Reduced risk through additional markets and customer groups
- Extensive use of existing production capacities
- Use and protection of existing raw material
- Benefit from cost advantages
- Closeness to markets and customers
- International linking alliances, coalitions, joint ventures
- Favorable currency relations and advantages
- From strategy to competitiveness
- Procurement and use of new know-how
- Avoidance of import restrictions
- Use of state and international support measures
- Use of support measures of host countries

SWOT Analysis

In order to perform the SWOT analysis, the team must hold interview meetings with company personnel. For these meetings to be successful, the team leader has to be very skilled, as the team will be asking deep and probing questions. Table 5.1 presents items and business areas suggested as topics for the interview meetings by division.

At this point, team members want to know exactly what they should ask. The detailed list of questions on goals, objectives, strategies, benefits, requirements has already been covered in Figures 5.1 and 5.2. If the

TABLE 5.1   Customer Participants for SWOT Discussions with the Project Team

Division 1	"c"-level personnel	Corporate-level goals, objectives, directions, etc.
	Controller and staff	Detailed financial
	Senior manager and staff for Area 1	Detailed questions on Area 1
	. . .	. . .
	Senior manager and staff for Area N	Detailed questions on Area N
Division 2	"	"
Division 3	"	"
. . .	. . .	. . .
Division N	"	"

team can perform the SWOT analysis from those answers, the problem is solved, and the meetings can serve as validation meetings in which to get information on unanswered questions. If these answers are not reliable or satisfactory, they can become the items to talk about. An effective technique is to ask questions in the broad categories:

- What are your (not the enterprise's) critical success factors (CSFs)?
- What are inhibitors to your achieving your CSFs?
- What are the enablers to your achieving the CSFs?

By the time you come to the enablers, you will have a pretty good idea of the answers. From there, you can go to the SWOT format and ask the customer team leader to give three answers to each of the strengths, weaknesses, opportunities, and threats.

It is recommended that each team member write down notes from each day's meeting. The project leader consolidates the answers daily, so that the findings can be circulated to the customer representatives for validation.

All of these steps should be repeated before the realization phase begins. At that time, the emphasis shifts from strategy to realization-oriented items.

Case Example

This case presents the results of SWOT analysis and resulting strategy (needs) for a client in China. Results of the SWOT analysis carried out are presented first.

(Continued)

(Continued)

SWOT Analysis
- Strengths
  - Management
  - Practices
  - Relationships with vendors, dealers, partners
  - Design and engineering
  - Lean cost structure
  - Capacity
- Opportunities
  - Exploding markets in China
  - Exploding markets globally
  - Strengths the company possesses
  - New tools and technologies, such as SCM, PLM, CRM, and the Internet, can give the company muscle to compete in the high-volume world of tomorrow
- Threats
  - World Trade Organization opening up the local market to global powerhouses
  - Global multinational corporations have high-class practices supported by IT
  - Local competition could take the new-market share to become the high-volume market leader
- Weaknesses
  - None

No weaknesses were found with this company. Two years after our work, this client had become so good that it bought the entire PC business of an iconic U.S. firm.

Translation to strategies resulted directly from the opportunities identified. They are repeated for the sake of completeness:

Strategies
- Increase market share by 7% per year.
- New tools and technologies such as SCM, PLM, CRM, and the Internet, can give you the company muscle to compete in the high-volume world of tomorrow. This was on top of the full function enterprise resource planning working completely.

The rest of the work on this assignment, such as KPI determination, benchmarking, scorecarding, value determination, and business case establishment, was a result of the strategies established here. If we were to operate at a lower level, the strategies would be more operational.

So far we have discussed the business scope, goals, objectives, requirements, strengths, weaknesses, opportunities, threats and strategies. With the validated write-ups, we have a basic strategy document and are ready to drive the next sections of the strategy.

Key Performance Indicators

Introduction

Key performance indicators are the measure of the business goals. Contrary to most projects that concentrate on IT-oriented KPIs, we are concerned here with the KPIs of the stakeholders' business goals. There is a slowly growing trend towards using the business KPIs. I was once a guest lecturer at the University of Southern California in the master's Product Development and Program Management course. After I presented my KPI-based opportunity assessment case study, I was surprised to learn that no one in the class had been taught this kind of KPI-based approach in project management.

Characteristics of KPIs

Figure 5.3 is based on the Supply Chain Operations Reference (SCOR) model and the unique business environment of a client company. It shows the hierarchical nature of KPIs and also how they are changed by the process. Level 3 KPIs, such as forecast accuracy and schedule adherence, which belong to the planning area, are the most independent by nature; they are

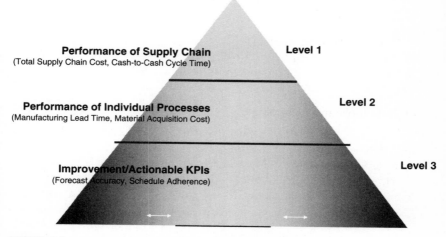

FIGURE 5.3 SCOR Model Representation of a Business Environment

actionable and show their impact on Level 1 KPIs, such as total supply chain cost and cash-to-cash cycle time. Level 2 KPIs will vary by the process area and have an impact both on Level 1 and Level 3 KPIs.

How to Establish KPIs

The three essential steps to the establishment of KPIs are:

1. Identify KPIs translatable from the business goals.
    a. They should be measurable and quantifiable.
    b. They should be dependent variables that respond to some independent variables. For example, inventory is an independent variable that affects the supply chain cost as a dependent variable.
2. Identify in the value-driven tree the independent variables that affect the subject KPIs or the dependent variables. This is done because these independent variables can be adjusted to have a desired effect on the subject KPIs or the dependent variables.
3. Identify all such KPIs that form a natural cluster.

Table 5.2 summarizes results from an engagement from the farm equipment sector of an automotive client company. Here the process areas are on the extreme left-hand side, in which rows provide the quantifiable and actionable goals/KPIs that the company wants to achieve. Columns 2 and 3 provide the as-is and to-be values of each KPI. Column 4 gives the delta between the as-is and to-be values. Note that the process area KPIs are enterprise-wide KPIs that generally every company in manufacturing wants to achieve.

KPI Value Trees

Figure 5.4 shows the value tree of KPIs for the total supply chain costs.

As the value tree shows, you can reduce the total supply chain cost by reducing the order management costs, material acquisition costs, inventory carrying costs, finance and planning cost, plus the supply chain (SC)–related management information system (MIS) costs. Each one of these is in turn dependent on many other variables that can be modulated. Hence, if the business goal is to reduce the cost of goods sold, you can attempt to reduce the total supply chain cost. However, since this SCM cost is impacted by many other independent variables, you may look for the heavy hitters, which most of the time turn out to be are inventory carrying costs and transportation costs.

Table 5.3 takes the supply chain total cost of KPIs, identifies the source variables that impact it, and clusters the KPIs. The table provides a good

TABLE 5.2   The Delta

Area	As-Is	To-Be	"Delta"
Inventory			
XYZ	99 MUS$	51 MUS$	45.5 MUS$
Dealers	10 MUS$	3.5 MUS$	6 MUS$
Inventory savings	—	—	16.9 MUS$
Cycle time	39 Days	19 Days	20 days
Market share	28%	35%	7%
Practices	"Push driven"	"Demand Driven"	Idealized and practical practices consistent with strategic considerations
KPIs	Localized	Integrated Clustered	Supporting the above practices
IT infrastructure	Limited IT infrastructure to support outbound logistics	Integrated IT systems across the entire Supply chain	Timely availability of data for real-time decision support
Customer responsiveness	Focus on selling to dealer	Focus on end customer sales and service	Focus on wholesale as well as retail demand

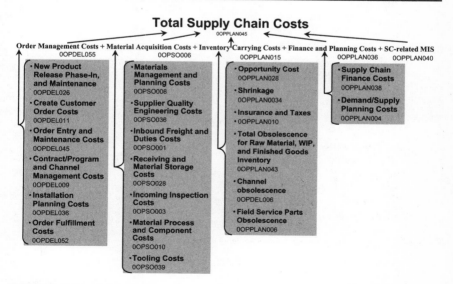

FIGURE 5.4 Total Supply Chain Costs

TABLE 5.3   Clustered KPIs Leading to Total Supply Chain Cost

No.	Metric	Client Company	Best in Class	Average in Class	Median
1	**Order Fulfillment Days** Days to order Days to make Days to deliver				
2	**On-time delivery to committed dates (%)**				
3	**Total inventory (days of inventory)** Supplier-side finished goods inventory (days of supply) Branch inventory (days of supply) Dealer (days of inventory)				
4	**Supply chain management cost (% of revenue)** Total supply chain costs (% of total product revenue) Order management costs Material acquisition costs Inventory carrying costs Supply chain–related financial and planning costs Total supply chain–related management information system costs Sum of supply chain costs components (% of total product revenue)				

example of SCM cost cluster, which summarizes the 96 SCM KPIs. However, note that the four items listed make up the SCM cluster. Item 1 concerns the cluster of order fulfillment days, which includes days to order, days to make, and days to deliver as the independent variables. This cluster is not related to cost but to quality.

Conclusions

Through examples of the case work, we have seen:

- How to establish measurable and quantifiable KPI clusters
- How clusters essentially mean related KPI chunks; generally they mean independent and dependent KPIs
- How value trees provide examples of KPIs, and how you can form clusters by selecting chunks of them as per items 1 and 2 in Table 5.3

KPIs from the SCM and PLM domain are given in detail in Part II. All of them can be used as needed for further work with KPIs for value creation.

Benchmarking

Benchmarking is the activity that is driven by KPI clusters. Here we compare the company KPIs with the ones of industry at large and also the best in class. Benchmarking is the process of determining who is the very best, who sets the standard, and what that standard is. Until recently, Dell was the best in running supply chains, because its inventory and cash-to-cash cycle was the very best in the industry.

A lot of services provide benchmarking services. Some are legitimate and others are not. If your budget is low and manpower is abundant, you may start on your own path to estimate the best in class (in your industry) and median in industry. You can do this through surveys. However, you may run into difficulties because your competitors may not want to share their KPIs with you. Another approach is to plow through the company annual reports and glean whatever you can from them. One thing you certainly will get is inventory levels in dollars, from which you can calculate inventory carrying cost. This is the annual interest on the value of the inventory that appears as an asset on the balance sheet. Without surveys, it is almost impossible to find a good set of benchmarks. Hiring a consulting company and telling it which KPIs you want benchmarked is your best bet.

The results of a benchmarking study done for a client in the automotive sector are shown in Figure 5.5. The "Metrics" column lists the KPIs we gave to a consulting company to benchmark. The column headed "Practical"

Metrics	As Is	Best in class	Ideal (norm-alized)	Prac-tical	Target 2001	Target 2002	Target 2003	How to Achieve
Order fulfillment lead time (days)	39	12.5	16	19	27	21	19	Planning in APO Satellite plants BPR implementation
Key components or material availability (days)	30	12.5	7	14	25	21	14	Procurement strategies and procedures
Direct labor availability (days)	30	3.3	7	14	25	21	14	Flexibility in deployment
Supply chain costs as % of revenue	24.7 (8.9)	2.1	22.9 (7.1)	22.9 (7.1)	24 (8.2)	23 (7.2)	22.9 (7.1)	Supply chain optimization Quality systems
On-time delivery to commit percentage	99	97	100	99	99	99	99	Demand-driven organization

FIGURE 5.5 Results of Benchmarking Study

gives the practical best-in-class values for the local environment based on my team's judgment.

Now the customer team and the project team are ready to select the annual improvement targets. The result is Figure 5.5, which, in the parlance of the Supply Chain Council, is also known as a SCOR card.

In the case of the subject client, the president had the scorecard enlarged, framed, and hung above his chair. I asked him why. He replied: "I want everybody on my staff that comes to see me to look at the best-in-class column, because that is where I want this company to go."

Benchmarking is an extremely useful tool. It serves as a basis to start making improvements that have been achieved by others in the same class or in a similar sector or if you want to exceed the best.

Value/Benefits Estimating

Introduction

Nick Carr, in his famous *Harvard Business Review* article,[1] wrote that IT does not matter. Andy Grove, who was Chairman and CEO of Intel for a long time was upset and wrote about it. I too was somewhat upset and also wrote to Nick Carr. I raised these points:

- IT by itself is more a menace than a solution.
- It is not IT but deft exploitation of it that delivers the value.

- Most of IT without the deftness does not deliver value.
- IT does not increase the top line, but judicious use of it can help improve the top line.
- IT can certainly act as an enabler to bottom-line improvements.
- Neither the vendors nor the users can properly quantify each tool and its benefits. All claim the same thing in a very hazy way. And this becomes a problem.

The goal of this chapter is to take care of these issues by establishing the business value from the pragmatic and business goal driven SCOR card.

Estimating the Value: PC Company Example

This chapter focuses on estimating the value that can be derived from the improvements achievable by improving KPIs. To demonstrate this, we will consider further the earlier referenced engagement done for a PC sector.

This study refers to the SCOR model shown in Figure 5.3. While our technique is applicable to any process area, supply chain redesign happened to be the engagement in this instance. For other areas/processes, the KPIs and therefore the benchmarks would change.

Consider the SCOR card in Table 5.4. The KPIs of the supply chain appear in column 1. Column 2 provides the as-is KPIs but recast to bring them up to international reporting standards. "Best in Class" and "Average in Class" numbers were determined by the client and our project team, as was the "Target Client Company" column. "NC" stands for "no charge," and appears whenever the line item was not included in the savings estimate. This company's supply chain cost was running at the extremely low level of 3.15 % of the revenue, so it would not be a candidate for further reduction.

The last three rows were going to yield low contributions to improvements. Because of this, we were left with only the material cost improvements as paid to the vendors, but company executives declined to squeeze their vendors (whom they considered partners) any further. After a great deal of soul searching, we thought of including the market share gain as a possible contributor. Based on the SWOT analysis, we were confident that the customer team could ramp up the production and supply chain. We discussed this with the client executives, and they accepted the idea. The calculations in Table 5.5 are included to illustrate how we estimated the value creation due to these items.

Based on the PC market growth estimated at 3%/year for the three-year time frame of the forecast and the client company's accepted market share of 8%/year, line 7 was computed. Line 8 gives the profit at the base rate of 6.66% of revenue at the baseline. This increases as per the volume growth; the assumption is that the base infrastructure would remain the same, and

TABLE 5.4   Client PC Company's SCOR Card

Important KPIs	As-Is Recast %	Best in Class	Average in Class	Target Client Co	Enablers/ Client Empowerment
Materials cost as paid to vendors	86.40	80	50	3%/Yr Red	Vendor-managed inventory
Wage cost	1.2	2		NC	
Total SCM cost	3.15	6.3	11.6	NC	
Order fill time days	7	1		2	Real-time ATP
Brand new products, time to market	1	2–>1		NC	
Manf paradigms	Push	Push>Pull		Pull	Assemble to order
Days of inventory	18	6	26	NC	
Material acquisition cost	0.64	0.86	2.18	NC	
Cash-to-cash cycle	−11	24.7	97.4	NC	
% Orders on time to customer requirment date	70	94.6	80.1	95	CTP
% Orders on time to commit date	64	97.1	89.9	97	Exeception management
Forecast accuracy %	75	?	?	90	Collaborative consensus

any incremental expense would increase in the same proportion as at the baseline. So line 9 was computed, which is simply the contribution due to volume growth. Line 10 gives the additional profit due to 3% material cost reduction. Line 11 aggregates all improvements, and line 12 gives the 300% of the base value creation.

Now, even if we do not want to take credit for material cost reduction and supply chain cost improvement, as management wanted to do, the cumulative profit improvement over the baseline comes at 44% for the three-year time frame assumption.

TABLE 5.5   Calculations of Value Creation

No		MRMB	2000	2001	2002	Total 3 Yrs
1	Revenue at the base of 99, if nothing else was done	7,969	7,969	7,969	7,969	
2	Profit at the base rate of 6.66 of 99, if nothing else was done	531	531	531	531	1593
3	PC market growth		35%	38%	40%	
4	Total # of units market	5,590,909	7,547,727	10,415,864	14,582,209	
5	XYZ Co market share, at the rate of 8%/year growth	22	30	38	45	
6	XYZ Co Volume As per market share growth rate and its own market share growth rate	1,230,000	2,264,318	3,958,028	6,561,994	
7	Revenue growth as per unit growth	7,969	14,670	25,644	42,514	
8	Profit at the base rate of 1999 of 6.66%, for the unit growth rate	531	977	1,708	2,831	
9	Additional profit due to volume growth		446	731	1,124	2,301
10	Additional profit due to 3%/yr material cost reduction as % of revenue		440	769	1,275	2,485
11	Total opportunity created = due to market share growth+reduced material cost		886	1,500	2,399	4,786
12	Net new value created as % of base					300

Conclusions: Principles of Good Value Estimating

Certain principles can be recommended for good value estimating:

- Go for heavy hitters/impact.
- Purists and academically oriented people try to make an exact science out of value estimating, but it is a crude patchwork of estimates-based benchmarks and a lot of industry knowledge.
- Emphasize large deltas and do not get stuck with precision.
- Realize that the business case is a lot more than a good number that you can derive by value estimates. This is illustrated in Chapter 7 in the section entitled "Business Case Development."
- Help client teams select target KPIs. They should not be so ambitious that the implementation teams get overwhelmed, nor should they be so easy that there is no challenge in achieving them.

Business Process Reengineering

Introduction

Business process reengineering (BPR) was a topic of great activity and scholarship in the 1990s. Everybody, every company, every country launched a BPR initiative. I was involved with many such initiatives at client companies to optimize operations and improve the bottom lines. Then came SAP with its Business Blue Print (BBP). If you look under its hood, it is the same as BPR. Nevertheless, SAP seemed to be more interested in creating a BBP reference model of to-be workflow models for all processes that could be customized (configured) by each vertical and each customer. This approach must have sold countless copies of SAP; many of the reengineering directors I talked with implemented SAP, because it would save them the drudgery of detailed business modeling and workflow modeling. For the purposes of this book, BPR can be defined as the BBP.

Basic Beliefs of BPR

The basic beliefs of BPR were to cut out the process steps that do not add value.[2] In a positive sense, this means to create value. Value, when tangible, can be created by reducing operating costs and also by reducing the costs of goods sold. Certain parameters can improve the bottom lines. To achieve this, greater revenue and better asset utilization has to take place.

In BPR, you must reduce the cost of goods sold, reduce material acquisition costs, and reduce production costs. Operating cost reduction can be achieved by reducing the logistics and administrative costs.

To improve asset utilization, both fixed capital investment and working capital investment have to be reduced. Revenue increase can be achieved in four ways:

1. Reduce lost sales.
2. Reduce order cycle times.
3. Increase margins on existing sales.
4. Increase on-time deliveries.

These four categories of value creation can also be looked at in light of these four categories:

1. Increase revenue:
   - Optimize demand fulfillment.
   - Increase forecast accuracy.
   - Improve inventory positioning.
   - Improve manufacturing responsiveness.
   - Optimize vehicle scheduling.
   - Improve supply chain responsiveness.
2. Increase asset utilization:
   - Rationalize the network.
   - Rationalize equipment.
   - Reduce finished goods inventories.
   - Increase forecast accuracy.
   - Reduce cash-to-cash cycle time.
   - Optimize batch runs.
   - Reduce raw/work-in-progress inventory levels.
   - Reduce damage obsolescence.
3. Reduce operating costs:
   - Optimize the network.
   - Reduce transportation costs.
   - Reduce transshipments.
   - Reduce inventories.
   - Increase forecast accuracy.
   - Improve processes.
4. Reduce cost of goods sold:
   - Optimize supply sourcing.
   - Increase forecast accuracy.
   - Reduce inbound transportation costs.

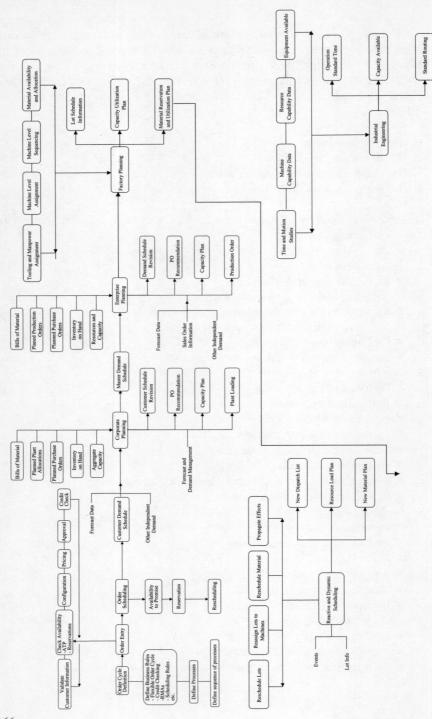

166

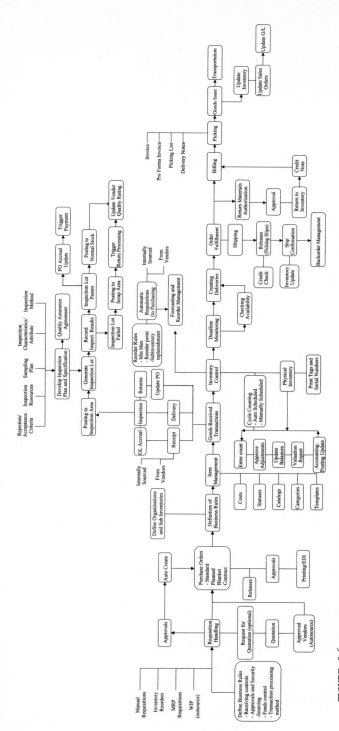

FIGURE 5.6 Overall Business Model

- Improve quality.
- Increase velocity.
- Improve manufacturing efficiency.
- Optimize changeovers.

Workflow Modeling

However, to approach business process reengineering systematically, follow these two steps:

1. Collect data from the business leaders and experts on
   - Goals and objectives
   - KPIs
   - SWOTs
2. From these data, prepare models:
   - As is
   - To be
     Prepare these models for each process area of the business in accordance with the project scope.

We already discussed what to collect and how to collect it. The only thing that has not been covered is as-is and to-be (workflow) modeling.

You can do workflow modeling (WFM) for a process, for a business unit, or for a corporation. The essentials are:

- Event that causes the model to come alive
- Organization performing a given function
- Function being performed
- Action it takes and trigger it creates
- Resultant information processing it does
- Report(s) it creates

Figure 5.6 is an overall business model of the semiconductor industry. It shows all the major processes, such as supply chain planning, manufacturing, industrial engineering, and dynamic scheduling. This model can be used as a reference model.

Using from the knowledge gained from the business model, you can easily create workflow models using tools such as Visio. Note that all the models we built used standard Microsoft Word.

We do not give all the other models here; our goal is just to show what a WFM looks like.

Reengineering

By the time you are done with the as-is and to-be WFMs and the overall business model, KPIs, and benchmarked scorecard, ideas will begin to flow for:

- Where the unnecessary steps can be eliminated
- Which processes can be eliminated altogether
- What the new practices will look like (to-be WFMs)
- What the value drivers are
- What IT technologies are responsive to the value drivers

The last step is validation and approval with customer teams. Customers may need to be guided because they may not fully understand the WFMs. In my engagement in the farm equipment sector, when the president finally understood the impact, he said, "It is not reengineering. It is innovation." That made my day.

Bibliography

Andrews, Dorine, and Susan Stalick. *Business Reengineering*. Prentice Hall, 1994.

Burn, Janice M. "A Comparison of the Views of Business and IT Management on Success Factors for Strategic Alignment," Edith Cowan University, Perth, Western Australia.

Carr, Nicholas. "IT Doesn't Matter," *Harvard Business Review* (May 2003).

Daum, Jurgen H. "Strategy: A Holistic Approach: Adding Value Through IT Investments," SAP AG, sapinfo.net.

Gartner Group. "10 Step Guide to Achieving Business Value of IT," 2003.

Hoque, Faisal. "The Alignment Effect: How to Get Business Value Out of Technology." *Financial Times*. Prentice Hall, 2002.

Jahnke, Art. "Why Is Business–IT Alignment So Difficult?" *CIO Magazine* (June 2004).

Scheer, A. W. *Business Process Engineering*. Springer Verlag, 1994.

Tieschendorf, Raymond. "Technology: Nothing More Than a Vehicle for an IT Strategy: Corporate Goals Set the Course." META Group Deutschland GmbH.

CHAPTER 6

Realization Phase

B y the end of Chapter 5, you should have a quantified scorecard that has been developed in full alignment with the company's investment strategy. Now is the time to drive the technology functionality to the architectural and implementation considerations.

Solution Architecting

Introduction

Some time ago, I read a good article and wrote some thoughts in reaction to it. These thoughts are about the characteristics of a good information (IT) architecture. They are, by the way, the notes I used to follow when architecting a solution:

- Compatible
- Migratable
- Portable
- Scalable
- Longevity
- Delivers good return on investment
- Intra- and intercompany world wide integration
- Functional support
- Intuitive to users
- Alerts, tracking, reports, workflow
- Linking business processes to the business bottom line

Serious examination of these notes shows that they are the highlights of good architecture, even today.

Solution Mapping

However, the task on hand is to go from Business Process Re-Engineering/
Business Blue Print (BPR/BBP) to solution architecture. From previous
chapters, we have the value drivers (key performance indicators [KPIs] that
drive the KPI variables measuring value). By mapping them on the solutions
provided by prospective vendors, we are able to create a solution map.
There will be no problem with higher-level functionality. Any problem will
be in the details.

Column 1 of Table 6.1 shows the opportunities identified with the PC
client with whom we had an engagement. Column 2 was carefully mapped
on the two opportunities. Care was taken so that column 2's items map
appropriately on the two opportunities, so that value drivers that can deliver

TABLE 6.1   Value Creation and Value Drivers

Opportunity 1: Value Creation	Value Drivers
Increase market share	
Innovative production introductions	New product introductions/special configurable products
Special configurable products	Collaborative engineering
Service and after-sales support	Know-how sharing with partners, dealers
Collaborative channel management	Life cycle costing
Delivery performance	Configuration management
Improved forecast accuracy	Variant pricing
Increased regional presence	**Value Drivers:** Channel Management
Direct sales model	Collaborative forecasting with dealers for long term, seasonal, and short term
Capacity planning	Promotional planning with dealers capable to promise (CTP)
	Value Drivers: Delivery Performance
	Reduction of order fulfillment lead time
	Real-time available to promise (ATP)
	Assemble to order
	Value Drivers: Forecast Accuracy
	Use of centralized database for consistency
	Employ casual and statistical methods
	Use collaborative planning with dealers
	Consensus forecasting process
	Automated system
	Use variant based forecasting
	Consider promotional planning together with product life cycle

TABLE 6.1 *(Continued)*

Opportunity 2: Cost Reduction	Value Drivers: Order-based Model Configuration
Reduce material cost Maintain supply chain (SCM) management cost	Challenge: Product knowledge management
	Wider variety of possible configurations
Planning based on improved forecast	Enhanced complexity without frequent engineering change
Reduce spot market/buying	Central knowledge repository & master data distribution
Product cost planning	More complex product / target costing
Alternate vendor program	Know-how transfer to dealers and service agents
Raw material (RM) quality	. . .
Vendor managed inventory	**Value Drivers:** Order-based model configuration
	Challenge: Planning
	More complex product/target costing
	Forecasting on basic model and variants
	Variant-based trend analysis on historical data
	Interleaved mix procurement planning for common/variant parts
	Variant-based forecasting for spare parts
	. . .
	Value Drivers: Order-based model configuration
	Challenge: Order Fulfillment
	Smaller lot size (customer order lot size)
	Customer order-based configuration and pricing/consistency
	Customer order pegging
	CTP instead of ATP (ATP on component level and capacity)
	Individual production lot tracking for warranty/call-back/repair
	More complex production scheduling (sequencing/line balance)
	More complex material preparation

opportunities 1 and 2 map correctly. On close inspection you will find that most of the items of column 2 belong to the supply chain management (SCM) domain, as can be ascertained by referring to the architecture and functionality of Chapter 3.Fig 3.1 Those not available in Chapter 3 call for practice change, such as smaller lot size, use of a central database, individual production lot tracking, and the like.

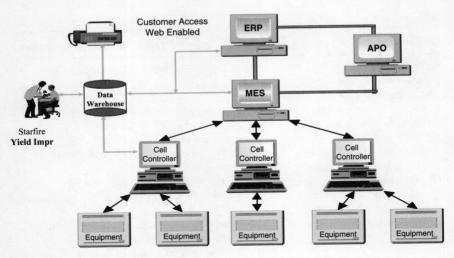

FIGURE 6.1 Full-Service Solution Architecture

Solution Architecting

By considering the items in column 2, you can envision a logical architecture of systems that will provide all the functionality demanded by the opportunities. Certainly most of the support will come from a modern SCM system, but what it will not be able to handle can come from other systems. This may require more than one vendor, or a gap will be created. This enables us to create logical architectures of support as shown in Figures 6.1 and 6.2.

Note that these solution architectures presume that a full-service support is required, based on the mapping. The functions that were not available from the SCM modules will come from the manufacturing execution system (MES), such as lot tracking, ability to handle smaller lot sizes, and so on. Others, such as enterprise resource planning, mail, file, and print servers were not part of column 2 of Table 6.1, but they are given as part of the legacy systems. Note that legacy systems predate SCM's introduction; hence most likely they existed. If not, they can be presumed to be a part of best practice in advanced manufacturing solutions. Figure 6.2 shows global network architecture.

The solutions architecture shown in the figures meet all the characteristics of a good architecture.

Gap Analysis

Introduction

Essentially, gap analysis involves the detailed mapping of system requirements, as derived from to-be WFMs. It is not based on the functionality

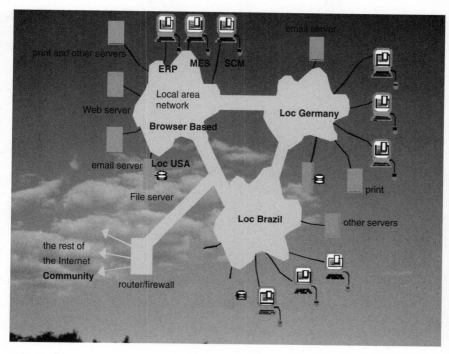

FIGURE 6.2 Full-Service Manufacturing Solution's Architecture

available in the vendor's literature and conference room presentations. Note that it is far easier to develop a gap list at a higher level than at the detailed level.

How Vendors Handle Gaps

When working with an SCM vendor at the early stages of product introduction, we found the following vendor-created ratings. Note these codes:

    − = gap (lacking in standard product)
    + = in standard product
    has required functionality
    has some functionality already
    $\frac{1}{2}$ = product has only half the desired requirements

- Binning: $\frac{1}{2}$. Need to improve coproduct functionality to make data maintenance easier
- Capacity measurements by starts and outs : +
- Lot genealogy: −

- Long lead times: +
- Repeated processes: +
- Multiple-step routings: +
- Yield by operation: + (Release 7)
- Outsourcing: +
- Strategic commodity relationships and volatile demand: +
- Allocation by customer and products: −
- Upgrades and downgrades: $\frac{1}{2}$ (need to enhance part substitution logic)
- Inventory allocation: −
- Product configuration: $\frac{1}{2}$
- Supply chain capable to promise—multilevel requirement: −
- Reprioritization or bumping: −
- Soft pegging: +

Note that this vendor was comparing his offering against the requirements cited by members of the semiconductor community as well as by us, the industry consultant. Therefore, the obvious question was: Why did anybody buy the vendor's system with its known gaps? The vendor supplied these answers:

- Buy the product. We know what you need.
- We will fulfill some of your needs in the next release.
- We are working on some updates in the lab, and they will be available to you before you go live.
- Yes, there are three gaps that our standard offering will not fulfill, so you must customize.

Another high-tech customer used this vendor and another vendor for ERP. The gap analysis had been done a long time before my team's involvement. Details of the requirements were different because this client belonged to a different vertical. However, the vendor response followed similar lines, and the results were similar.

And eventually, some of the problems in meeting the promises to fill the gaps after customization above may or may not happen. But the point is that gap analysis was done.

How to Deal with Vendors on Gaps

When there is any doubt about a vendor's offerings, you should insist on a conference room demonstration with live data before you select a vendor and award a contract. However, you must supervise vendor personnel very aggressively so that they show you a real demo, not a simulated one. In the heat of the performance and with little knowledge of the vendor's system, it is easy to get fooled. You need to be aware of this problem.

Some vendors are so new that most of your requirements will be fulfilled by custom development. This is what you may be told in response to your request for proposal questions. In this case, you will disqualify the vendor at this stage.

Best Disposition with Gaps

The best outcome beyond gap analysis is when you:

- Have selected a good vendor.
- Are ready to make gaps work in the most expedient fashion.
- Staff members who are familiar with the system and are able to manage either a work-around or do a little customizing

My Best Experience with Gaps

The best experience I had was with projects that were developed in-house, or we gave the document/system specifications to the selected vendor to develop according to our needs. In all these cases, which were in the semiconductor or high-tech industry, projects did very well. Not that it was the first time the systems behaved as envisioned, but they were made to deliver results with fewer hassles. So you could say the gaps were well satisfied.

Best Scenario with Gaps with Packaged Systems

With packaged systems, the best results happen when:

- The project team understands the processes well.
- They can do accurate WFMs with understanding.
- They also understand the functionality of the chosen system's repertoire, or you have a good consultant on your project team.
- The team is not under heavy fire of an impending deadline.

Roll-Out Planning

Introduction

When times were simpler, you developed and deployed. If others liked what you did, they came to you and you asked them what they wanted, customized their needs, and gave them the solution. But then corporations got smart and began demanding the roll-out to different businesses. In doing so the motivation would be to keep the basic functionality that had been developed the same but allow minimum changes as required. Then came the time when all these roll-outs went global. Now, in terms of complex systems and mega global systems, we have all of these issues to consider. This section is concerned with how to move the same solution to multiple locations with minimum rework or maximum reuse.

Why Work with Templates

These are the main reasons for working with templates:

- The use of corporate standards throughout the enterprise, including best practices, is mandatory.
- Templates reduce the time it takes to implement the system.
- Templates reduce the effort needed to maintain a major global solution.

Implementation/Roll-Out Strategies

The various implementation strategies can be grouped into:

- Global template
- Partial global template
- Full global template

Next we briefly define some of the possibilities and discuss a few of the implications that should be taken into consideration.

GLOBAL TEMPLATE   A template is a part of one or several systems/solutions that have been configured somewhat by the company, as per the process given in Figure 6.3. It is used in other parts of the company (or enterprise) as a template with predefined settings for the implementation of production systems. Global templates comprise customer-specific as well as vendor-delivered models, concepts, documentation, system parameters, developments (called add-ons), master data, and sample test runs as well as outline project structures (in order to structure and support implementation of the production system). However, it is a basic assumption that local adaptations always will be required to make a global template work in a local productive situation.

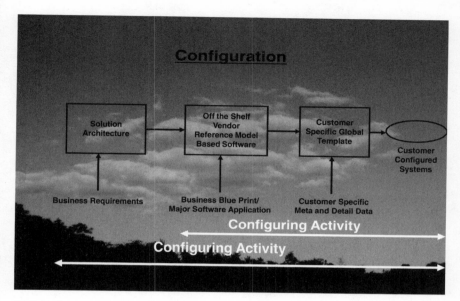

FIGURE 6.3 Configuring Activities

PARTIAL GLOBAL TEMPLATE   A partial global template includes all of the business processes that are intended to be global or regional/divisional in nature but not local. The template includes the global business processes that could subsequently be rolled out plus all other objects/transactions required to execute these global processes.

FULL GLOBAL TEMPLATE   The full global template includes extensive modeling of complete business units for subsequent complete roll-out into local units. It can be used for smaller sites that have very little time, capital, and resources available to achieve accelerated implementation of a productive system.

GLOBAL REFERENCE SYSTEM   All global templates being developed will reside in a global reference system, which can be composed of several physical distributed systems. This reference system is then used as the source for extracting the global templates, which will be sent to the local implementation sites and used only for testing, presentation, demonstrations, and training purposes of the entire global solution. By nature, the global reference system does not contain all existing local solutions and processes, only local processes which are required to make the global solution in the reference system executable. Note that in Figure 6.3, it is the result (i.e., customer-specific global template) from block 2.

Roll-Out Issues

The roll-out planning team has to address these issues:

- What is the impact of global requirements and approaches on the roll-out strategy and local units?
- What are the main elements for roll-out efficiency (e.g., early preparation, solution package, prepared project layouts, global roll-out core teams)?
- Are there political and psychological aspects related to a roll-out approach?
- What types of communications are required to include locals into the roll-out?
- What local specific pros, cons, drivers, and constraints exist for a specific treatment during roll-out?
- What preparations can be done for locals to ease the roll-out?
- What are the business-related roll-out drivers?
- What resource capabilities impact the roll-out approach?
- Are budgets available to perform the roll-out, and in what form?
- Is the corporate/regional/local IT support set up appropriately?
- On what quantitative and qualitative levels is local project execution possible?

Configuration Planning

Introduction

Configuring is defined as identifying the hardware and software components that make up the system. Generally speaking, this is the definition of solution/system architecture. However, here and specifically for the environments of off-the-shelf vendor-furnished business software, consider the explanation given in Figure 6.3.

Configuring

While the activities from solution architecting to the generation of customer-configured systems is generally classified as configuring, here the focus is on creating the customer-specific global template and finally the customer-configured system. As is shown in Figure 6.3, when business blueprint and major software application requirements are used to tailor an off-the-shelf vendor system, a customer-specific global template is created. When this template is used along with the customer-specific metadata and detailed data and business rules, the customer-configured system is generated.

Configuration Planning

Configuration planning can be done after completion of the tasks described in previous chapters, or overlapping right from solution architecting, or from the business process reengineering stage, if the teams are ready. However, configuration planning must not be started before the business process reengineering stage.

Important elements for the configuration plan include:

- The to-be model of the company with the enterprise segregations, the model-based reference software, and templates as defined earlier
- The agreed system topology as per the solution architecture
- For the modeling elements, the classification of distributed, globalized/standardized, and local elements together with the full setup of organizational elements in the vendor's system
- The company's historic solutions and their documentation state
- The agreed sequence and prioritization of implementing the reference systems and templates

The results of the configuration plan consist of:

- The strategy for the configuration of the global solution
- The concept and features for the appropriate link between the global solution model and its elements with the global solution configuration and its elements, and a mutual maintenance process
- A plan for the setup of one or several reference systems and a physically configured system setup of clients within the reference systems, supplemented with appropriate software
- The confirmation and firm definition of templates in terms of configuration—the configuration content plan broken down into:
  - Reference systems and clients
  - Distribution features to be used
  - Templates to be created
  - Relevant localization and internationalization issues
- A plan for the setup of global development environments (sandbox, development, delivery) and for the transporting/installation procedure

for local roll-out development systems (roll-out deliveries for the initial case and the follow-up)
- A fixed release for the start-up of the reference systems and a release schedule for them
- The main parameters (e.g., language, representative organizational units) and overall guidelines for the global solution configuration and local roll-out adaptations, including a check procedure for local coherence with the global settings
- General reporting and checking features for global and local level, and the according statistics

As configuration and developments depend on each other, these links have to be managed as well.

The major characteristics and options of specific configuration approaches are:

- Functional-oriented configuration versus process-oriented configuration
- Usage/application of configuration tools, including configuration documentation
- Handling of classes of customizing objects (client-dependent and independent, generating and generated objects, not transportable objects, etc.)
- Handling of other vendors' major applications
- Handling of "configuration" of e-commerce scenarios
- Handling of "configuration" of the role and workplace features
- Handling of vendors' industry-specific precustomization, if any
- Handling of customer-specific historic configuration
- Configuration related to distribution

Types of Configuration Documentation

Areas to consider include:

- Attributes of configuration: defined before and related to model objects
- Degree of freedom for configuration: global/mandatory, optional, local
- Conversion of configuration with respect to organizational units during roll-out
- Configuration and sample master data
- Configuration and test data
- Language-dependent configuration and dependencies on code pages
- Configuration related to country-specific functionality

Based on the definitions in the previous step, one or more dependent or independent configuration activities will start. As approach, environment, and methodology are defined, and skilled personnel are assigned, the additional activity here is to have an execution plan for each distinct configuration activity, which allows for reconciliation with the other configuration activities and groups. A questions-and-answers procedure is required to ensure that everyone sticks to the rules defined in the previous step. This applies to the global level if multiple templates are configured at the same time and to the local level to ensure that the global input is used and applied correctly.

Configuration Packaging and Transport, Installation, and Verification (Roll-Out)

The concept of solution packaging is associated with the detailed creation of global templates. It incorporates practically all results and objects that appear during a global implementation. The preparation of solution packaging goes along with the configuration and testing process. The (local) installation and verification process is considered to be the initial step during roll-out.

Bibliography

Parkinson, John. "The Limits to Good Architecture," *CIO Insight* (July 2003).

CHAPTER 7

Human Factors

This chapter describes the most obscure but important reasons that can cause project failure or success. Perhaps everyone knows that you should have good project managers, but how many know and believe that every successful project must have a project champion who acts as a facilitator when the project runs into heavy headwinds? And while the prestart return on investment was found to be quite high the project was still not started. These are some of the situations for which human factors considerations are important, hence they are described in this chapter.

Project Management

Introduction

Although the literature is replete with books on project management, none deals with all the aspects of this complex subject. Each author has his or her own strong perspective to offer. It is hoped that this volume succeeds in providing a holistic and complete view of project management science. It is based on this author's 41 years in project management, which encompasses multiple products, development projects, off-the-shelf projects, novel initiatives, and global projects. They varied from small to global implementations, and most were successful. The experience covers a period when there were no tools, up to the present when we are inundated with project management tools and technologies.

This is not intended to be a primer on project management. Rather, it is an advanced treatise on the subject. It avoids elementary topics such as project planning and focuses on the items that make the projects successful in delivering on the promises of the technologies. Hence, success is not viewed as the working implementation but the stakeholders' satisfaction that they got the best value for their dollars.

In this chapter we discuss implementation of a software solution and all the activities in this phase that should be done to deliver the business benefits of product technology.

Why Projects Fail

When a new technology is first implemented by a group of trailblazer companies, its success is far from guaranteed. Success and satisfaction are seldom achieved. However, as the technology ages and becomes commonplace, its success rate can increase. It has been found that the larger the company and the larger the project, the more likely project failure is. Larger projects (more than $3 million in application spend) routinely need harsh turn-around measures or they get stalled, and eventually killed, by the weight of their own bureaucracy.

Chapter 1 covered why projects fail in detail. However, in the context of project management, there are some important, additional reasons for product failure:

- User requirements are not firmly nailed down and/or may have changed midway.

    The requirements gap can go unnoticed until the project is late, overbudget, and the scope is still creeping toward the horizon. Projects get this way because:
    - The business requirements definition was simply a series of capabilities statements and thus too vague to implement data flow.
    - Business rules behind these requirements were never discussed and captured.
    - The templates used by the company could not be populated by the business managers and received only cursory attention.

    No amount of project management can fix a project where requirements are poorly defined. A failing project eventually dies under the weight of user frustration and antipathy. Fixing the problem of poor requirements, however, means getting four times as much information in one quarter of the time.
- On large projects, too much information is made available with inadequate details as required by the implementation team. Take for instance the case of President Obama's stimulus plan which is great on broad vision and extremely poor on details. Same was the case with previous treasury secretary Hank Paulson's troubled asset relief program (TARP)
- If the project is under time pressure, the amount of time available to digest, critique, and get buy-in does not exist. So the problem related to requirements definition raises its ugly head.

In my experience poor requirements definition is a copout. Even when company and user community are responsible for the requirements, they may not be able to provide them. It is the project manager and his or her team who need to get them defined. Of course, the project manager has to beg and influence the user/customer community to provide what is needed. This task is never easy, but it will make or break the project. It is not wise to expect the customer community to provide a well-written document that the project team can follow and implement. Besides, customers sometimes change the scope and requirements on the fly. Good project managers have to take these kinds of problems in stride.

MEASUREMENTS OF SUCCESS AND FAILURE   Generally accepted criteria for success by the project team are:

- On time
- Within budget
- Meeting all the functional requirements

But the stakeholders may have a different view of success and complain:

- It does not do what I want today.
- No, no, that is not what I meant; you misunderstood my needs during the requirement gathering time.
- The cost was far more than the tangible benefits received.
- From the time you started, the business has changed so much that what you are giving us is obsolete.
- Ah but . . . etc.

When the perspectives vary this wildly, it is incumbent on the project team to firmly nail the definitions of success, failure, and conditions on when to pull the plug. Preparing a scorecard, as defined in Chapter 5, and business key performance indicators (KPIs) serve everyone well and eliminate the subjective perspective. The solution is discussed through all sections of Chapter 5.

Methodologies of Project Management

Efforts by corporations to systematize the project/program management processes have been under way for some time. Project management offices (PMOs) were created first, with many more methodologies added. The Department of Defense (DOD) was the early mover to establish and legitimize these efforts. The DOD's aim was to gain control of how projects are conducted by project/program managers, with the hope of increasing their success rate. Note that for a PMO to succeed, it must have the support and buy-in of top management as well as the project managers, who may consider the PMO heads unhelpful bureaucrats. If these efforts are to succeed, they have to be sold as true value adders to the firm's top management as well as to their practitioners. Proponents of PMOs tend to consider them indispensable, which they are not. However, companies that have a senior-level title overseeing the PMO have had greater project success rates (projects completed on time, on budget, and with all the original specifications) than those that do not. PMOs that were formed at a corporate level take on a greater number of the company's projects, and the projects managed are larger in terms of dollars invested. Some of these practices/methodologies are:

- Project/program management office
- Portfolio management
- Life cycle approaches
  - Generic enterprise management system (GEMS)
  - Methodology given in this book
- Fast prototyping

PROJECT MANAGEMENT OFFICE   As a company goes about establishing the PMO office, it may recommend these practices for greater success:

Implement in Incremental Phases
- Start with one or two non–mission-critical systems.
- Begin with minimal application integration.
- Understand roles and responsibilities for all affected organizations.
- Conduct workshops or storyboarding sessions to gather requirements and educate.
- Include business and technical representatives.
- Identify key technical challenges and risks.
- Include all communities in test planning and execution.
- Plan the work, utilizing a project definition document.
- Create a planning horizon.
- Define project management procedures up front.
- Look for warning signs.
- Ensure that the sponsor approves scope change requests.
- Identify risks up front.
- Continue to assess potential risks throughout the project.
- Resolve issues as quickly as possible.

BEST PRACTICES OF PROJECT MANAGEMENT OFFICE   A PMO must strive for the listed best practices. However, a PMO insisting on these practices without getting the buy-in of project managers will run the risk of alienation. The PMO must mentor, generate trust, and prove that best practices can benefit the organization. If the resources are tight, hardcore project tasks get done and the nice to-do PMO directives fall by the wayside. Nonetheless, the best practices of project management are:

- Organizational practices
  - Knowledge management
  - Continuous improvement
  - Corporate policies and governance
  - Scalability of practices
  - Cross-functional teams
  - Edification
- Team practices
- Focus
- Team members
- Team processes: front-end planning
- Team life
- Good communications
- Risk registration and documentation
- Individual practices
- Personal processes
- SAP (sociology/anthropology/psychology) implementation

ESTABLISHING PROJECT MANAGEMENT OFFICE   Establishing a project management office is like establishing any new department that is perceived not to have a direct value-added function. Hence, you should take these steps to ensure PMO success:

- Prepare role and charter.
- Define the scope of the projects it will support.
- Define the resources required.
- Define the expected benefits the incremental staffing will produce.
- Define measurements of success and failures.
- Define your competition with and without PMOs.
- Strive to have the highest level of buy-in.
- Define and build the best practices that will be supported out of this function.
- Prepare training programs for different levels of people.
- Establish communication sessions for stakeholders at major project milestones.
- Establish a tradition of mentoring.

Portfolio Management

Proponents of portfolio management believe that companies have projects in start-up or implementation mode, over which the chief information officer (CIO) has little control or little oversight. The CIO and his or her staff may not have bought in to the projects. These projects typically:

- May represent an overload condition
- May have been approved due to the persuasion of a head of a business unit
- May not be aligned with corporate strategy
- May not have enough of a business justification
- May not have measurements in place to quantify success or failure
- Lack processes to monitor progress or the lack thereof

In other words, these projects are begun and implemented without adequate up-front preparation and oversight of those who know the business better, i.e the IT staff and its CIO.

To overcome these problems, a portfolio of projects by the department or the business unit must be put together and monitored, similar to what you would do with a stock portfolio. Portfolio projects would be selected by:

- Previously agreed-on rules of business justification
- Monitoring on a fixed schedule or based on an event
- Predetermining whether to continue or shut down rules of the project

These benefits, and others, can be achieved as a result of sound portfolio management:

- Maximize value of information technology (IT) investments while minimizing the risk.
- Improve communication and alignment between the information system and business leaders.
- Encourage business leaders to think "team," not "me," and to take responsibility for projects.
- Allow planners to schedule resources more efficiently.
- Reduce the number of redundant projects and make it easier to kill projects.

There is no right or wrong way to accomplish portfolio management; however, some of these methods have been observed to be helpful:

- Gather: Do a project inventory.
- Evaluate: Identify projects that match strategic objectives.
- Prioritize: Score and categorize your projects.
- Overcome: Hurdles to portfolio management.

Other Approaches

Under the life cycle approach, there are the following three major methodologies:

- Generic Manufacturing Sysems (GEMS)
- Scorecard methodology
- Fast prototyping

Because trillions of dollars are being spent on project management every year, budgets ought to be so huge that project management best practices could be deployed easily. But what I have seen does not corroborate that. Heavy methodology efforts are sustained as long as the champions were in place; sooner or later, however, the stakeholders get fed up with spending money on methodologies and begin demanding real results. If they do not get these results, their science and technology boards encourage them to go for real business benefits. It seems that as long as methodology is well hidden under the actual implementation efforts, it has a chance of being adopted.

How I Accomplished Successful Project Implementations

I grew from a simpleminded process engineer doing small but complete projects to solve vexing business problems, to highly complex global implementations. All my training in project management methodologies was acquired to defend my methods from hostile program management offices or the proponents of portfolio managers to systems engineering and integration divisions that espoused the use of structured techniques. The need to defend my methods arose because I was always a hard-nosed project manager, oriented toward exploiting the business benefit. My business sense was keen, and I would take whatever shortcuts necessary to deliver the benefits of the technologies promised. By the time I became a management/business consultant, I had become well versed in analyzing business problems and defining the solutions. If clients would not define the requirements adequately, I would define them and get their buy-in. As a result, I gained the trust of senior management and business unit heads. Supporting all this was my methodology, refined over 25 years, with the core still intact.

By doing all this, my role as project/program manager/director expanded to project champion and, at times, even to expert user.

First let me enumerate my fundamental beliefs in doing the projects:

- The project's objective is to solve a business problem and deliver the maximum benefits to the business.
- Have a keen understanding of the business, and rank order the priorities, in terms of their ability to deliver the biggest value for the money.
- Project management techniques in themselves are not the deliverables, so concentrate on the real deliverables of the project.
- Develop a system of backup and redflagging.
- Do not fight the problem; avoid it.
- Work with users to guide them through the requirements definition.
- The real solution is a working system based on user need, not one based on the signed-off requirements document.
- Modify the solution if for any reason users do not buy it.
- Users alone do not own a solution. They share it with the project management. Therefore, make sure the solution is workable and will not collect dust.
- The project team needs to be guided and mentored and their hands held.
- Develop a strong team sense.
- Your teams, users, and senior management need periodic progress reviews.
- Keep the champions and executive sponsors in a close loop and provide them with an unvarnished view of status and problems.

Items that I would pay attention to every day are:

- Running list of a few critical show stoppers
- Urgency versus bureaucracy
- Innovation versus plodding
- Circumventing the problems
- Backup plans

How "did I do it" steps are:

- Strategy formulation and alignment as covered in all sections of Chapter 5
- Business case
- Sell, if required, to executive sponsor or the board
- Revisit business case and each other item, such as:
  - Quality management

- Change management
- Risk management
- Training
- Communications
- Scope management
- Team formation
- Team recruiting
- Project kickoff
- Team building
- Work breakdown structures
- Microsoft (MS) Project or SAP Project
- Follow-up and keep current
- Budget and spending control
- Reporting to stakeholders
- Reports from the team
- Develop or configure
- Escalation process
- Leverage the technology
- Fast prototyping
- Test plan and test procedure

Although project critical success factors (CSFs) have been mentioned elsewhere, in my experience, these are the ones that matter the most:

- On time
- Within budget
- Happy team
- Motivated team
- Support of project champion
- Support of stakeholders
- Collaborative end users

Role and Responsibilities of a Good Project Manager

Project management is a set of tools, processes, and competencies utilized by people to enhance an organization's services and practices.

According to the Code of Practice of Project Management 2000[1]: "The key role of a project manager is to motivate, manage, coordinate and maintain morale of the whole project team." However, in this book, we extend the definition to include the producer of business results that the stakeholders are expecting based on the business case.

CHARACTERISTICS OF A GOOD PROJECT MANAGER Whom would you like to
have as your important mission control project manager? As off-the-shelf
solutions have proliferated, a common tendency is to ask the vendor. In-
evitably, the answer is someone who knows the product well. This is true
if the projects are small and the number of project personnel is limited.
However, when considering mission-critical large projects, what the project
manager needs is a combination of business (domain) knowledge, people
skills, and product knowledge. Product knowledge should take a back-
seat for the project manager, as others on the team can supply this. The
project manager must marry the solution with the project requirements to
deliver the promised benefits of the technology and keep everyone—from
the project team to champions and sponsors—motivated, empowered, and
enthusiastic.

People Skills Management needs to be able to plan and control the activities
of the organization. At the same time, people run organizations—whether
they are senior management, project managers, or team members who can
perform with higher or lower levels of efficiency, creativity, and job satisfaction. In the past, project management focused on "management," which
implied a top-down view of how projects are conducted.

However, studies of weaving mills in India and coal mines in England in
the early 1950s discovered that work groups could effectively handle many
production problems better than management if they were permitted to
make their own decisions on scheduling, work allocation among members,
bonus sharing, and so forth. This was particularly true when variations in
the production process required quick reactions by the group or when the
work of one shift overlapped with the work of other shifts. These findings
apply, although not always directly, to the people who contribute to large-
scale, complex, often-distributed projects such as those typically scheduled
by tools like Microsoft Project and Palisade's @Risk. But these people do
not work in a vacuum.

At one end of the spectrum, opposed to the "autonomous" work groups
just mentioned, are toxic project managers—those who tightly control and
manipulate others for their own aggrandizement. They can actually degrade
the quality of work, morale, and even the stability of an organization. Organizations that tolerate or reward toxic behavior are heading for an inevitable
fall, because it usually creates tension between labor and management that
consumes the energy of both.

In contrast to the effective work-group members are the solitary problem solvers who excel at figuring out how to handle "nontrivial" tasks who
are found throughout many organizations. Forcing these loners to work by
team rules can neutralize their potential contributions.

What has all this talk about "good" team members and "bad" project managers got to do with project management software and systems? Just this: The savings of time (a.k.a. money) made possible by the proper use of today's powerful project management software and systems can be dwarfed by the economic losses that can occur from not considering the wants, needs, and psychological makeup of the people who do the actual work that your software attempts to model and the behavior of the project managers who run these applications.

Peter Drucker and others have written extensively on the leadership attributes of successful leaders, many of which apply to project managers. The essentials consist of:

- Interpersonal skills
- Creative thinking
- Empowerment
- Active optimism
- Determination to improve
- Encouragement of delegation
- Real potential

Interpersonal Skills Interpersonal skills are the communication-oriented skills that make a good project manager a great leader. They encompass the ease with which a successful leader can get the team or an individual team member marching in sync with him or her. With these skills he or she can easily plan, organize, schedule, brainstorm and problem-solve a complex problem as well as get the team motivated by the excitement and challenge of the opportunity rather than dragging it down into a blue funk. He or she is skilled at both the positive and negative reinforcement to the team or the individual member, depending on circumstances and judgment. His or her ability to relate with the people is so good that any interaction is invariably enjoyable.

As been expressed by Leyton W. Collins[2], the acronym CARE for this good project manager stands for:

C: Clear and concise direction
A: Adequate and appropriate training and support
R: Recognition and reward
E: Empathy

The good project manager is a true believer and practitioner of CARE and, by makeup, perspective, and style, is a truly interpersonally skilled person.

If the company does not emphasize interpersonal or communication skills, it is looking for a project manager with the know-how to lead projects in that field or a subject matter expert who knows something about project management. If the latter is true, the company may view project management professional (PMP) as just another accreditation, and the projects in their organization tend to finish late, cost more, or have lower quality.

Also note that anyone can learn how to plan, use MS Project or Primavera, and develop work breakdown structures and a project plan. However, no matter what the person in charge of the project is labeled, his or her aim, in a nutshell, is to reach the project's defined objectives. How you get there within the required time, cost, quality, and performance parameters and then close out the project defines the professional maturity of both the project manager and the organization. And, unless the project team is a team of one, objectives are achieved through the performance of other people.

Creative Thinking A successful leader is a master problem solver, someone who can think out of the box, dissect a problem, and achieve a unique solution. Analytical capability along with intuitive ability is the hallmark of this person's problem-solving ability. His or her approach is flexible because it is not bound by any previously learned norm of problem solving.

Through lateral thinking, project managers try different perceptions, concepts, and points of entry. They consider multiple possibilities and approaches instead of a single approach. The key benefit of this kind of thinking is that it is enables users to solve difficult project challenges more successfully.

Empowerment Usually people run to claim ownership of a solution, ignoring the real problem solvers. They do not encourage initiative or give recognition when deserved. Contrary to this, a good leader motivates and energizes not only himself or herself but the whole team. The good leader looks for positive reinforcement at every opportunity for every team member. The result is the whole team feels empowered to take initiative and solve problems. Morale is up, camaraderie is high, and results are positive.

The ultimate paradox of project leadership power is that to be an effective leader, project managers must help all team members develop into leaders. In this way, processes (such as relationships and the issues of leadership) and empowerment become important. Successful leaders are able to motivate, energize, and empower others. When people are excited and empowered, it affects both their task initiation and task persistence. In other words, empowered people get more involved, take on more difficult situations, and act with more confidence.

Active Optimism   Leaders are optimistic. They think positively. Positive thinking is more than just avoiding negative emotions. It translates into actions that are forward thinking and involved. When negative events happen, excellent project leaders focus on the positive aspects of the event. They look at a problem as an opportunity for learning and team development—for the team and for themselves.

Determination to Improve   A successful leader is always ready to improve. This continuous improvement bias is visible in all project processes, problem solving, team communication, and relationships. This leader is constantly aware of others and will ask "How can I help?" By asking this question, leaders focus on challenging themselves and project team members. Further, the question sets into motion ongoing self-evaluation and achievement. In turn, this focus on continuous process improvement reaps results.

Encouragement of Delegation   Good leaders know that their time is limited, as is that of the team. Nevertheless, leaders' control span is far wider than that of their reports. So leaders are constantly and systematically delegating decision-making, initiative-taking, and problem-solving opportunities to the team and positively encouraging the delegation of work. Thus, by delegating tasks and authority, leaders spend less time fighting fires and correcting errors and more time on vision development, motivation, project change, control, and goal setting.

Delegation relieves time pressures, provides team members with an opportunity to expand their decision-making and problem-solving skills, and encourages creativity and initiative while motivating them to achieve their potential.

In addition, delegation forces leaders to spend time with team members, thus developing interpersonal relationships. Leaders' feedback and attention will encourage the team to attain higher levels of responsibility. Delegation helps set performance standards based on team members rather than purely on their activity. Leaders who encourage delegation are able to step back and look at the bigger picture rather than be caught up in the minutiae of the project.

Real Potential   To meet future challenges, leaders must be inspired by real potential and strategies for the future. Only then can they set a vision with reasonable goals and promote the process of developing effective strategies to achieve them. Considering the organization's potential and future enables leaders to think constructively about what could be and what would be necessary to achieve a vision. Proactive and realistic "future-oriented" thinking can lead to greater project success. For leaders, a successful future requires real planning now.

Proactive and future oriented visions for a company are the skill that will propel them to understand and participate in the transformation of the company's business. This is the attribute that will let them deliver the business results, not just technically successful projects.

The next list presents statements by project managers to their teammates, along with the personality traits of the project managers.

If you get in my way, I'll kill you!—ideal project manager
If you get in my way, you'll kill me!—somewhat less than ideal manager
If I get in my way, I'll kill you!—somewhat misguided project manager
If I get in your way, I'll kill you!—tough project manager (eats glass, cats, etc.)
If get kill in will way I you!—dyslexic or functionally illiterate project manager
I am the way! Kill me if you can!—messianic project manager
Get away, I'll kill us all!—suicidal project manager
If you kill me, I'll get in your way!—thoughtful but ineffective project manager
If I kill you, I'll get in your way!—project manager who has trouble dealing with the obvious
If you kill me, so what? If you get in my way, who cares?—weak, uninspired, lackluster project manager
If I kill me, you'll get your way!—pragmatic project manager
If we get in each others' way, who will get killed?—an utterly confused manager
Kill me, it's the only way!—every project manager to date

CRITICAL SUCCESS FACTORS OF THE PROJECT   Chapter 5 discussed the business-level CSFs. Suffice it to say that not doing any of the items listed next well will jeopardize project success. Hence, take extreme care that these items remain in place for the entire duration of the project:

- Business case
- Strategic alignment
- Risk management
- Change management
- Training
- Test/Risk/QA
- Project champion
- Executive sponsorship

Project-level CSFs are given next. As I have already explained what they are and what can go wrong with each one of them, I do not offer a detailed description here:

- Project manager
- Project team
- Technology
- Time availability of users
- Time availability for parallel runs

There is some overlap between the project-level CSFs just mentioned and the ones listed next, but for the sake of clarity I am listing them here:

- **Control and coordination.** In this category, the problems can arise due to unclear or shifting project goals and managerial intentions, unresolved congruence between project benefits and personal aspirations, uncontrolled change propagation and cross-checking, brittle technical architecture, and inadequate availability of user resources when needed.
- **Communication.** In this category, problems can arise due to lack of coordination of resources and activities, ambiguous and imprecise communication/follow-through, unclear understanding of stakeholders and their wants, needs, reactions, and satisfaction.
- **Tools and training.** Problems here include insufficient knowledge of the customer industry or internal processes, insufficient skill with the technologies used, and insufficient tools (automation).
- **Team building.** Problems occur here when the skills and backgrounds of team members are unidentified and underutilized, festering resentment among team members.
- **Conflict management.** Problems in this area include undetected inconsistencies in requirements, designs, or implementation; inadequate quality assurance/control, resulting in the delivery of products that are unacceptable or unusable; failure to realistically and courageously attack risks.
- **Negotiation.** The problems here are lack of flexibility or openness to improvement, overwhelming complexity.
- **Risk management.** In this category, problems can arise due to insufficient metrics measuring process effectiveness, product tolerances, and project impact; poor estimation of duration and costs, leading to projects taking more time and costing more than expected.
    Other CSFs that some people feel very strongly about are:
  - Have a clear objective.
  - Pick the best people.
  - Support them with the best team.

- Support them with the best equipment and technology.
- Train constantly.
- Prepare for the unexpected.
- Never consider defeat.
- Improvise.
- Take risks.
- Turn failure into success.

Requirements

The literature is full of articles and stories about requirements definitions, processes, best practices, and what will happen if users do not own the requirements and there is no consensus on them. Having worked with brick-and-mortar companies as well as with consulting companies, I have found that most of the time:

- Users do not have a firm grasp of the requirements.
- They do have a hazy end product in mind but do not know how to get there.
- The business processes are so bad that they need to be reengineered or, in case of start-ups, they simply are not there.
- Project teams may have a high complement of younger systems people.

In any of these cases, a fundamental belief should be that while the users own the requirements, the systems folks have to help the users to define and refine them.

Even if the requirements are well defined and the final product is not accepted by the users, this unfortunate situation should be fixed. It does not matter whether the project team is a captive team of the company or from the outside consulting company. In the first case, if the solution is not accepted by the user you would need to redo it or you will be made to. In the second case, if the situation is not fixed, litigation could follow.

- **Conventional way to define requirements.** Starting with the detailed list of domain requirements, ask questions about them in interview sessions with users. However, users seldom have time to give answers to elaborate questions. If this is so, you may be tempted to go to the published requirements documents on enterprise resource planning or whatever else the project is about and get the user sign off. But this does not work well all the time.
- **Storyboarding way to define requirements.** I successfully practiced storyboarding on many projects as a method to define requirements. However, every client company I suggested it to did not accept adoption of this methodology. Results were very good with those clients who

accepted it and participated. The method is a very effective way to define requirements and benefits.

- **Fast prototyping way to define requirements.** My initial success with fast prototyping was so good on a mission-critical but small database project that I adopted this technique for all my subsequent complex and global projects. This methodology entails:
  - Defining the requirements crudely enough to do a prototype along with a workflow model
  - Making as-is and to-be views of the workflow model to clarify complexity
  - Doing the prototype as quickly as possible to demonstrate the basic
    - Look and feel
    - Process flows based on the workflow models
  - Revising the prototype as per the user comments
  - Iterating the process until the user is satisfied

The rest of managing the development of requirements entails the usual attention to managing the scope, budget, schedule, and user reasonableness. A skilled project team has to strive to achieve all of this. If the project manager has good credibility with the users, all the better. If not, his or her chances of success will improve if the users realize how proactive the project team is. Nowadays, project managers are being assigned business analysts. A good business analyst will go a long way toward establishing business benefits and business KPIs.

Technology and Tools

Perhaps the earliest tool to facilitate project management by scheduling was the critical path method (CPM). However, lately a great many project software tools have proliferated. Among the best-known and most widely used tool sets are:

MS Project from Microsoft
Project software from SAP
Project software from PLM suppliers (Matrix One, etc.)

An in-depth discussion of each one is out of the scope of this chapter. However, it is obvious that the advent of the Internet has created tools that facilitate, among other things:

- Virtual teams
- Global collaboration
- E-mails
- Video conferencing
- Project message boards

Each Internet tool is intended to improve communication among the team members regardless of location. While technology serves as the enabler of the virtual project, the specific nature of technology could become a source of conflict. Team members must strive to reach agreement as to the purpose of each tool and the procedures for its use. Otherwise, the lack of common norms can lead to conflict that could damage working relationships. For example, one team member might feel that e-mail is a tool to be used for urgent business, while another might feel e-mail is to be used for documentation of information, with urgent business to be conducted by phone.

Current Issues of Project Management

GLOBAL COLLABORATION AND OUTSOURCING   Due to the global nature of businesses, the need for global collaboration has arisen. This is true whether you are a project manager on the in-house developmental project of IBM or a project manager of an outsourced effort. In both these cases, two critical issues have to be dealt with deftly:

1. International cultural differences
2. Communication tools

International cultural differences exist because a person in India acts, reacts, expects, and needs differently from a person of U.S. origin. This produces a great burden until the team has been through a storming period and everyone understands the expectations, behavioral norms, and quality standards.

The *Wall Street Journal* had a fine article[3] on how it is managing an in-house project in the Websphere domain. The project team comprised 50 people in three different countries. To remain current with each other, they used a Web-based collaborative communication software known as Wiki. (See the Section entitled "Communications Management" in Chapter 8 for further discussion.) This sort of tool is available for anyone's use.

MISSION CRITICAL   It is common for all applications to be considered mission critical; nevertheless, some are more critical than others. Furthermore, the boss's predisposition on any such issue defines its criticalness/priority. In summary, if the project is of a critical nature, then the project manager and team have to be extra careful about schedules and down time. Testing and test time availability becomes a major factor during the project's complete life cycle.

WHEN YOUR VENDOR DOES NOT PERFORM   No matter how careful you may be, one day you will find that the vendor has not performed, and finally, either the vendor has sued your company or your company has sued the vendor. When this happens, you do not need not worry as long as you have been honest and up front with the vendor, have provided plenty of opportunity to remedy the deficiency, and have good documentation. While documentation sounds bureaucratic, it is a fact of life today that a hierarchy of complete project documentation is necessary. At a minimum, you must maintain requirements documents, requests for proposals (RFPs), RFP responses, minutes of meetings, and change management documents. Thus, even if a suit arises, you can defend your position. In such an event, maintain your composure and ability to articulate if you have to give a deposition. The lawyer will do the rest.

Project Champions

Introduction

The champion has been said to be the spark plug that starts the process. He or she is a catalyst, a facilitator, a person of high credibility with top executives and stakeholders. This person may conceive the initiative or be convinced of its merits by lieutenants and then come to personify the initiative. From then on, there is no stopping until the implementation succeeds through the postaudit stage.

In the actual practice of successful projects, there is always a champion. It is of utmost importance to have this person on board, as projects will cut through every department of the corporation. Without a champion on board, preferably from the start, lightweight personnel should think twice before embarking on such arduous journeys.

The champion can come from any area of the business. However, a high-level product or engineering person is the best fit for the job. If a top IT executive has enough passion, it could work, but this person must have the confidence and respect of the business community of the enterprise.

This section explores:

- Who champions are
- Essential characteristics of champions
  - Commitment/time
  - Influence
  - Proactive
  - Relations
  - Trust of senior management
  - Power
  - Rising star
  - Big-picture guy
  - Team builder

- Roles they play
  - Advocacy
  - Roadblock removal
- Why project champions succeed
  - Organizational belonging
  - Champion versus project manager
- How to recruit champions
- When to recruit a champion
- Champion needs a sponsor

Who Are They?

Successful project champions are the catalysts who start the process and take it through to success. They are the change agents who cause the change to take place. They can come from any part of the organization. But the higher they are, the better will be their effectiveness. If a project's stakeholder can be a champion, the project will be well served. By definition, strong champions have these characteristics:

- Personal and profession commitment to the endeavor
- Understanding of the larger process or activity that is being undertaken
- Trusted of the campus community and the president
- Power
- Keen interested in building and working through the planning or action team

Essential Characteristics of Champions

The appropriate individual should fit the scope and range of impact as well as the visibility the project will have within the organization. A champion should exhibit these characteristics:

- **Commitment/time.** The champion must be fully committed to the process at hand. As part of this commitment, the champion must have the time to accomplish the task. It is important to understand this point. At most institutions, champions often are the go-to people, the people who get things done. As a result, there is a strong temptation to keep heaping tasks on them until they collapse beneath the burden. Not only does this reduce their overall effectiveness, but it imperils the larger project that is being undertaken. It is essential that they have time to perform. They must be able to manage their own time for the project if the synergy with the project manager and the team has developed.
- **Influence.** The individual needs to carry weight in organizational decision making. That is why most successful project champions are found in mid- to senior-level management.

- **Proactive.** This person must be someone who will be a proactive initiator, a charming persuader, and diligent when actively pursuing project support within the organization.
- **Relations.** Successful champions are skilled relationship managers and effective bridge builders.
- **Trust of senior management.** The champion must be trusted by the larger campus community. Issues involving change, whether they are PLM, marketing, strategic planning, or brand building, make people and the organizations they inhabit nervous. Any change initiative often involves issues related to budget, staffing, and even performance. Tensions sometimes may run high. A basic level of trust is essential.
- **Power.** The champion must have power. There is no such thing as a weak champion. If the champion is given responsibility for leading an initiative, then he or she should be given authority to get the job done. It is always a mistake to designate someone who is not a senior player as champion. He or she typically does not have the experience, the clout, or the staying power. And once again, the initiative may be imperiled. I do not want to belabor the point, but I do want to repeat it: The champion must be powerful. There is a temptation—often a very strong one—to put an assistant of this or that in charge. This is almost always a mistake. Major initiatives cannot be led from below. If what you are doing does not warrant a true champion, you should rethink your overall strategy.
- **Rising star.** Many successful champions are current employees whose careers are on the rise or who are already organizational leaders.
- **Big-picture person.** The champion must have a general and conceptual understanding of what is happening and why. Champions work at altitudes. They understand the big picture of where they are and where they are going. They do not need to be the technical expert of the initiative, but they must know well its strategic alignment with the corporate strategy and its strategic and tactical benefits. They must know and understand how the project will go through the realization process, at least, at a conceptual level.
- **Team builder.** Finally, because champions work best through teams, the champion must be a team builder. As team builder, the champion must:
  - Have a clear sense of the overall project goal(s).
  - Maintain a sense of urgency and direction.
  - Select team members by skills and skill potential, not personality. Skills of special value include technical, functional, problem solving, and interpersonal.

- Set up clear rules of behavior. The most critical rules pertain to attendance, discussion, confidentiality, constructive confrontation, contributions, and reporting.
- Challenge the group regularly with fresh ideas.
- Reward the team periodically.

Roles They Play

Project champions often provide assistance in two areas:

1. **Advocacy.** The primary role of the project champion is to advocate and promote the benefits of pursuing the project. The champion actively seeks project support from management and other organizational leaders. The aim is to ensure that senior decision makers view the project as necessary.
2. **Roadblock removal.** All projects run into barriers at some point. Whether it is project funding, resource allocation, or any of a number of other issues, the project champion is often able to grease the wheel to get the project moving again.

Why Project Champions Succeed

Projects thrive when two people take the time to talk, interact informally, and learn more about each other's perspectives. The best opportunity to exchange important information may be out of the office while sharing a meal, a beer, a ride, on the golf course, or on an airplane flight. At such informal encounters, information about the project and its benefits to the company and details about the new approach can be best communicated and eventually lead to buy-in.

Champions can act as mentors. They can be grilled about competing opportunities or initiatives the company may be exploring, or about the fit of your work with the overall corporate strategy. At these meetings, conceptual strategic alignment can take place, and the advocacy person is born who can learn to trust you, work as your ally or true partner, and listen well.

ORGANIZATIONAL BELONGING Project champions can come from any part of the organization and any level. Generally, the higher their position, the more effective they will be. Their homeroom may, or may not, be the project organization, depending on the company preferences.

CHAMPION VERSUS PROJECT MANAGER This is the most crucial issue of project organization with champions: Do not confuse the role of a project champion with that of the project manager. The project manager is also a project advocate; his or her focus is to plan, schedule, organize, and manage the execution of the project. The champion, however, may not be a member of the project team but will strive to help the project succeed.

If the project champion is not the project manager, when the project comes to an end, the champion should be thanked for his or her help in leading the project to its successful completion. No matter how they are thanked—by being taken out for lunch, acknowledged for their efforts in a company meeting, or in some other fashion—champions should know that the project recognizes and appreciates the role they played in its success.

HOW TO RECRUIT A CHAMPION   Once a champion is identified, work should begin to gain the person's support and enthusiasm. Project managers or team leaders can initiate this, or the champion may emerge by him- or herself. Hold meetings with the champion for candid discussion about project goals and objectives. Be sure to provide your champion with the opportunity to suggest enhancements to the project plan even if the ideas do not bear a direct relationship to the champion's primary job functions.

WHEN TO RECRUIT A CHAMPION   The best time to recruit a champion is during a project's definition phase. Not only does this provide the champion with a ground-up approach, but it also provides an opportunity to rally support from upper management early on.

CHAMPION NEEDS A SPONSOR   Even a champion need the helping hand of someone in the organization who is more powerful than they are and is willing to use that power to move things along. Like the champion, the sponsor must be personally committed to the success of the undertaking. However, the champion is seldom involved in the day-to-day business. In almost all cases, the sponsor is someone more senior in the organization than the champion—the company president or a major stakeholder. The sponsor clears the way, lends political and budgetary support, and makes tough decisions that are above the champion's pay grade. The sponsor is an advocate, not a meddler.

Case Example: Boston technology highway route 128 company

The next example compares and contrasts the concepts about champions just discussed. In this example, I was involved as the champion and project director. This case is from a Boston technology highway route 128 company's New Bedford facility, where it made all the negative film used to produce a film pack that would go in an instant camera.

(Continued)

(Continued)

Who are They (Champions)

This author was hired by the company to lead a Process Control Systems group. The environment for IT and automation was not conducive to any megaproject because earlier efforts undertaken by the company had failed.

However, due to my passion for creative and state-of-the-art work in advanced manufacturing, I was not satisfied with the status quo. So I developed a strategy blueprint for the entire operation, singlehandedly, without much support from my group. The proposal and details were reviewed by the company's senior management and eventually were blessed by the board.

A key point to mention is that I emerged as a champion; I was not appointed by the management but was accepted in the role of the champion. I continued as the project director as well.

Essential Characteristics of Champions

- **Commitment/time.** As far as time goes, bosses did not control my time. I was a responsible member of the management team and as such, in the fine tradition of this Boston technology highway Route 128 company, was allowed to manage my own time. However, the key decision I made was to organize and delegate day-to-day management duties within my staff. Next I dedicated with full fervor my time, attention, and energies to flesh out the strategy document that I had authored, as per the requirements of the senior management. I guided senior management as they reviewed the document and became comfortable with the ideas and concepts, and prepared them for the cognitive leap they were asked to take for this mega-initiative.
- **Influence.** I grew in influence as the project progressed from a mere concept to a well-thought-out executable plan of action. Competing organization heads set up many roadblocks that I had to overcome.

    But ultimately, only one senior manager failed to agree to the project. The rest of the team was on board to support it and move forward. At this time, the executive sponsor challenged the dissenting senior manager to either flesh out his objections beyond "I think" or just keep quiet and let the project be blessed unanimously. Compare this situation with the first presentation that I made at the senior management meeting, when the boss caustically greeted me, saying "He has a God-damned automation project proposal that he wants your buy-in." In this company, opinions had no place. Only objective and provable hypotheses were accepted. Without total influence and credible arguments, I would not have completed this megaproject successfully.

- **Proactiveness.** I worked proactively. The project had become mine, and I had unflinching motivation and passion. I would go to any lengths to convince anyone, anytime on any aspect of the project.
- **Relations.** The relationships with the entire senior management team were cordial but not personal. However, I had made a place among them and was respected for my knowledge and motivation. I was considered the horse on which they were betting, and I might be the only one who would lead them to success. After this, I won the project from the board and execution began. There were no roadblocks from senior managers or others.
- **Trust of senior management.** I enjoyed tremendous trust from senior management. However, it was not a blind trust. I faced strong questions and arguments all along, but full preparation and work with unflinching motivation was crucial to the continued trust. The trust situation was tested time and again over the course of the project, but solid and powerful arguments continued to build the trust.
- **Power.** While deep knowledge of the concepts and thorough familiarity with the strategy were my real power bases, my executive sponsor was the real power that supported me. As a result, I overcame any resistance from any quarter of the company amid full political pressures from various corporate groups, such as IT and Engineering. I actually never lost a battle.
- **Rising star.** I got promoted twice within five years. I was responsible for expanding, restructuring, and revitalizing the IT and automation efforts not only of my division but of the entire corporation through the computer review board.
- **Big-picture person.** I truly was a big-picture guy here. I conceived, justified, and sold the plant-wide automation initiative through a business strategy blueprint document that I authored myself. However, I left the individual systems planning and implementation for the project teams and team managers.
- **Team builder.** I built the team by expanding, restructuring, and merging several groups. I built the team through organizational development (OD) sessions and careful hiring. I was involved in every hire and one that I fired. Mentoring took place through one-on-one

(Continued)

(Continued)

meetings, weekly project team meetings, and ad hoc issue resolution meetings. The core principles of my championship practice were involvement in problem resolution and passion for individual team members and the project's success.

Roles They Play

These issues have been covered before.

- **Champion versus project manager.** As mentioned, I was both the project champion and the project director. There were project managers, team leaders, and teams. Project managers reported to me in my role as project director. There were no problems due to this dual role. Actually, once there was an opportunity to separate the dual role, but no other project manager was found acceptable to the management team. Hence, I continued in my dual roles.
- **How to recruit champions.** The circumstances surrounding this category have been described. I came into both roles based on my own efforts and passion.
- **Champion needs a sponsor.** The need for an executive sponsor cannot be overemphasized. The secret of my success was the synergy between me and the executive sponsor. This person was the head of the film manufacturing facility, and as such was a major stakeholder in the project. He, along with the champion, wanted to run the business without the interference of the corporate IT, engineering, and other groups. So he fully cooperated with me. Whenever I approached him for help or an issue, he would discuss it thoroughly, convene all the right parties, and settle the issue objectively. The key behind this synergistic solution was that both he and I always had the same goal: a goal that would be beneficial to the film manufacturing facility.

Business Case Development

Introduction

Earlier we discussed the vision, goals and objectives, KPIs, scorecard, cost and value created, value drivers, solution architecture, and business process reengineering as well the project managers and project champions. Now the time has come to get the final nod from the boss. The nod may or may not come. If it does not come, it will be because of several issues that you will never be told directly, nor will they get the required sign-off from the boss. I faced these issues while implementing megaprojects around the world for major multinationals. The projects were in product life cycle management, supply chain management, manufacturing execution systems, computer-integrated manufacturing, enterprise resource planning, IT, and manufacturing automation domains. Generally, I was both the project champion and the project manager, acting as the project director. Sometimes the champion was from the client companies and I was called the project director.

If the senior management of the company is unimaginative, reactionary, complacent or risk avoidant, it will be unresponsive to innovation and hence to the new project/initiative. Unless the competition or the market forces change them, they will not listen to anyone.

In another situation, unless the senior management is predisposed to implement the subject innovative technology, it has got to be justified. I found this to be true even in the most justifiable high return-on-investment (ROI) projects. If the projects are justifiable, what is management asking for? The truth is they are asking to answer the softer issues. This is what the bulk of this chapter is about.

After a long involvement in business case development (BCD), I have noticed that certain issues stand out, either from the perspective of the senior management or from the perspective of the BCD team. These issues are described in the next sections.

Issues

Unless bosses are subject-matter experts, they are concerned with these issues:

- Is due diligence done?
- Is the project truly justifiable?
- Who is competing for funds?
- Is there a champion?
- Is there a sponsor at the senior executive level?
- What is the risk to the sponsor or to the company?
- Is the subject initiative under this BCD better than product development programs?
- What level of comfort does the sponsor have with the champions, the technology, or the teams?
- Can I trust the leader, the team?
- How does it link with our strategy?
  - Does it conflict with any of the goals my boss/company has?

- Does it help any of the product, process, material or yield-improvement programs?
- Does it help any of my critical problems with people, material, space, and profitability (i.e., does it lower my direct or indirect costs)? If so, can I live while implementation of the promised technology is developed and completed?
- Can the operation deal with the innovation during implementation and after?

IS DUE DILIGENCE DONE?   A question usually asked is: Is due diligence done? Are all the staff groups in agreement, and are they supportive?

When the senior management is approached for review and support, sometimes they may begin questioning the proposer. Not that they know the subject technology better than the proposer, but by asking this question, they can learn and also judge how comfortable the proposer is while answering. At the end of this session, if you, the proposer, did well, most likely you will be told to seek the support of the staff groups. This command can take many forms. However, in all cases the meaning is the same. Generally the staff groups are, accounting, industrial engineering, and all relevant operating and support departments. Once again, senior management is looking for a consensus opinion that the plan is well thought out. While the opinion may lack precision, all angles must have been considered.

Before reviewing with the staff groups, you must do the planning and design. Doing this entails collecting functional requirements and translating those requirements into systems requirements and responsive architectures. You document these findings and send them to generate the RFPs, if appropriate. System requirements and the architectures form the basis of the cost and schedule estimates. You must think out and put in place training and technology transfer plans and procedures. While doing the requirements definition, you can also make a benefits compilation. Compile all of this work in a general design document and present it to senior management.

Time permitting, it is prudent to review the proposal with the staff groups. They will express their support, disagree with it, or argue. If they point out a problem and you agree, you must take care of it before proceeding further. If they argue, politely back out of it. If, however, disagreement is genuine and you do not agree with it, you should note it and still proceed. It may have to be resolved with senior management during the review process. You have at least an even chance to win your case.

Having reviewed the proposal with all the staff groups, due diligence can be considered done and you are ready to go to senior management.

IS THE PROJECT TRULY JUSTIFIABLE? Compiling the benefit was mentioned during the due diligence process. Staff groups for this task are the same as in the last section.

However, when staff groups are asked to provide an estimate of the savings, they may not be able to come through due to a new technology. One reason for this is that they genuinely do not understand how the subject technology's incorporation will produce savings. Even you may not know, or you may be unable to articulate it. In such cases, seek outside help from consultants or friends, if they have the necessary experience. Even after this, if the department manager does not want to participate in estimating the savings, either he or she is not capable of doing so or he or she does not want to risk upsetting the status quo. In such a case, approach accounting and/or industrial engineers. They may help or may decide not to. In any event, now you are ready for senior management review.

Having gone through all relevant departments to be affected, you must prepare a summary of benefits and compute an ROI. The next step is to review these with the accounting and the industrial engineering groups. The main purpose here is to be sure that they will give their support and that there are no systematic errors in the proposal that may cause it to be shot down in the final review.

Exercise utmost caution against the temptation to pick savings estimates from some published article or book. The main point of this exercise is not only to estimate the savings but to gain the commitment of the department manager. He or she must know what will be gotten and how to use it to achieve the estimated savings.

An ROI of 40% or better is generally considered good. However, if the company is cash starved, good ROI does not matter. Also, if alternative investments are producing much better ROIs, then the subject plan may not be attractive. In such cases, you must consider intangibles, such as the cost of lost opportunity, lost market share, and the like.

WHO IS COMPETING FOR FUNDS? It is the job of the senior management to weigh all the facts, factors, and constituencies. You may not know who else is competing for the funds and what their strategic importance of investments in them is. Competing projects may be producing even better ROIs. See Figure 7.1 for an example.

Five cases are shown in the figure. Each bar graph shows direct material, direct labor, and overhead costs. When added together, these costs make up the total cost to manufacture the goods. Case 1 is of an electrical assembly plant cost in 1980. Case 2 shows the same plant after CIMing it completely. Case 3 is that of oil industry averages, representing the best cost structure among the five compared. Case 4 is of a metals company average, and case 5 is of electrical industry averages. In case 4, direct labor is 25% of the costs.

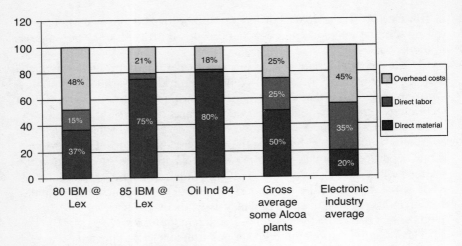

FIGURE 7.1 Collapsing Overhead and Direct Labor

The high labor component is not due to a high number of people employed but to the high wages and benefits paid to them. In this plant, cost to further automate in order to reduce labor would be very unproductive. Of the 25% overhead costs, 18% were recurring costs due to allocation of depreciation and the like. As such, they are not easily impacted by automation. Consider the outcome if another plant were built in this scenario. However, if this plant is built elsewhere, where the cost of labor is a quarter or less, and where due to corporate rules 18% recurring cost is not allocated to the plant, simple math shows a savings of 37%. These savings are very easily realizable, especially if a new plant is to be built. No wonder so many companies have gone to areas of lower labor costs rather than improve existing operations with advanced technologies.

If this is going to be the case in a retrofit situation, it is very hard to refute the alternative. In a greenfield case, however, the argument would be on the basis of cost avoidance and building even a healthier enterprise from the cost point of view. Consider asking the staff groups these questions during the due diligence process. Most likely they will tell you about "who/what else." This may prepare you to argue with senior management. They may or may not allow such debate or even be disposed to listening to your side. But you lose nothing by trying. Actually, you gain more knowledge of the company's business (as I said before what is the cost structure and what are the plans to improve it) and its plans by asking these questions.

IS THERE A CHAMPION?   Most big projects have a champion, a person who is fully and personally committed to seeing the project through. Senior management likes to have one person of this kind for every major project.

If a major innovation project is going to be undertaken, a champion has to come forward. A committee head is not a good enough champion. A true zealot would be one. Contrary to popular opinion, even if this person is from the subject technology area—say a manager or a subject matter expert with enthusiasm and commitment—management will accept him or her. In my experience, major innovation projects are seldom approved without a champion.

What are the credentials of such an integral member of the team? Needless to say, this person must have unquestioned credibility with senior management and be well respected within the peer group for his or her knowledge or vision. He or she should also be a can-do kind of a change agent. Technically, if this person is capable of doing all the due diligence and justification compilation and analysis, the project will benefit immensely. Above all, this person has to know the company's business and the division's manufacturing strategy. He or she should be in a communication loop that is well informed of the changes to the strategy taking place. Of course, this person has got to be a good project manager.

IS THERE A SPONSOR AT THE SENIOR EXECUTIVE LEVEL?   A champion alone will not do. There has got to be a sponsor who is either a mentor to the champion or is personally committed to the subject innovation. The best candidate would be the head of the manufacturing division. This person may not know how to implement the subject innovation but feels a strong need to do so. He or she is well aware of the virtues of the innovation and knows that, without it, the operation will face tough times. This person wields enough influence to meet his or her superiors for the champion and the project team. This person also will provide support when the project runs into tough yet resolvable times. In short, he or she is the top management person without whose support, the champion is powerless. This person walks the project through the company's fiscal processes and can arbitrate priorities for his or her division for capital spending and expense budgets.

WHAT IS THE RISK TO THE SPONSOR OR TO THE COMPANY?   This is a very subjective issue. If asked, every sponsor may deny any practice of it. However, the fact is everyone practices it. They may not want to accept it, may not want to admit there is any determinable risk that they cannot deal with the subject, either due to financial or personal loss of some type. Uncertainty of benefits or project cost control may bring about a bad name. Supporting very unpopular company projects is another category of risky ventures. Every sponsor evaluates and walks with a certain amount of trepidation in unfamiliar personal areas.

The champion's task is to allay most of these concerns in a very unobtrusive, courteous, pithy, and objective manner. Personal relationships or outside education and training done with finesse can alleviate some of these problems. If there is a genuine risk, you should be candid and up front about it. The executive sponsors will appreciate it. Do not hide any of the facts. But then offer an explanation, and be prepared to deal with the uncertainties and the risks.

IS THE SUBJECT INITIATIVE UNDER THIS BCD BETTER THAN PRODUCT DEVELOPMENT PROGRAMS? If the project is compared to some other product development programs, the going will be very tough. Comparisons are not fair for the project either, especially because of innovation project's placement in the value chain. However, most good companies will have the sense not to compare these initiatives to the product development programs but look at them in the category of manufacturing upgrade, facilities upgrade, equipment modernization, productivity improvement, or something similar. If the staff person responsible for review does not categorize appropriately, try to reason with him or her. This is another place where the champion's relationship and credibility can pay off.

WHAT LEVEL OF COMFORT DOES THE SPONSOR HAVE WITH THE CHAMPIONS, THE TECHNOLOGY, OR THE TEAM? If the sponsor is the least bit uncomfortable with any of the champions, technology, or the team, the discomfort has to be changed. If the sponsor is uncomfortable with all three, the champion has to alleviate that discomfort. Usually sponsors are mostly uncomfortable with the technology, even though in their heart of hearts they know that they have to adopt it. Here again the champion can pay his or her dues. Teach the sponsors, if they provide you with an opportunity to do so, and convert their discomfort into a comfortable experience.

CAN I TRUST THE LEADER, THE TEAM? The trust issue is much more prevalent if the champion is new. In such cases, often he or she is not given a chance. They do not believe what he or she says. They do not know the technology themselves and are not ready to accept what the champion is telling them, especially if it is in conflict with the opinions of long-term employees. The situation is difficult, but a good champion can take care of it using candor, sincerity, knowledge, desire to help, and above all the need to work the process with patience and perseverance.

HOW DOES IT LINK WITH OUR STRATEGY? Questions on the minds of senior management are: What does it do for my image, plan, or future? Does it conflict with any of my bosses' goals? Does it help any of our strategic product, process, material, or yield improvement plans? Does it help any of our critical problems with people, material, machine, space, or profitability by impacting direct or indirect cost? Essentially, the main question, whether debated or not, is: What does it conflict with, if anything? What does it support, if anything? The linkage they are trying to establish is with the company business or division manufacturing strategies.

The champion's challenge, obviously, is to relate as much of the innovation plan to the "strategy" as possible. Doing this involves knowing, understanding, articulating, and translating the company strategic plans and then relating all, or parts, of the innovation plans to it. Innovation plan functionality has to be responsive and supportive to the company/division strategies. In addition to functionality, the plan implementation and performance time must be consistent with that of the company/division's strategies. Once the innovation's project plan is successfully done, it must be kept in sync with the company's strategies at all times.

If the strategic linkage is well established, it should be highlighted at all available opportunities to win friends and support. If communicated and articulated well, it will satisfy most of the mind-rattling queries in the minds of the management, and they will be highly supportive.

CAN THE OPERATION DEAL WITH THE INNOVATION DURING IMPLEMENTATION AND AFTER?   The last of the hurdles the management has to cross is to reach a level of comfort that the subject innovation will not impact the operation harmfully during, and after, the implementation. Managers who are not subject-matter experts are dealing with a new set of implementers and are highly suspicious in these areas. This is a very natural human reaction to the unknown. The best the team or the champion can do is to provide a line-by-line analysis of the worries management has expressed. Not paying attention to them, or ignoring them, will be counterproductive. In the analysis, the champion should explain how a given worrisome scenario will be handled satisfactorily. When done well and with conviction, the champion will win support even from the most skeptical.

Worried plant managers often cannot articulate their fears. Yet sometimes they are saying: Can you explain how my operators will use the system? How will *I* use it? Most of these issues can be taken care of with the team simply developing and presenting the current and future Operations models. However, neither the management nor the team may be able to articulate what the other is saying. The gulf keeps increasing instead of shrinking. If this is the case and the sponsor does not show buy-in, the champion should stop all support for the project; the time for it obviously has not arrived.

TECHNOLOGISTS' SENSITIVITIES TO SENIOR MANAGEMENT NEEDS   Some basic points the team and the leader have always to keep in mind, as they deal with the manufacturing and company management, are:

> *These guys are under the gun for relentless reduction in time to market. Quality revolution has added another quantum or two of troubles. Then there are higher yields and reduced cost of doing business. If they cannot*

achieve all of these, their job will be done for them. They will be divested, sold, or shut down. In any event, there are dangers to the jobs. Downsizing and restructuring is now a constant happening in practically every country.

In this scenario, business and manufacturing management can become hard-nosed and less patient. They want to upgrade, modernize, and streamline their facilities, equipment, and plants. Innovation can help. They are not the subject-matter experts. They rely on staff groups—accounting, industrial engineering, and relevant operations groups—to do staff work. These groups, over the years, have developed language and matrices that are commonly understood. So there is a common language for the operational problems, such as yield, ROI, capacity, quality, control, time to market, and the like. Hence, subject-matter experts have to translate their message to the language and criteria that the management understands. The experts have to go more than halfway here. You need this sensitivity in all phases of the project as you deal with the business/manufacturing management.

TECHNOLOGISTS' PERSPECTIVE   A young technologist with little experience in dealing with management could get a serious jolt if subjected to the justification process. Seniors not only have to shield and support but also have to train and educate junior team members. Various emotions during these exercises have been: Justification is a subjective process. Nothing could ever get justified, filtering through the various group's objections, as laid down before. It is an exercise in futility. I do not know the company strategy; worst, they themselves do not know it. Still worse, it changes too often. Our management is complacent; they cover themselves. The manager is reactionary.

The fact is, all of these opinions, and more may be correct. But they may not. It is believed that if one follows the justification process and works it, one will find either success or a real explanation. If management does not accept the plan, the reason behind it is subjective, as has been observed many a time.

Undoubtedly, due to the placement of innovation in the value chain, justification of innovative technologies is harder. But it is not impossible. It can be done and has been done, provided that you follow the process completely.

Realize, however, that even though the proposer/champion wants to do CIM, there is no reason why management should want to do it. It is the job of the champion to articulate why and how the project is a tremendous enabler of the company goals. Align CIM strategy with the company and business's manufacturing strategy, both for functionality and time frames. Innovation strategy is subordinate and responsive to the company, business, and manufacturing strategy.

Lessons Learned

These next issues must be positively resolved up front. Otherwise, the success of the project is questionable.

- Availability of the senior executives and key operating personnel
- Availability of the time required
- Readiness of finance managers to share the cost data
- Readiness of operating personnel to share the KPI goals
- Availability of good benchmark data (they can be expensive, if to be obtained from outside)
- A perfectly logical and accurate BCD is no reason for the senior management to follow through due to the the above issues

Case Example: PC Company

I developed and applied a methodology to develop business cases widely during my tenure at SAP in the high tech, automotive, and oil gas verticals, in the domain of supply chain optimization. The methodology was derived from my previous experiences in the chemical and semiconductor industry. It can diagrammatically be described as shown in Figure 7A.

Figure 7A maps into the BCD major activities as shown in Figure 7B.

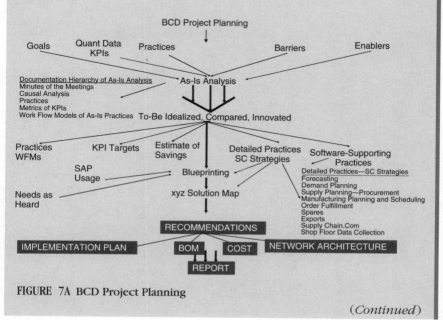

FIGURE 7A BCD Project Planning

(Continued)

(Continued)

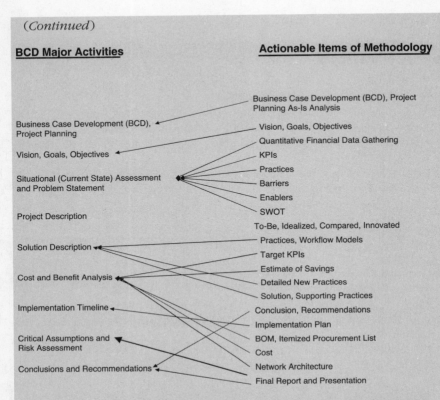

BCD Major Activities   **Actionable Items of Methodology**

Business Case Development (BCD), Project Planning As-Is Analysis

Business Case Development (BCD), Project Planning

Vision, Goals, Objectives

Quantitative Financial Data Gathering

Vision, Goals, Objectives

KPIs

Practices

Situational (Current State) Assessment and Problem Statement

Barriers

Enablers

Project Description

SWOT

To-Be, Idealized, Compared, Innovated

Practices, Workflow Models

Solution Description

Target KPIs

Estimate of Savings

Cost and Benefit Analysis

Detailed New Practices

Solution, Supporting Practices

Implementation Timeline

Conclusion, Recommendations

Implementation Plan

Critical Assumptions and Risk Assessment

BOM, Itemized Procurement List

Cost

Conclusions and Recommendations

Network Architecture

Final Report and Presentation

FIGURE 7B Mapping Actionable Items of Methodology on BCD Major Activities

The next example is from one of the largest personal computer (PC) companies in China. It succeeded so well that it eventually bought the PC divisions of one of the largest U.S. companies.

I was contacted by our China office to do a business case for the subject company. Table 7A presents the key questions asked of the China office personnel along with their answers.

TABLE 7A   Preliminary Questionnaire

Questions	Answers
Who is the client?	Chinese PC Company
What is the scope of the operations to be studied?	All of the supply chain
What is the scope/level of the work?	2-week level 2 business case development
Will they adhere to the study's requirements? Etc.	Yes

While preliminary answers were adequate, an initial meeting was set in China. The purpose of the meeting was to acquaint the client's champion and his executive team with:

- Our methodology
- The detailed agenda of activities to be followed
- The personnel involved in the project
- When they will be involved, and for what activities

Essentially our goal was to give the client a good feel for what the BCD team could do and would do to address their queries. Table 7B provides a schedule of activities, potential times involved, and the participants. Note that the activities are exactly as per the methodology given in Figure 7B and description of the activities to be performed as given earlier in Chapter 5 and 6. Also note that all the questions raised under BCD project planning had been answered by the end of the second day. By this time, we had explained to the client company everything that it had to do. We had given them the list of KPIs and financial questions on which they were supposed to gather data.

TABLE 7B   Activities for Business Case Development

Activities	Estimated Time	Participants
Day 1		
Introductions	.5 hr	BCD Team + Client Co. Personnel
Expectations from this opportunity assessment workshop	.5 hr	BCD Team + Client Co. Personnel
Scope		
Deliverables		
List of topics client company would like to be covered	.5 hr	BCD Team + Client Co. Personnel
KPI explanation	6 hr 7.5 hr	BCD Team + Client Co. Personnel
Day 2		
Presentation of opportunity assessment methodology	2 hr	BCD Team + Client Co. Personnel
High-tech solutions: Overview	2 hr	BCD Team + Client Co. Personnel
Discussion on KPIs already furnished	4 hr	
Finance		BCD Team + Client Co. Finance Personnel

(Continued)

(*Continued*)

TABLE 7B   (*Continued*)

Activities	Estimated Time	Participants
Supply chain		BCD Team + Client Co. Supply Chain Personnel
	8 Hr	
Day 3		
BCD team preliminary off-line analysis	4 hr	BCD Team
Feedback on KPIs furnished by XYZ Corp.	4 hr	BCD Team + Client Co. Finance and Supply Chain Personnel
	8 hr	
Day 4		
BCD team off-line analysis	4 hr	BCD Team
Vision and objectives of client company: Discussion and interview	2 hr	BCD Team + Client Co. Supply Chain Head: "c" level
Vision and objectives of client company: Discussion and interview	3 hr	BCD Team + Client Co. Executive Team of "c" levels
	9 hr	
Day 5		
1. Design and engineering: Discussion and interview of practices	2 hr	BCD Team + Client Co. Design and Engineering
2. Demand planning and forecasting: Discussion and interview of practices	2 hr	BCD Team + Client Co. Product Department
3. Production planning	2 hr	BCD Team + Client Co. Material Management
4. Sales logistics and distribution	2 hr	BCD Team + Client Co. Sales and Marketing
	8 hr	
Day 6		
1. Manufacturing and shop floor	2 hr	BCD Team + Client Co. Factory Team
2. Analysis of client company opportunity	10 hr	BCD Team
	12 hr	

TABLE 7B *(Continued)*		
Day 7– Day 10	32 hr	
1. Complete solution description		BCD Team
2. Complete project description		"
3. Change and risk management		"
4. Project planning: Timelines		"
5. Cost		"
6. Complete cost and benefits		"
7. Final report		"
8. Final Presentation		BCD Team + Client "c"-level Management + Other Teams
Total	84.5 hr	

At the end of Day 2, the BCD team returned to its home base and client company personnel began gathering data, calling me occasionally for clarification. Upon completion of the data-gathering phase and as previously planned, our BCD team returned to China. Then, from Day 3 (not a sequential calendar day 3, but the team's 3rd day at the client's facility) to Day 10, work began along three parallel streams:

Stream 1. Concentrate on meetings with client personnel as per Table 7B. Here the aim was to understand and build the vision, barriers, enablers, solutions, SWOT and opportunity.

Stream 2. Complete the data gathering, facilitating the gathering process, finalization, and normalization of the data on financials and KPIs.

Stream 3. Perform as-is and to-be analysis as well as all the desktop analysis, leading to the costs and benefits, solution, program planning, change and risk management considerations, final report, and gearing for final presentation.

Significant results of these activities are provided next, with client-sensitive details removed. For further questions, please contact the author.

Overview

The emerging market conditions in China as a result of its entry into the World Trade Organization and the pace of Internet penetration are bringing new globalization pressures on businesses there to be

(Continued)

(Continued)

the best world-class players. The existing competitive structures and the established basis for competition are no longer entirely valid, even for major and established players like the client company. Also, seen from a different view, this is an opportunity to be an early mover and reestablish the dominant position in the market as the new economy arrives in China.

The subject BCD was carried out in the light of these facts to look at value creation opportunities for the client company operating in the domestic market. The results, methodologies, and recommendations are given next.

Objectives

The objective of the study was to assess the supply chain value creation opportunities that exist for the PC business from a long- to medium-term perspective of three years and to arrive at a KPI scorecard for the next three years to lead the client company to realization of the value.

Scope

The BCD project was done for client's PC business in the domestic market. This is a core business that contributes to 90% of the client company's revenue.

The BCD project involved analysis of KPI data and interviews with functional teams and C-level teams and a factory visit.

No detailed process analysis and workflow modeling was done during this study. Nor was any detailed cross-validation of KPI data done. The KPIs as given to the client are given in Table 7C. The client response is not presented to honor client confidentiality.

TABLE 7C   KPIs to Collect

Key Performance Indicator	Definition	Data Requirement
Cycle time: Cash to cash	Payment made for materials received until payment received for goods sold	Yearly average: last 2 years

TABLE 7C *(Continued)*

Key Performance Indicator	Definition	Data Requirement
Supply chain management costs as a % of total revenue	Transportation, distribution, warehouse, inventory carrying cost, related cost of manpower, administration expenses, any depreciation on capital expenses/total revenue, by month, last 24 months	As on month-end: last 24 months
Order entry time and full-time equivalents (FTEs)	Time to prepare an order based on dealer's requirement; FTEs involved in order acceptance	Yearly average: last 2 years
Inventory turns: Finished goods	Total no. of working days in a year/total finished goods inventory at year-end	As on year-end: last 2 years
Inventory turns: Raw material	Total no. of working days in a year/total raw material inventory at year-end	As on year-end: last 2 years
Inventory turns: Work in progress (WIP)	Total no. of working days in a year/total WIP inventory at year-end	As on year-end: last 2 years
Inventory: Total days supply of finished goods	Total inventory of finished goods at year-end/average daily production	As on year-end: last 2 years
Inventory: Total days supply of raw material	Total inventory of raw material at year-end/average daily production	As on year-end: last 2 years
Inventory: Total days supply of WIP	Total inventory of WIP at year-end/average daily production	As on year-end: last 2 years
Inventory level: Finished goods	Total inventory of finished goods at year-end	As on year-end: last 2 years
Inventory level: Raw material	Total inventory of raw material at year-end	As on year-end: last 2 years
Inventory level: WIP	Total inventory of WIP at year-end	As on year-end: last 2 years

(Continued)

(Continued)

TABLE 7C *(Continued)*

Key Performance Indicator	Definition	Data Requirement
Inventory accuracy	Stocks as per physical verification /stock on books in %	As on month-end: last 24 months
Distribution costs as a % per vehicle	Total distribution costs/annual production	As on year-end: last 2 years
Forecast accuracy	Actual demand/Forecast demand in %	As on month-end: last 24 months
Number of supply sources	As on month-end	As on month-end: last 24 months
% of single-sourced parts of total parts	No. of parts having single source/total no. of parts in %	As on month-end: last 24 months
Order fulfillment lead time	Order acceptance from dealers to delivery of product to the dealer	Yearly average: last 2 years
Delivery performance to customer request date	No. of times dealer's request date met with same model mix/total no. of dealer's orders in %	Yearly average: last 2 years
Delivery performance to scheduled commit date	No. of times area office committed date to dealer met with same model mix/total no. of dealer's orders in %	Yearly average: last 2 years
Incoming material quality	% age rejects of incoming materials	As on month-end: last 24 months
% of local (indigenous) content parts	No. of indigenous parts/total no. of parts in %	As on month-end: last 24 months
% of parts handled by logistics providers	No. of parts handled by logistics providers/total no. of parts in %	As on month-end: last 24 months
Capacity utilization (see: The difference between maximum possible productivity and planned productivity level)	Agreed capacity/capacity defined by machine specifications or industrial engineering norms	As on month-end: last 24 months
Inventory obsolescence as a % of total inventory	Total nonmoving inventory/total inventory	As on month-end: last 24 months

TABLE 7C *(Continued)*

Key Performance Indicator	Definition	Data Requirement
Lead time: Production	Production cycle time: Start of production from the time order is taken	Yearly average: last 2 years
Back orders as a % of total orders	Committed orders but not yet fulfilled as on month-end	As on month-end: last 24 months
Customer credit check processing time	Average time to check credit status of a dealer	Yearly average: last 2 years
Cycle time: Order to cash	Time from placement of order by dealer to realizing money from dealer	Yearly average: last 2 years
Lost sales due to unavailability		As on month-end: last 24 months
Days sales outstanding	Total outstanding/ average daily sales	As on month-end: last 24 months
Delivery date predictability	(Actual delivery date − committed delivery date)/committed delivery date, in %	As on month-end: last 24 months
Delivery performance	(Actual model mix − committed model mix)/committed model mix, in %	As on month-end: last 24 months
Inquiry response wait time	Time to respond to an inquiry and commit a delivery date	Yearly average: last 2 years
Inventory: Obsolete as % of sales	Nonmoving: Finished goods, WIP, raw material separately as % of total sales	As on month-end: last 24 months
Invoices generated through EDI/Internet/R/3 as % of total revenue		Yearly average: last 2 years
Savings due to Web-enabled order entry, order inquiry, parts availability for spare parts		Yearly average: last 2 years

(Continued)

(Continued)

TABLE 7C *(Continued)*

Key Performance Indicator	Definition	Data Requirement
On-time pricing requests to customers		Yearly average: last 2 years
% of inquiries taken over the Internet		Yearly average: last 2 years
% of orders taken over the Internet		Yearly average: last 2 years
% of orders taken via EDI		Yearly average: last 2 years
% of inquiries taken via EDI		Yearly average: last 2 years
% of invoices paid in full	Total no. of invoices realized/total no. of invoices	As on month-end: last 24 months
Sales cost as a % of revenue		Yearly average: last 2 years
Market share		As on month-end: last 24 months
Spares: Inventory days of supply		Yearly average: last 2 years
Spares: Inventory turns		Yearly average: last 2 years
Warranty/claims costs		Yearly average: last 2 years
Internet orders		Yearly average: last 2 years
Elapsed time between product production and sale		As on month-end: last 24 months
Lead time for customer custom-built order		Yearly average: last 2 years

Interviews

Group discussion sessions were held with functional teams of the client company to understand the processes, critical success factors, barriers, enablers, and KPI data explanations for four processes:

1. Demand planning and forecasting
2. Material planning
3. Order fulfillment
4. Design and engineering

To preserve client confidentiality, I do not summarize the interviews here.

Supply Chain Key Performance Indicators

KPIs as per SCOR model were used to measure the characteristics of the client company's supply chain. We analyzed these characteristics of the supply chain:

- Total supply chain cost
- Supply chain performance in terms of delivery performance and inventory
- Supply chain agility in terms of lead times and capacities

We explained the definitions and formula for arriving at the KPIs to the client teams. We used the data on KPIs as provided by the client teams for the analysis; no cross-validation was possible due to project scope/time constraints.

The data on total cost as provided worked out to 102.2%. This was rationalized to 100% by reducing certain other expenses with the client's consent. The other exception was that there was no interest cost and hence no opportunity cost on inventory. Table 7D gives the details on the supply chain costs of the client company on as-is and as-is-recast basis.

TABLE 7D   As-Is and Recast Supply Chain Costs

Metric of Key Performance Indicator	As-Is %	As-Is-Recast %
Material cost as paid to vendors	86.84	86.84
Wage cost	1.20	1.20
Transportation cost	0.85	0.85
Warehouse cost	0.69	0.69
Others	2.60	2.60
Advertisement	3.36	1.16
Profit	6.66	6.66
Taxes	0.00	0.00
Inventory Carrying Cost	0.00	0.00
Total	102.20	100.00
Supply chain cost, without inventory carrying cost, without associated wage expenses	**1.54**	
Total supply chain cost = Above + inventory carrying cost + material acquisition cost		**3.15**

(Continued)

(Continued)

Supply Chain Scorecard

Table 7E gives the supply chain scorecard done as per the SCOR model of the Supply Chain Research Council:

TABLE 7E   Supply Chain Scorecard

Important KPIs	As-Is-Recast %	Best in Class	Average in Class	Client Company Target	Enablers
Material cost as paid to vendors	86.40	80	50	3%/Yr Red	Vendor-managed inventory
Wage cost	1.2	2		No charge	
Total SCM cost	3.15	6.3	11.6	No Charge	
Order fill time days	7	1		2	Real-time available to promise
Brand-new products, time to market	1	2–>1		No Charge	
Manufacturing paradigms	Push	Push > Pull		Pull	Assemble to order
Days of inventory	18	6	26	No Charge	
Material acquisition cost	0.64	0.86	2.18	No Charge	
Cash-to-cash cycle	−11	24.7	97.4	o Charge	
% of orders on time to customer required date	70	94.6	80.1	95	Capable to promise
% of orders on time to commit date	64	97.1	89.9	97	Exception management
Forecast accuracy %	75	?	?	90	Collaborative Consensus

Findings Opportunity Assessment

Based on the KPIs data analysis and interviews held with the client team, the characteristics required for the supply chain of the PC market are:

- Agility
- Support new product introductions

- Low cost
- Low order fulfillment lead times

Value creation opportunity could arise from lowering of cost and improvement in market share in a fast-expanding market. Some of these opportunities are tangible via cost reductions; additional revenues through increase in sales are tangible benefits. Examples of intangible benefits are increase in market share, improvement in customer loyalty, and better dealer relationships.

The client's existing supply chain can be characterized as a low-cost supply chain. The supply chain cost is not a key issue for the company. Moreover, due to availability of low-interest credit, there is almost no inventory carrying cost. However, the material cost of this client is at 86.4%, much higher than average. So there is an opportunity for value creation through lowering of material cost. This should be viewed as one of the goals. A target reduction of 3% per year has been taken for assessing the benefits.

Given the client company's strengths, many of which are world class, and the expected expansion and activity in the marketplace, it is recommended that the *client company should take the high market-share growth route to additional value creation.*

Assumptions
1. The time horizon considered for the calculations is three years.
2. The domestic PC market growth rate has been taken as 35%, 38%, and 40% for those three years.
3. The current market share at 22% is targeted to increase 8% every year. Accordingly, the market share for the company should be 30%, 38%, and 45% for the next three years.
4. Based on the overall market growth and this client's market share, the volume growth rate for the company works out to be 84%, 75%, and 66% for each of the three years respectively.
5. All sales value figures have been worked out using last year's prices of PCs as the basis.

Business Case Development Results
1. Based on the market-share growth, the total cumulative value creation potential for the three years is 1,699 million RMB.
2. Through material cost reduction, the additional cumulative value potential is 2,485 million RMB.

(Continued)

(*Continued*)

3. The total value creation potential for the next three years is 4,183 million RMB.

These computations are presented in Table 7F.

TABLE 7F   Summary of Improved Potential Benefits

	(in million RMBs)			
	Yr 1	Yr 2	Yr 3	Total
Profit at base year	531	531	531	1593
Additional profit due market share growth	195	512	991	1699
Additional profit due material cost savings	440	769	1275	2485
Total additional opportunity for increased profits	635	1282	2266	4183

The rest of the items in the project were completed as per the methodology given earlier and the Final Presentation and Final Report given to the Client Company's "c" level management. The results of Improved Potential Benefits were discussed at length and both the Cost and the Benefit assessment recommendations were accepted as given.

The Client went after Market Share, improving their share value at the Chinese Stock market and became very successful as the BCD SWOT analysis had learned about their strengths, etc. They continued to progress as recommended and subsequently acquired a major US based PC Company.

Bibliography

Alliance for Project Innovation. "Harness the Power of Project Champions," home page 2005.

Bansal, Sam. ALCOA's CIM Showcase, Advanced Manufacturing Systems (AMS 86), Chicago, April 1988.

Bansal, Sam. "Computer Integrated Manufacturing: A Greenfield Paradigm Implementation," *Industrial Automation Journal* (Singapore) (October 1993).

Bansal, Sam. "Developing a Framework for Plant-wide Control Investment Strategy," *Computer Integrated Manufacturing Systems* 4, No. 4 (November 1991).

Bansal, Sam. Federation of Automatic Controls, Barcelona, Spain, July 2002.

Bansal, Sam. Framework for Plant Wide Process Control Investment Strategies, Control, Chicago; January 1991.

Bansal, Sam. "Impact of IT on the Human Roles in Manufacturing in the Next Century," Paper presented at the International IT Human Resource Conference, Singapore, October 1993.

Bansal, Sam. "Issues of International Users of CIM," Paper presented at the FAIM 1995, Stuttgart, Germany, June 1995.

Bansal, Sam. "Management of Plant-wide Automation," *Industrial Automation Journal* (Singapore) (March 1994).

Bansal, Sam. "Managing Innovations in CIM Environments: Justification and Implementation Paradigms," University of Torino, Italy, 1995.

Cai, Sunny Ghali, Michael Giannelia, Aaron Hughes, Adam Johnson, and Tony Khoo.

Code of Practice for Project Management (2002). AllPM.Com, February 2005.

Collins, Leyton W. "Interpersonal Skills and the Effective Project Manager," allPM.com, June 2003.

Cosgrove Ware, Lorraine. "Best Practices for Project Management Offices," *CIO Research Reports* (July 2003).

Datz, Todd. "Portfolio Management Done Right," *CIO* (May 2003).

Ellis, Keith. Getting Consensus on Business Requirements, January 2004.

"Exchange 2000 Migration: Project Management Best Practices," *Tech Republic*.

Gulesian, Marcia. "Project Management Issues to Consider," marcia.gulesian@verizon.net.

Teplitzky, Victor A. "Attributes of Successful Leadership," allPM.com, February 2003.

Wilson. Project Planning Strategies and Tools, March.

Withrow, Scott. "How Project Champions Can Rally Support for Your Team," Builder.AU.Com (November 2004).

Yongxue. Identifying Best Practices in Information Technology Project Management.

CHAPTER 8

Umbrella Considerations

Umbrella considerations are some of the most important life cycle considerations that a new practitioner does not even know about. To ensure the success of the project, you have to know and plan for each one right from the start, even if for no other reason than that they impact the project budget considerably. Clients have asked me to plan and forecast the costs associated with each consideration at the inception stage in order to establish an accurate budget estimate. It is actually the lack of accurate budget estimate that is behind the cost overruns and missed start-up dates.

Change Management

Managing change in today's business environment is part of everyone's job, whether you are in a management, professional, or nonmanagement position. Managing change includes change management planning, understanding stakeholders, risk analysis, and effective communication to support change initiative.[1]

Change management is the process of developing a planned approach to change in an organization. Typically the objective is to minimize disruptions to the normal flow of activity. Change management can be either reactive—in which case management is responding to changes in the macroenvironment (i.e., the source of the change is external)—or proactive—in which case management is initiating the change in order to achieve a desired goal (i.e., the source of the change is internal). Change management can be conducted on a continuous basis, on a regular schedule (such as an annual review), or when deemed necessary on a program-by-program basis.

Change management can be approached from a number of angles and applied to numerous organizational processes. Its most common uses are in organizational development, information technology (IT) management, strategic management, and process management. To be effective, change

235

management should be multidisciplinary, touching all aspects of the organization. However, at its core, change management is primarily a human resource management issue. This is because implementing new procedures, technologies, and overcoming resistance to change are fundamentally people issues.[2]

Psychology of Change

Attitudes toward change result from a complex interplay of emotions and cognitive processes. Because of this complexity, everyone reacts to change differently. On the positive side, change is viewed as opportunity, rejuvenation, progress, innovation, and growth. But just as legitimately, change can also be seen as instability, upheaval, unpredictability, threat, and disorientation. How employees perceive change—with fear, anxiety, and demoralization; with excitement and confidence; or somewhere in between—depends partially on an individual's psychological makeup, partially on management's actions, and partially on the specific nature of the change.

An individual's attitude toward a change tends to evolve as he or she becomes more familiar with it. The stages a person goes through can consist of: apprehension, denial, anger, resentment, depression, cognitive dissonance, compliance, acceptance, and internalization. It is management's job to create an environment in which people can go through these stages as quickly as possible and even skip some stages. Effective change management programs often are sequential, with early measures directed at overcoming the initial apprehension, denial, anger, and resentment but gradually evolving into a program that supports compliance, acceptance, and internalization. I fought these issues at every company I worked at, if the technology I was delivering was novel. What won over the skeptics was the successful demonstration that the new technology could deliver better results than what they were capable of delivering themselves.

Management's Role

Management's first responsibility is to detect trends in the macroenvironment so as to be able to identify changes and initiate programs. It is also important to estimate what impact a change likely will have on employee behavior patterns, work processes, technological requirements, and motivation. Management must assess what employee reactions will be and craft a change program that will provide support as workers go through the process of accepting change. The program then must be implemented, disseminated throughout the organization, monitored for effectiveness, and adjusted where necessary.

In general terms, a change program should describe the change process to all the people involved and explain why the changes are occurring. The information should:

- Be complete, unbiased, reliable, transparent, and timely.
- Be designed to effectively implement the change while being aligned with organizational objectives, macroenvironmental trends, and employee perceptions and feelings.
- Provide support to employees as they deal with the change and, wherever possible, involve them directly in the change process itself. If the change involves vendors and customers, effective communication will make change smoother.

Change Management in Information Technology

Change management considerations during the implementation phase of an enterprise project are concerned with the "best practices" to manage changes in the plans, procedures, scope, or specifications of any type. They also are concerned with making the organization capable of absorbing the change productively and creatively. Next we focus on two issues:

1. How to enable the organization to absorb the change (new technology)
2. How to manage the change (in, and with respect to, technology)

HOW TO ENABLE THE ORGANIZATION TO ABSORB THE CHANGE (NEW TECHNOLOGY)
This aspect of change means preparing the organization for the change, i.e., the new technology, that is being brought into the organization. The key aspects of this are:

- Communication
- Training

These are covered in subsequent sections later in this chapter. They are mentioned here for the sake of completeness

HOW TO MANAGE THE CHANGE (IN, AND WITH RESPECT TO, TECHNOLOGY)   Although the next best practices are generally applicable to a technology initiative, some aspects are more useful for IT-oriented initiatives. Given next are the best practices that deal with change management in the context of information technology (IT) projects.

- **Change management best practices.** They can be grouped into three areas: General, Change Request Management, and Deployment Management.[3]
- **Communicate roles and responsibilities**. Communication of roles and responsibilities of the project team to the enterprise participants belongs to the IT area's responsibility. The enterprise and team ensures that change management policy, procedures, and standards are integrated with and communicated throughout the IT area with all the business management functions. Doing this entails:
  - The existence of a written policy for change management that defines all roles, responsibilities, and procedures related to change management, approved by the chief information officer/IT director and the business information security manager.
  - Communication of change management procedures and standards that define the techniques and technologies to be used throughout the enterprise in support of the change management policy.
  - Periodic review (at least annually) by IT management of policies, procedures, and standards to ensure suitability and completeness.
- **Define Roles and Responsibilities**. Roles and responsibilities affecting change management are defined, designated to qualified personnel, communicated to the organization, and enforced throughout the change management process. Specifically:
  - Infrastructure support personnel are appropriately assigned with regard to the complexity of the organization, the complexity and performance of the organization's applications and networks, and the criticality of these systems to the business.
  - Personnel responsible for business analysis are competent and/or fluent in the organization's IT systems and have exposure to the organization's management policies, procedures, and people.
  - Personnel responsible for technical analysis are skilled in the organization's IT systems and have experience and/or have been trained in project management for these systems.
  - The "major-impact" change management team has sufficient business management authority to analyze, prioritize, and allocate all resources for project implementation.
  - The "minor-impact" change management team has sufficient IT management authority to analyze, prioritize, and allocate resources for change design and implementation.
  - Configuration/release managers are assigned the responsibility to maintain the integrity of IT system environments. A release management function monitors and controls the deployment of changes between logical environments, allowing development and testing

teams to focus on their specialties. Personnel with configuration/ release management responsibility are not assigned to develop or test infrastructure changes that they are responsible for promoting.

- Developers are assigned in teams and managed according to projects and business priorities.
- A separate testing organization is assigned the responsibility for quality assurance of all developed software and network changes.
- Systems/production control teams are assigned the operation and administration of all production systems.

MANAGE CHANGE MANAGEMENT PROCESS VIA KEY PERFORMANCE INDICATORS

This general area of best practice relates to managing change management via key performance indicators (KPIs). KPIs about the entire change management process are captured periodically and are used by management to alter or adjust procedures and practices. Doing this entails:

- Capturing metrics about the request management processes, identifying bottlenecks and successful techniques to management for continuous improvement of this process.
- Periodically capturing metrics about the deployment management process, indicating to management the successes and obstacles in this process. Baseline metrics should be captured for the solution/system at solution conversion or roll-out.

KPI metrics cover each of the next areas by period, category, and risk level:

- Volume of change processed
- Average turnaround time of a change
- Number of requests received
- Number of requests rejected
- Number of change back-outs
- Number of changes that generate follow-on requests
- Number of changes that do not pass acceptance testing
- Number of emergency changes requested and implemented

Metrics also convey the number of resources required for each enhancement and project as well as any technical or system maintenance issues that can be improved to make the process more effective and efficient.

AUDIT SYSTEMS
Systems are monitored for integrity by an internal organizational unit. Specifically this means that applications and networks are

monitored for their functionality by an internal business unit that effectively represents a user population and makes change requests on their behalf.

SPECIFICATION CHANGE REQUIREMENTS   This best practice relates to the design domain and is concerned with the enhancements and/or bug-fix requirements that are developed, documented, and coordinated with all parties. Doing this entails:

- Documenting requirements and specifications relating to the business (functional, market, regulatory, etc.) and technical needs of the solution.
- Coordinating design work with system users, testing personnel, and the information security function to ensure a sufficient understanding of the business and technical requirements and the impact on current production systems.
- Submitting solution prototypes to the organization's project management for approval prior to final design and subsequent build/configuration/integration work.
- Integrating design of the solution with the requirements of processes, users, technology, and data elements in compliance with service-level agreements.
- Creating solution designs within organizational standards for development, architecture, engineering guidelines, naming conventions, and security requirements.
- Producing an implementation plan that outlines resources, time, and coordination points for the solution, including building/configuration/integration and testing of the solution.

REVIEW REQUESTS FOR SPECIFICATION CHANGE AND BUGS   This best practice relates to the request management domain and is concerned with infrastructure support. It is about the enhancement requests and bug-defect reports that are captured and submitted to business and IT management for review. Specifically it entails:

- Charging personnel responsible for infrastructure support roles with the responsibility to capture, prioritize, and submit change requests to the appropriate change management process.
- Assigning a business sponsor for change requests; this person is notified as requests are captured.
- Infrastructure support personnel categorizing change requests based on priority as enhancements, bugs, patches, updates, and any other "emergency" need. The subsequent routing of the request is expedited based on this priority.

MANAGE ISSUES AND REQUESTS This best practice relates to the request management domain and is concerned with infrastructure support. It is about the issues and requests that are managed throughout the change management life cycle. In particular it ensures that infrastructure support personnel have the ability to manage the request management process, including:

- Measuring process performance criteria
- Escalating inactive requests
- Prioritizing "emergency" fixes
- Reporting progress of requests to users

REQUEST ANALYSIS, BUSINESS ANALYSIS The best practice of the request management domain is concerned with request analysis support. Business analysis is performed to determine likelihood of success, significance to business, resources required, and business justification. In particular, this best practice makes sure that:

- A business analyst analyzes requests to assess risks of solution implementation and to determine minor/major impact to the business.
  - If minor impact, the business analyst routes requests to technical analysis for further action (including bug reports).
  - If major impact, the business analyst performs business justification in conjunction with technical analysis, including likelihood of success, significance to the business, resources required, and system interdependencies.
- When analysis is complete, the business analyst prioritizes based on the analysis and routes to business management for decision making.

TECHNICAL ANALYSIS This best practice relates to the request management domain and is concerned with the technical analysis support. Technical analysis is performed to determine system dependencies, technology resources/techniques required, and project estimates.

- For bug-defect reports, a technical analyst function assesses and routes the report to appropriate development teams for immediate action.
- A technical analyst function identifies the technical feasibility of change requests, including impacts to existing infrastructure and development, testing, and release schedules.

REQUEST REPORTING: LIFE CYCLE REPORTING FOR VISIBILITY This best practice relates to the request management domain and is concerned with reporting request support. It concerns the organization's ability to retain visibility on the status of requests and projects as they are analyzed, prioritized, designed, developed, tested, and deployed. Doing this entails:

- The ability of infrastructure support tools to retain visibility and status for submitted requests through every phase of the change management process, including details about the deployment of the change.
- Integrating infrastructure support people and tools into help desk and enterprise management tools, to quickly analyze and prioritize requests.

PROJECT MANAGEMENT: BUSINESS MANAGERS REVIEW MAJOR IMPACT   This best practice relates to the request management domain and concerns project management support. A team of business managers reviews "major-impact" requests and prioritizes them based on business needs. Specifically:

- The team (business managers and the project team) reviews change requests determined to be of major impact to the business and prioritizes initiatives for design and implementation.
- The team regularly exchanges analysis and opinions and reaches decisions related to major change requests at a pace commensurate with business needs.

IT MANAGERS REVIEW MINOR IMPACT   This best practice relates to the request management domain and concerns the project management support. Specifically:

- The team reviews change requests determined to be of minor impact to the business and prioritizes initiatives for design and implementation.
- The team analyzes and prioritizes change requests at a pace commensurate with business needs.

PROJECT MANAGEMENT OFFICE (PMO) ALLOCATES AND REDISTRIBUTES RESOURCES
This best practice relates to the request management domain and concerns the project management support. The organization's project management office is involved in managing and allocating resources between "major-impact" projects and "minor-impact" requests. Doing so entails enabling the business to streamline projects and reallocate resources as necessary during the change management process, within business requirements.

Deployment Management

This aspect comprises aspects of logical environments and process and technology leveraging.

LOGICAL ENVIRONMENTS: IT ENVIRONMENTS   This best practice relates to the deployment management domain and concerns logical environment support. Here the organization defines separate IT environments, each with its own configuration, operational responsibility, and access controls. This means:

- The organization has, at a minimum, three primary separate functional environments—development, test/quality assurance, and production—each consisting of the appropriate tier components (client, server, database, etc.).
- Release/configuration managers may have access to all environments, depending on process needs.
- Multiple environments of each primary type may be used, provided that they are separated logically.
- Development, test/quality assurance, and staging environments may be defined to share the same physical equipment but should be logically isolated, so that system access for one environment does not allow the same access to another environment on the same hardware.

LOGICAL ENVIRONMENTS: DEVELOPMENT ENVIRONMENTS   This best practice relates to the deployment management domain and concerns the development environment support. The development environments are used to build, configure, and integrate infrastructure changes. Specifically at the platform, database, and network levels, developers do not have access to environments other than their assigned development environment.

LOGICAL ENVIRONMENTS: TEST/QUALITY ASSURANCE ENVIRONMENTS   This best practice relates to the deployment management domain and concerns the test/quality assurance environment support. The testing/quality assurance environments are used to ensure the functionality, performance, and business acceptance of solutions prior to deployment. This means:

- Only testing team personnel have access to their assigned test/quality assurance environment.
- The organization help desk administers and supports the test/quality assurance environments.
- A test/quality assurance environment is configured to replicate (as closely as practicable) the performance of the production environment for which solutions are implemented or changed.

LOGICAL ENVIRONMENTS: STAGING ENVIRONMENTS This best practice relates to the deployment management domain and is concerned with staging environment support. Staging environments are used to assemble solution changes into releases for which the business is prepared.

- The organization may use a stage environment for staging solution changes until the business is prepared for infrastructure release.
- Doing so may prevent process bottlenecks and configuration problems in a rapid pace of development but may add complexity to release administration.
- Access is limited to those users who have a business need to access the stage environment for its designed purpose.
- The organization may use a stage environment for user training or other purposes required by the business.

LOGICAL ENVIRONMENTS: PRODUCTION ENVIRONMENTS This best practice relates to the deployment management domain and concerns production environment support. Production environments are used to support the business's IT infrastructure requirements.

- Access to the production environment at the application level is limited to those users authorized to use the production system.
- Access is highly limited to those personnel who are authorized to configure and/or administrate it.
- The production environment is not physically collocated with any other environment. It has its own hardware and network connectivity to ensure availability in the event of a development, test/quality assurance, or stage system crash.

PROCESS SUPPORT: CHANGE MANAGEMENT PROCESS This best practice relates to the deployment management domain and concerns process support. The change management process follows a logical order and is controlled to ensure the logical evolution of effective enhancements to production environments. This means:

- "Major-impact" projects are first built/configured as prototypes to demonstrate to management their business justification and feasibility. Preliminary testing (including functionality and performance), business acceptance, and adjustments to design are used as specifications for solution development.
- Infrastructure changes are first built/configured/integrated in the development environment(s), followed by testing in the test/quality assurance environment, and are deployed to the production environment in

intermediate steps as business needs require. These steps may include staging, training, approvals by affected parties and management, or other activities and environments after testing but prior to production.

- Infrastructure component purchases (software, hardware, and network components) are coordinated using requests for proposals and vendor proposals to determine the best fit for the business needs based on solution requirements and specifications.

- Procedures are in place to ensure that system changes can be immediately demoted or restored to a prior state in the event of an unsuccessful or undesired deployment of infrastructure changes to production environments.

- Business units that will be directly affected by an enhancement are given right of approval/disapproval/delay prior to a particular change's deployment into production. This may include end user training, documentation, and staging, as the business unit's needs require.

- Production deliverables are released concurrently or prior to solution conversion/roll-out. Deliverables should include all applicable editions or updates to user and administration manuals, configuration references, topology diagrams, support procedures, and business continuity plans.

PROCESS SUPPORT: TEST/QUALITY ASSURANCE PROCESS   This best practice relates to the deployment management domain and concerns process support. Here testing/quality assurance is conducted to ensure reliability and performance of all components of the organization's technology infrastructure.

PROCESS SUPPORT: EMERGENCY REQUEST HANDLING PROCESS   This best practice relates to the deployment management domain and is concerned with process support. Here emergency requests are handled in a manner similar to normal requests, with minor differences to allow for expedited development, testing, and release.

- Emergency/bug changes are verified by business and technical analysis and then are expedited through a simplified promotion and deployment process. Emergency releases must be authorized by a predetermined manager and logged into the appropriate system for audit purposes.

- All emergency build/configuration/integration changes must be tested in all sufficient phases to ensure quality performance without adding additional disturbances to the current systems.

- Emergency releases should be communicated to the user and administration population to alert them to the need and impacts of the emergency changes.

PROCESS SUPPORT: CONFIGURATION/RELEASE MANAGEMENT PROCESS   This best practice relates to the deployment management domain and concerns process support. The configuration/release management function provides administration and control over deployment management. Specifically:

- A release management function has the responsibility to control the deployment of changes from one environment to the next. No other role should be allowed to "push" or "pull" changes from one environment to another, and the release management function has the authority to approve or deny change promotions and/or deployments. This function may utilize different personnel for each promotion stage, depending on business requirements.
- Release management administers and oversees version control and program libraries and other systems software that automate the change deployment process.
- All changes made for deployments to each environment are logged for solution module versions, date/time stamp, identification of user deploying the change, and execution steps for the deployment.
- Changes that fail in their deployment to the production environment are analyzed for root causes, and these findings are documented for organizational reference.
- Availability of infrastructure components is maintained within service-level agreements and business requirements. If availability of these components must be interrupted, downtime for deployment is scheduled appropriately and users of the affected systems are notified in advance of the change deployment to ensure business continuity.

TECHNOLOGY LEVERAGE   This best practice relates to the deployment management domain and concerns technology leverage support. Technology leverage is possible through the technology tools to provide audit ability, versioning, and automation throughout the deployment process.

- Version control systems and/or program libraries are used to maintain all copies of software and configuration ever developed, tested, or deployed in the enterprise.
- Version control systems control the check-in/check-out of software and subsequent deployment throughout the deployment process. It does so by ensuring that these concepts are possible:
  - *Either* no two users may check out and check in software for changes at the same time
  - *Or* if simultaneous check-outs are allowed, a tool or process for reviewing and merging changes is used prior to check-in.

- Check-in of previously checked-out software always changes the version label in the system, so that no two versions are labeled alike.
- Only new software modules are allowed to be checked in without checking them out first
- Version control systems are used as the source for all deployments of software to test/quality assurance, stage, and production environments.
- Selection of deployed versions is controlled by version labels.
- Automated tools are utilized to enhance and enforce the organization's change management policy and procedures, including messaging, workflow, and push-button deployment capabilities.

Implementation Time Risk Analysis and Mitigation of Risk in Enterprise Systems

Risk management at a business level has always been the subject area and focus of top managers and executives. Those who anticipated risks and took great care of them did well and thrived; those who did not did not advance in their careers. Figure 8.1 presents a historical perspective.

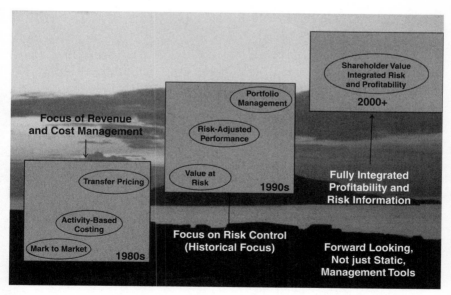

FIGURE 8.1 Evolution of Risk Decision Making

IT and systems have become so mission critical that risk estimation, measurement, and management have assumed significant importance. Today's project management processes emphasize project risk management. Its objective is to identify risk conditions; prioritize them based on their impact on project goals; identify, plan, and execute mitigation steps; and track risks during the project life cycle. Doing this ensures that you are always apprised of project risks and measures that can be taken to mitigate them.

Since systems have become an intimate part of the business processes, risks can be found in one or all of the areas: financial, operational, supply chain, image areas.

Given the fact that today's enterprise systems are serving most of the company's business processes, it is not difficult to imagine how a nonfunctioning or malfunctioning application could put the entire enterprise at risk.

In the context of IT systems the risk scenario can be divided into two phases:

1. System implementation phase
2. System operational phase

Here we cover the implementation and operational phase aspects of test planning and test procedures, with a greater focus on implementation phase aspects.

Implementation Phase Risk Planning

In the implementation phase, the risks that you have to be concerned about are different from those that exist when the systems are operational. However, some of the operational time considerations with respect to risk begin in this phase. The implementation time risks are due to:

- New technology (hardware, software, networks, sensors)
- Security and access control
- Undersizing
- Inadequate backups
- Vendors
- Poor project/program management and poor tools
- Bad estimates of life cycle costs and benefits of customizing an enterprise application
- Not involving external resources
- Not doing a good business case
- Lack of champion and executive sponsors
- Strategic mis-/nonalignment
- Nonacceptance of installed system

- Inadequate training
- Poor communications
- Poor change management
- Staff turnover

Next we describe each risk, how it manifests, its impact, and how to mitigate it.

RISKS DUE TO NEW TECHNOLOGY (HARDWARE, SOFTWARE, NETWORKS)   If new technology is selected, risks have to be considered because the support required will be for mission-critical applications. Because the technology is unproven for robustness, user friendliness, and fault tolerance, risks must be evaluated. The technology can cause difficulties in testing and later in going live and then even in stabilization phases. The consequences are not only financial but also the loss of credibility of the project team, sponsors, stakeholders, or even customers. There might also be the case of lost opportunity costs. The plans and ways to mitigate each risk item must be put in place.

RISKS DUE TO SECURITY AND ACCESS CONTROL   Many enterprise systems replace old, obscurely coded, disparate applications running on proprietary operating systems with modern, integrated systems built on relational databases on UNIX and Windows NT platforms. One of the gotchas in this architectural transition is the loss of security by obscurity. These popular operating systems are vulnerable to security attacks from within and without. And modern powerful query tools, combined with integrated data warehouses, increase the risk that even authenticated users might be tempted to browse data they are not authorized to see. Also, these modern systems require equally modern and sophisticated security architectures. Important security considerations include constructing firewalls to protect the databases, encrypting passwords and possibly all user transactions, and protecting end users' computers. Careful attention must also be paid to access control provisions because enterprise packages, as delivered, may not provide the level of interdepartmental privacy demanded in some higher education institutions. Note that making changes in a vendor-supplied access control infrastructure can lead to costly customizations.

RISKS DUE TO UNDERSIZING   Advanced relational databases, complex graphical interfaces, ad hoc query capabilities, sophisticated authentication and authorization protocols, and hundreds of simultaneous online users all combine to chew up as much hardware as you can afford to allocate to a new enterprise application. Rule 101 of computer science used to be that capacity is consumed the day it is installed.

Accurate estimates of how much disk space, processor capacity, and network bandwidth will be required are difficult to make, because of the switch from old paper-based processes to new online methods when historical data is not available. In the marketing cycle, software vendors tend to downplay the need for adequate hardware, because it increases the costs of implementing their systems. In addition, users can be unhappy about the performance of a new system compared with an older one, because highly tuned, terminal-based legacy applications, although hard to learn, often have very good performance characteristics. New applications usually require a great deal of tuning to meet performance expectations. All this creates risks that have to be considered and mitigated. The rule of thumb is to have more than adequate capacity and bandwidth. Also, the selected system should be highly scalable so that when problems do show up, it can be upgraded. Tuning, training, and system user friendliness in context will be the other remedies.

RISK DUE TO INADEQUATE BACKUPS   If the application is not mission critical, systems do not need to be backed up. However, with growing complexity, seldom are systems not mission critical, although some may be more critical than others. Therefore, a judicious level of backup must be considered right from the selection and evaluation stages. Both financial and customer-facing systems that used to be thought of as pretty harmless systems can bring the entire enterprise to its knees if they fail. Hardcore process control systems cannot be allowed to go down in the midst of production. Thus, depending on the business processes, criticality backup has got to be considered.

The threat to the risk can be eliminated by considering levels of backup. Automatic backup with shared resources, analog backup in some applications, and manual backup are the modes that can be used. Backup methods must be considered for all elements of the entire system. Thought must also be given to readiness exercises after the go-live time, so that operating people do not forget to run the system in backup modes.

RISKS DUE TO VENDORS   "Marketers" often promote future versions vaporware. However, in all fairness to vendor sales teams, usually they do not mislead customers. Due to inadequate information and the push to make the quarterly quotas, they may oversell their systems. Even the best usually are focused on the promises of release $n+1$. Intense competition can drive a vendor to concentrate on the bells and whistles of future versions rather than focus on the mundane but critical issues of quality and supportability of the current version. As a result, the project team may plan on doing something that is unachievable. And usually by the time it gets known, it is already too late.

You must begin to mitigate the impact of vendor overselling at the very start of the selection process. Thoroughly investigate the functionality, architecture, and future upgrades. Identify and discuss gaps with the vendors' reps and customers. Contact customers who are in production with the subject systems and ask about the functionality, features, gaps and their level of satisfaction with the system. Talk with product developers and consultants with significant experience to understand the current status of the products to be installed. On-site visits to similar institutions of vendor customers are perhaps the most valuable evaluation techniques available. Good reference sites from lists of peer institutions are better than those provided by the vendor. When possible, carry out a trial period or a prototype demonstration using live data in as realistic a setting as possible. Recognize the potential instabilities that are likely when you become involved in a beta test for the next generation of an application. In other words, try to "open the box" as early as possible before making the buying decision.

RISKS DUE TO POOR PROJECT/PROGRAM MANAGEMENT AND POOR TOOLS   There is an organizational tendency not to pay attention to the best practices, tools and personnel required to do enterprise projects. This is based on the fact that these projects are supposed to save money; so, to spend while implementing them is anathema to many organizations. This kind of thinking can develop into a serious problem.

Risks can be mitigated by a good project manager or a good champion. Effective risk assessment and sound contingency planning is of paramount importance. Most enterprise projects are very expensive, and investing in good project management tools and personnel early in the project is money well spent. A good project manager with good tools can deal effectively with the potential risks.

RISKS DUE TO BAD ESTIMATES OF LIFE CYCLE COSTS AND BENEFITS OF CUSTOMIZ-ING AN ENTERPRISE APPLICATION   A good project manager will be very realistic about the costs and benefits of customizing an enterprise application. He or she will be twice as careful if the development is completely customized. However, some project managers can get talked into tough requirements by influential customers and can embark on a path that will prove to be fatal. Also, if this practice (cost/benefit analysis based customizaion) is not followed, the benefits—such as ease of initial and future release installations, remote customer support from the vendor, low-cost maintenance, and economical feature acquisition—vaporize when an application is tailored to fit the unique requirements of the institution. In the real world, few large organizations with functional units and strong customer-focused goals have the discipline to accept a given package as is. As soon as important users see what really comes out of the box, the pressures mount exponentially to make just a few important changes. This process is a very slippery slope that leads directly to a highly customized, hard-to-maintain, and very expensive solution.

To minimize or eliminate these risks, customizations ideally should be kept to zero. If that is not achievable, then they should be kept to the bare minimum. All effort and communication with the customer base should be to point out the cost benefit of an all-vanilla system. If the customization is substantial and the organization is large and cost benefits are there, the vendor might be persuaded to undertake the customization effort, at cost. However, the cost of choosing a customized path is very high and usually not well understood by senior management. Customization proposals should be escalated to a high level in the decision-making framework.

RISKS DUE TO NOT INVOLVING EXTERNAL RESOURCES   The organization will need additional staff to implement a major new enterprise system. Normal production work needs to continue at the same time that the new system is developed, tested, and introduced. External consultants and contractors, although very expensive, can play invaluable roles in the implementation process, but project managers must understand how to manage and utilize them in the organization's culture. The consultants will have a tendency to bypass the project management team and go directly to the senior management. Often they do not understand the organization's unique business processes or the culture. So the system they implement will be less than desirable, and the local project team will end up maintaining a nonmaintainable system. Worse still, the system does not provide the major functional support that customers will demand later from the project team.

To alleviate these problems, project managers must understand that even if their organization is not doing the implementation, it is their leadership in IT that the organization will look to when the consultants have departed. Best practices in this area are strong leadership and open communication with company management, with the consultant, and with the project manager. In these communication reviews, the project manager sets the agenda to review the requirements, progress, and problems. Doing this will satisfy the needs of the senior management contact's consultants. Also, while external consultants can fill key roles, often faster than might be possible by recruiting permanent staff members, they do not solve the problem of who will fill these positions when the consultation is over. A good guideline is to use consultants as much as possible for temporary assignments that will not continue throughout or after the implementation. In other words, try to use them as true consultants, not as long-term additions to the IT staff.

Another strategy is to use outside review teams. They should be viewed as an integral part of large-scale enterprise projects. They can be used to great advantage at several stages of an enterprise system's implementation cycle. Many noncompeting institutions have completed significant segments of major new systems; for some purposes, consider inviting such peer teams as an alternative to professional consultants. Members of peer teams not only contribute to the subject environment but also learn from it. Their advice can be just as valuable as the more expensive words of wisdom from consulting firms. Obviously, you must seek a balance between the skills desired from a consultant or a visiting team, their experience, and the cost of the engagement. The track record of peer advising visits has been reported to be very positive.

RISKS DUE TO NOT DOING A GOOD BUSINESS CASE   Even steady-state cost savings are difficult to achieve. Legacy environments are perceived as costly: Software is idiosyncratic and most likely heavily modified by long-departed programmers; operating systems are proprietary; ancient hardware consumes space, electricity, and maintenance dollars; time is wasted on duplicate data entry; data access is a trial-and-error exercise for all but a few gurus; and so forth. Moreover, there are substantial opportunity costs and risks to an institution lacking accurate data for planning, decision making, and service delivery. That said, most companies find that replacing legacy systems with modern client-server applications will not result in immediate direct and measurable cost savings. However, that is not universally true, as it has been shown that many well-done enterprise projects do deliver the promised benefits.

The reasons for some companies saving but most not saving, as much as anticipated are many: Client-server systems require more powerful desktop computers, often with larger monitors and more memory and disk storage. Relational database systems consume enormous amounts of server disk storage and processor capacity. Hundreds of users exercising new query tools will stress all of your computing and communications resources. Servers will proliferate, with concomitant increases in systems management overhead. Relational database systems require additional administrators, open systems require security architects, and confused users require local handholding and more sophisticated help desks. License and support fees for state-of-the art software are substantial, as are compensation levels required to recruit and retain staff to operate and maintain the new environment.

You can mitigate these risks via a good business case based on the recognition that new systems will add substantial functionality and information access for more users. But at least in the short run, you will lack both the systems management tools and the experience to operate them at the same or lower costs as the legacy environments they are replacing. You will find the benefits of these systems in improvements to the fundamental business processes and the ability to provide better service. However, the benefits will not be gained from cost reductions in the computing

254 Umbrella Considerations

infrastructure or in distributed departments. A good business case will take into account all the incremental costs and all incremental benefits involved.

Another risk mitigation strategy that is often employed is underpromise and overdeliver. Enterprise projects are arduous and costly; do not increase pressure on the project team and provide fuel for the skeptics by promising the sun, moon, and stars at the outset. Too many projects are launched with lofty rhetoric about "enhancing" and "transforming," "state of the art," "client-server," "reduced costs," and "service quality." In this overheated atmosphere, even valuable early wins can look puny while delays and cost overruns can foment company-wide resistance, even ridicule. It is better to target narrower and shorter-term accomplishments, achieve them while garnering the concomitant goodwill and momentum, and then expand the scope to include more customers, additional software functionality, or thoroughgoing reengineering. Enterprise projects are best understood as foundations for long-term improvements, not short-term panaceas for decades of deferred maintenance of legacy systems.

RISKS DUE TO LACK OF A CHAMPION AND EXECUTIVE SPONSORS Champions and executive sponsors play crucial roles in the success of an enterprise project. Their absence can be very risky from the success point of view. The path to a successful implementation is strewn with conflicting demands from many quarters. Compromises must be made along the way, and not everyone will be happy with decisions that are made. For example, testing, training, and performance tuning are obvious areas where, with additional time, more can always be accomplished to make an implementation go more smoothly. However, no matter how much testing is done, some bugs will remain in a large application when you go live. The only true test comes when hundreds, and perhaps thousands, of users begin stressing the system in production. The same observation holds true for training and tuning; there is no such thing as too much of either. Nonetheless, you must decide when enough has been accomplished to make the go-live decision.

Another trade-off example is the decision of whether to allow a deadline for a milestone to slip a modest amount to avoid project staff burnout. In many ways, an enterprise implementation is a highly political process, and just as in politics, the art of negotiating good compromises is essential. Technical and functional project staff should be shielded as much as possible from the many political issues that are sure to arise. Their jobs are difficult enough to begin with.

In this environment, the true mitigators of the risks are the champions and executive sponsors who can make realistic compromises, knowing well that the best can be the enemy of the good.

RISKS DUE TO STRATEGIC MIS-/NONALIGNMENT Many times, large-scale projects lack alignment with the strategies of the organization or simply are misaligned. Also, the organization's strategy may change, and due to poor communication, the project has not remained aligned with corporate strategy, objectives, and goals. This situation creates a catastrophic risk for the project as well as for all those who are concerned with it.

Communication and access to the top management who are responsible for strategy settings serves to mitigate this risk. Having a good line of communication with the executive sponsor can ensure that you will not have to deal with this sort of risk situation.

RISK OF NONACCEPTANCE OF INSTALLED SYSTEM Apart from developers and implementers, systems users must be active project participants. Recognized departmental leaders should participate in both the selection and the implementation processes. They are needed because selecting and implementing a new enterprise system calls for the best, brightest, and most dedicated staff. A successful enterprise project requires detailed knowledge of how an institution operates, clear-headed analysis of current shortcomings, creative vision for improvement, ability to bridge business requirements and software features, and willingness to work for months, even years, on a team under intense scrutiny and pressure. If the team members are not involved in any or all enterprise projects, the finished system will have gained little acceptance. In such situations, money will have been spent but no benefits will accrue. This creates a serious risk situation.

Alleviate this risk by recruiting and seeking the participation of all users, present and future. You must identify, recruit, and involve these individuals early in the selection and evaluation activities to ensure their buy-in later in the process. People will not cooperate fully if they feel that a new system was forced on them. In addition, be sure that several technical experts are part of the selection team, so that marketing claims can be balanced against the technical realities faced during the implementation. Note, however, that some of the most knowledgeable functional and technical staff may be too wedded to the status quo to make effective project participants. They might be better deployed on the important tasks of maintaining legacy systems.

RISKS DUE TO INADEQUATE TRAINING It goes without saying that a new software system cannot be deployed successfully without significant end user training. But how will the users be trained: classroom style and/or computer-based training modules? How long will the training take place before roll-out? If the training is done too far in advance, much will be forgotten; if left too late, it will leave users unprepared. And how do you schedule the training as roll-out deadlines slip? Will users have to learn a new operating system (perhaps their first experience with a mouse)? Beyond software, how will they be trained on the new chart of accounts, new or revised operational policies, the more rigorous password scheme, and the penalties for perusing another department's data? Will training be mandatory? If so, what about management members who may also need training? Departmental support providers, help desk personnel, and data center staff will also need thorough training. When visiting reference sites during the software evaluation stage, ask not only project managers but also end users how effective the training was and how it could have been improved.

Risk of inadequate training is underusage of the system or no usage at all. Training is a critical success factor for the project. Hence, the mitigation of this risk is in adequate planning and budgeting for all required training. Many times it has been noted that budget is there, people have been identified, trainers have arrived, but the trainees are busy fighting fires. If this is about to happen, the project manager, the champion and the executive sponsor should influence the trainees' bosses to let them take the training. These situations are all too common, so they must be managed; otherwise, you face a huge risk.

RISK DUE TO POOR COMMUNICATIONS   Implementing a new enterprise-wide application is one of the most complex software projects in which a person can be involved. The technical components of the project are complicated, but most of the really hard issues will arise from the functional process changes and organizational adjustments inherent in these implementations. Most individuals on the periphery of the project will not understand the intricacies of such a large effort. Management teams who may be involved in various review committees are likely to be very critical of the amount of time, effort, and money required to rebuild a major part of the organization's systems infrastructure. Even if they are part of the communication process, they are likely to be unhappy about any large investment of their departments' time. Poor communication can prevent the project from getting off the ground or result in nonusage, ultimately resulting in money spent with no benefits achieved.

Resolution of this risk involves constant communication. A coordinated communication plan is a good way to explain the goals, timelines, benefits, and problems of the project. An up-to-date Web site and extensive electronic mailing lists are helpful, and many projects find that a periodic newsletter is very popular. Regular reports to the executive levels of the enterprise are absolutely essential.

RISKS DUE TO POOR CHANGE MANAGEMENT   One of the more common mistakes enterprise project managers make is to underestimate the magnitude of the changes that a new system will spawn and to overestimate the ability of the organization to absorb these changes. At any point in time, a particular organization has a certain amount of resistance to change procedures that have been standard operating practices for years, or even decades. Even if there is general agreement that these practices may not be working well, a built-in inertia makes change difficult. Just as with Newtonian physics, an external force is needed to overcome this inertia, and for each action there will be an equal and opposite organizational reaction. This situation can create all the barriers to the success of the system being implemented.

Recognizing these underlying organizational "laws" can help managers pave the way for change, thereby reducing or even eliminating the risk. Good change management seminars and workshops available, and several universities have reported good experiences in using them. An organizational readiness framework should be an important part of the overall implementation strategy.

RISKS DUE TO STAFF TURNOVER   Working on a major enterprise implementation is a great way for functional and technical staff members to increase their market value. People who have the right set of technical and organizational skills and the temperament to perform under pressure and to stay engaged in these projects are very valuable. They will receive outside offers, and headhunters will be recruiting all levels of the project team. Larger companies in India and China became enterprise systems' implementation service providers with the help of the staff who did their first implementations. However, if it is perceived that the organization has no upgrade path, the individuals will seek their own highlands (different job, better job), creating a risky situation for the company.

Therefore, it is important for both functional and technical departments to have recruiting, retention, and retraining plans already formulated when the implementation process begins. Stipends, reclassifications, significant pay increases, temporary assignments, training packages, bonuses, team and individual awards, and term contracts are some of the tools that are commonly used. Retraining senior employees is a good investment because they are strongly committed to the company and its benefit program. Many of these techniques are not part of the standard human resource programs at companies and may require effective negotiation with the human resources department.

Impact of Risks
- Loss of cost of systems expenditure
- Loss of operational people's time cost
- Loss of benefits that could have been achieved
- Lost opportunity cost
- Loss of image
- Loss of customers

Operational Phase

Since today's enterprise systems are so intimately interwoven in the fabric of the enterprises they serve, these next risks can be caused by nonfunctioning or malfunctioning enterprise software application.

Financial Risk
- Capacity/credit risk
- Default risk
- Downgrading risk

Market Risk
- Price risk (interest rate, equity, commodity)
- Curve risk
- Basis risk
- Correlation risk
- Option-specific risk

Liquidity Risk
- Funding risk
- Market lliquidity

Physical Risk
- Physical assets
- Real estate
- Manufacturing process
- Supply chain

Operational Risk
- Jurisdiction risk
- Settlement risk
- Systems risk
- Employee risk
- Strategic decision risk
- Purchasing risk

Sales Risk
- Competition risk
- Elasticity risk
- Predictive risk

Strategic Risk
- Regulatory risk
- Tax risk
- Catastrophe risk
- Currency policy

In the context of this effort, implementation phase risks are more relevant. Hence they have been discussed more thoroughly. However, regarding operational risks, enterprise risk management systems have started to appear. Some are quite robust and offer lot of analytics. Depending on the enterprise's risk mitigation desires, such systems should be seriously considered.

Risk Management

Any major project is a story of hope, inspiration, and perseverance. Management of risk is all about a very careful evaluation of what can go wrong and how to recover from it. As mentioned before, factors that minimize the risk are:

- Having a clear objective
- Picking the best people
- Supporting them with the best team
- Supporting the team with the best technology
- Constant training
- Preparing for the unexpected
- Improvising
- Taking risks, but only after careful review of options, alternatives, and how to recover from them
- Turning failure into successes

The process of risk management embodies careful evaluation of what can go wrong in the domains of:

- Schedule
- Budget
- Scope
- Technology being implemented

These difficulties can be induced by any or all of these situations:

- Lack of trained personnel
- New software-related unknown glitches

- New hardware causing unknown difficulties
- Bad planning causing more time and resources than planned
- Project manager, champion, and executive sponsor support not available when required

And those problems can be exacerbated by:

- Lack of a backup plan during implementation
- Lack of a backup plan during maintenance
- Project manager did not foresee the problems that would arise and was not taking early actions to avoid/fix it.

All of these issues are easier to handle if the systems being developed are not mission critical. If they are of mission-critical nature, the business risks assume an undue proportion. As one who has been involved in mission-critical global projects, I can only say that you should plan on everything going wrong, because it will. Hence the best defense is a backup plan.

Case Example

Risk analysis and risk mitigation are areas of concern to every head of systems, as they were to me. Some examples of the deliberations that arose during my experience with a Route 128 high-technology company in Boston area are worth reviewing.

Backup and saving off-campus copies of records is a pedantic exercise that every chief information officer commands staff to carry out. But in the case of mission-critical systems, certain stringent considerations have to be followed. If you do not follow them, you invite trouble. The next examples are over and above the normal risk management considerations that prevail in the IT industry because they relate to mission-control applications.

This plant was built with a PCP 88 dual-control redundant system. If the primary computer failed, the secondary (supervisory) would take over. A drum (today's disks) shadowed the primary disk and could provide the bumpless transfer if the primary computer failed. The situation was great when the technology was invented. When I confronted it, however, the main question was what if the drum (disk storage of today) failed. If so, the whole manufacturing would come to standstill. This was obviously not acceptable. So I began searching for the drum replacement and found a vendor in San Diego that could replace the drum with new technology disks with practically no downtime. I am mentioning this to impress upon you how the risk was mitigated.

Another example from the same company is: a hurricane was going to hit our plant. My computer center was huge and had glass walls facing the street. If the winds would get bad, they could tear through the walls and ruin the computer systems. The director of risk asked me if the plant could come back in operation even after the computer center is destroyed. My answer was no. After enough investigations and talking with production superintendants, the risk director concluded that I was right. As a result, all those glass walls were reinforced with bricks. Such was the risk mitigation strategy at this company.

Another example at the same company is when we were buying a new control computer system. Not only was this a new control computer; it was a way to obsolete the old system and migrate its functionality to the new control computer. The new control computer was scalable so we could grow new functionality as required on it. . During deliberations to write specifications for the new control computer, I met with stakeholders to iron out the issue of:

- Redundancy (two computers working simultaneously)
- Backup

Obviously backup is required, but redundancy is expensive. We settled on an option that was known as hot backup, which means you keep a hot device (CPU) ready to be swapped with the failed device. In hindsight, this strategy proved to be the most economical solution.

Example after examples from mission-critical systems prove that you should plan for as many modes of backup as the project can afford. However, if the system works well, you do not need multiple levels of backup. With technology getting more robust, these back up or redundancy considerations are overblown. But situations like Hurricane Katrina in New Orleans change the whole premise of risk management. *Do your risk planning well and adequately*.

Quality Management

Quality Context

From Juran Joseph M and Deming Edward W we got the quality revolution. Then came quality assurance and quality control, followed by total quality management (TQM). And then the ISOs were introduced. All these initiatives found homes in the manufacturing industries at the start. But their messages of benefits were so powerful that in the 1980s, even the software industry began to embrace quality as applied to software engineering. Today, IT managers have a bewildering array of quality disciplines to choose from, including Six Sigma, ISO 9000, and the Malcolm Baldrige program. Others, such as Control Objectives for Information and Related Technology (CobiT), may be imposed by your auditors. And IT-focused disciplines may originate in your own shop, such as the capable maturity model for software development and the Information Technology Infrastructure Library for IT operations and services.[4]

However, in the world of business software, quality is about quality planning, quality assurance and quality control; whereas software management is an integrated, formalized strategy for complete management of software assets, including project planning, change management, debugging/testing/quality assurance, application deployment, fast problem resolution, and security. Figure 8.2 clearly illustrates these concepts.

Quality planning, quality assurance, and quality control are applicable to all phases of a software enterprise project. Of course, the larger and more complex the scope of the project, the more important these processes become.

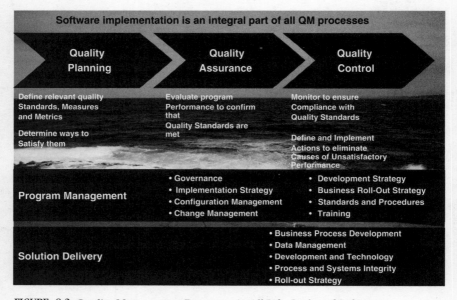

FIGURE 8.2 Quality Management Processes in All Life Cycles of Software Implementations

Quality Benefits Achievable

APPLICATION AVAILABILITY   Most of the unplanned outages that I have seen are due to application failure or operator error. Gone are the days when hardware systems used to be unstable. One such incidence that I watched when a printed circuit board came loose due to vibrations and the IBM's first mini computer's communications will not work Traditional system management techniques do nothing to help you if a poorly managed software change brings your system to its knees.

SOFTWARE QUALITY   Similarly a majority of the projects are missing a lot of specified features. Comprehensive software management gives you the means to track requirements and the extra efficiency to make sure you get to them before you exceed a project's cost and deadline.

ERROR REDUCTION   A formalized software management strategy greatly reduces the risk of errors by automating error-prone tasks and formalizing debugging, testing, and deployment procedures.

PROJECT SPEED   As per Chapter 1 we have seen that there are lots of time overruns. The true cost to your company can run into the millions. With software management, your projects are well organized, communication and other tasks are automated, and your software quality is higher so you have fewer interruptions. More time is spent on development, and less on spinning your wheels.

CUSTOMER SERVICE   Software management should include automated systems that let you detect and see end user problems, significantly speeding resolution of those problems. You will also improve customer service with reliable, consistent procedures for collecting, tracking, and implementing user enhancement requests.

CUSTOMER SATISFACTION   When customer service is fast and accurate, customer satisfaction soars. Corporate management, your "other" customer, appreciates software implementations that are on time and within budget. Nothing boosts user confidence and cooperation more than a well-oiled software management strategy.

SOFTWARE PROTECTION   A software management strategy begins with securing your software assets and ensuring that only people authorized to work with them can do so; and then only as prescribed by policies you set in your change management system. Software is your company's most important asset. A change management system lets you set the balance between access and security; between the demands to make changes rapidly and maintaining the reliability of your applications.

Quality Costs

Quality costs are the costs associated with preventing, finding, and correcting defective work. These costs are huge, running at 20% to 40% of sales.[5] Many of these costs can be significantly reduced or completely avoided. One of the key functions of a quality engineer is the reduction of the total cost of quality associated with a product.

Useful definitions, as applied to software products, follow.[6]

PREVENTION COSTS   Prevention costs are costs of activities that are specifically designed to prevent poor quality. Examples of poor quality include coding errors, design errors, mistakes in the user manuals, and badly documented or unmaintainable complex code.

Most prevention costs do not fit within the testing group's budget. This money is spent by the programming, design, and marketing staffs.

APPRAISAL COSTS   Appraisal costs are costs of activities designed to find quality problems, such as code inspections and any type of testing.

Design reviews are part prevention and part appraisal. To the degree that you are looking for errors in the proposed design itself when you do the review, you are doing an appraisal. To the degree that you are looking for ways to strengthen the design, you are doing prevention.

FAILURE COSTS   Failure costs are costs that result from poor quality, such as the cost of fixing bugs and the cost of dealing with customer complaints.

Internal Failure Costs   Internal failure costs are those that arise before your company supplies its product to the customer. Along with costs of finding and fixing bugs are many internal failure costs borne by groups outside of product development. If a bug blocks someone in your company from doing his or her job, the costs of the wasted time, the missed milestones, and the overtime to get back onto schedule are all internal failure costs.

For example, if your company sells thousands of copies of the same program, you probably will print several thousand copies of a multicolor box that contains and describes the program. You (your company) often will be able to get a much better deal by booking press time with the printer in advance. However, if you do not get the artwork to the printer on time, you might have to pay for some or all of that wasted press time anyway, and then you may have to pay additional printing fees and rush charges to get the printing done on the new schedule. This can be an added expense of many thousands of dollars.

Some programming groups treat user interface errors as low priority, leaving them until the end to fix. This can be a mistake. Marketing staff need pictures of the product's screen long before the program is finished, in order to get the artwork for the box to the printer on time. User interface bugs—the ones that will be fixed later—can make it hard for staff members to take (or mock up) accurate screen shots. Delays caused by these minor design flaws, or by bugs that block a packaging staff member from creating or printing special reports, can cause the company to miss its printer deadline.

Including costs like lost opportunity and cost of delays in numerical estimates of the total cost of quality can be controversial. J. Campanella[7] does not include these in a detailed listing of examples. F.M. Gryna[8] recommends against including costs like these in the published totals because fallout from controversy over them can kill the entire quality cost accounting effort. I include them here because I sometimes find them very useful, even though it might not make sense to include them in a balance sheet.

External Failure Costs   External failure costs are those that arise after your company supplies the product to the customer, such as customer service costs or the cost of patching a released product and distributing the patch.

External failure costs are huge. It is much cheaper to fix problems before shipping a defective product to customers. Some of these costs must be treated with care. For example, the cost of public relations efforts to soften the publicity effects of bugs is probably not a huge percentage of your company's public relations (PR) budget. You cannot charge the entire PR budget as a quality-related cost. But any money that the PR group has to spend specifically to cope with potentially bad publicity due to bugs is a failure cost.

TOTAL COST OF QUALITY   Note that the sum of all costs is equal to the costs of Prevention + Appraisal + Internal Failure + External Failure costs.

Project Quality Planning

The definition of software quality can be gleaned by defining the:

- Product and process quality
- Concept of software quality function deployment
- Quality agreement
- Quality agreement deployment
- Delivered quality measurement

- Quality assurance techniques
- Walkthroughs, technical reviews, and other techniques
- ISO 9000 and AS3562 standards

Quality Assurance Technique

A comprehensive quality assurance methodology may entail a methodology designed to address the software quality issues faced by the implementation project teams. This quality assurance methodology must directly map to each phase of a project's life cycle, such as strategy, blueprinting, realization, and support. To achieve an implementation faster, at a lower cost, and with less risk, the quality assurance technique is recommended. It aims to:

- Jump-start and define the quality assurance process and identify the on-site consulting and training from the vendor's software quality assurance experts if they are not available in-house.
- Reduce implementation risk by identifying potential performance problems before the software solution goes into production.
- Define the software quality assurance process and assign responsibilities earlier in the implementation cycle to ensure that critical business processes are thoroughly tested.
- Lower implementation costs by automating the repetitive testing and application maintenance tasks that must be performed both before and after the go-live phase.
- Have a solution that improves system quality and reduces maintenance costs throughout the life of the new application solutions.

Considerations of Quality Assurance Methodology

SOFTWARE QUALITY ASSURANCE PLANNING   Simultaneously with to the initial project preparation phase, the quality assurance team should begin to apply the quality assurance methodology to identify key project participants, perform test organization planning, and define quality assurance goals, processes, and standards based on overall project objectives, schedules, and budgets.

QUALITY ORIENTATION   During this phase, product training, test case creation models, and assistance should be sought. You also need help to define the test cycle criteria for each critical business process that the software solution must support. This quality assurance phase may parallel the business blueprint phase by identifying the unique business requirements and then delivering the appropriate training to your implementation and quality assurance team members.

BUSINESS PROCESS ASSURANCE During the realization phase, the automated functional and integration testing on new application and legacy systems are performed. During this phase, ensure that the key application functions perform as intended and that the application supports the business requirements identified in the business blueprint phase.

SYSTEM ASSURANCE As the new solution is fine-tuned and adjusted during the final preparation phase, the vendors' quality assurance team should provide the business consultants, technology, and support required to effectively automate the volume, stress, interface, and user acceptance testing necessary to ensure a successful implementation. The selected quality assurance methodology's tool kit should provide automation capabilities, an enabler to complete the final preparation phase in a condensed time frame while still maintaining a very high degree of quality assurance.

QUALITY IMPROVEMENT CONTINUATION Once the project implementation and go-live with the new software solution is completed, the quality assurance processes enable the software to perform the ongoing regression and performance tests required for every upgrade and system modification consistently, reliably, and cost effectively. It can also link production monitoring data (using the performance measurement module, if available) back to your test environment so you can pinpoint performance bottlenecks and fine-tune the new solution.

BENEFITS OF QUALITY Most organizations include a quality assurance component in their software implementation efforts. But all too often, the implementation of quality assurance procedures is relegated to testing within a compressed time frame at the end of the development effort, where, unfortunately, the effectiveness of the procedures to increase software quality and shorten development cycles is greatly reduced. Take the utmost care to avoid these pitfalls.

ACTIVITIES OF QUALITY ASSURANCE DURING THE LIFE CYCLE PHASES OF A PROJECT
Quality management and risk management activities are recommended toward the end of each phase of the implementation. Quality management is a major task for the program leadership team who will conduct a management review to assess whether sufficient progress has been made for the program, or project, to begin the next phase. The quality of work will be an important consideration in the decision-making process.

The quality assurance management review assesses:

- Adherence to the project implementation strategy and use of the available methodologies and tools
- Program progress compared to plan; milestone achievement

- Deliverables quality and conformance to the documented approval process
- Program/project team, steering committee, and any other program dynamics; for example, assessing the team structure and performance

Additionally, it is recommended that the experienced outside consultants conduct these reviews. Per definition, reviews are done by an external specialist, not by the project team. Specialists who are not involved in the day-to-day business of the project visit as independent and objective auditors to assess the status and progress of all activities. They identify potential risks to the project goals and recommend appropriate corrective actions.

Summary

Starting with the context of quality and establishing the benefits achievable, the costs of non–quality-based software implementation have been discussed. Here the universe of discourse was software implementation based on quality-based practices. Items related to project quality planning were mentioned. Special emphasis was given to quality assurance techniques, including considerations fundamental to this technique. Finally, the activities pertaining to the quality assurance tasks throughout the life cycle of a project were discussed.

Case Example

For quality of software, I believe in:

- Structured walkthroughs
- Periodic major milestone reviews
- Review of test results
- Review of permission to go live

These following examples from the Route 128 Boston area company stand out as having more to do with inventiveness than with quality methodology.

At the company, we had a quality problem. If it was not solved, the penalty would be huge. A certain range of film products was behaving poorly. It was determined that the problem was with the products of our plant. The plant's process engineers pored through the data from the relevant time frame. Nothing seemed to have gone wrong with the manufacturing with that batch of product, but a problem existed. Our process engineers continued searching. Ultimately they found that in the finished goods warehouse, during the summer months, temperatures were very high and were not controlled. That situation would create the quality problem we were having. The culprit, which was not under the control of the computer, was easy to bring under control. Since then we have never had any similar problem. Innovation in quality prevailed.

In the same process in the same company, if you wanted to do feedback control, you had to have some quality parameters indicating the product was good. If the product was bad, the processing conditions up the stream would have to be modulated to correct for the problem. The defect detection technology perfected by our engineering group took care of the problem. But it was an innovation that we had to make. Numerous examples of this type bolstered our quality regimen, and they go far beyond the realm of software quality. Hence it is important to add inventiveness to quality methodology.

Communications Management

In any human endeavor between two or more people, communication and its management is paramount. It is one of the most important reasons why successful projects succeed and failed projects fail.

In complex business software projects that are global in nature, communication is vital. Without it, results can be disastrous. In such projects, communication is more important than any other initiative. Some tasks, such as research and development in secretive labs, may have survived in the past but not in the environments we are talking about here. Constant communication is required in these environments. Fortunately, modern technology is on our side. Even so, communication has to be the master selling point of the project manager and the team. Next we examine all those areas of the project where communication is required, what needs to be communicated, how it is communicated, tools for communication, and the resulting communication environment.

Situations that Need Communications

The success of each of these activities depends on communication:

- Enterprise strategy
- Key performance indicators
- Benchmarking

- Value estimating
- Business process reengineering
- Blueprinting
- Detailed solution architecting
- Gap analysis
- Roll-out planning
- Configuring
- Project management
- Champions
- Business case
- Change management
- Risk management
- Quality management
- Communications management
- Test plan and test procedures
- Training
- Maintenance

What to Communicate

In each of these areas, communication is required

- Before launching the activity, to scope it out
- In the middle to discuss progress and at the end to provide results
- To receive critiques from the stakeholders as necessary
- For detailed validation by the relevant expert users of the respective areas

How to Communicate

Utmost attention should be given to the following:

- **Innovation and creativity.** While job number 1 for the project manager is to get the project done on time and within budget, the issue of creativity and innovation is very important. He or she must not only remember this but also foster it proactively.
- **Ad hoc meetings.** If meetings are prearranged, they should have an agenda. If they are impromptu, they may or may not have an agenda and are therefore specific on any one item or free flowing.
- **Agenda for meetings.** Each meeting should have an agenda, which should be published well in advance of the meeting, if possible. These items should be included for discussion:
  - Highlights of the last meeting if appropriate

- The objective of today's meeting
- Discussion of item 1, action plan
- Discussion of item 2, action plan
- ...
- Discussion of item N, action plan
- Any other item that anyone from the audience wants to talk about
- Go around the table and ask each attendee for honest feedback in two sentences as to how the meeting went.

- **Minutes of the meeting.** Although they are bureaucratic in nature, minutes can prevent a lot of problems. So I highly recommend they be drawn up. They should contain a summary of the issue, the discussion, the conclusion, and who was assigned to any given task as well as the task's completion date. The minutes should be circulated to those concerned or put on the project's Web page.

- **Chairing the meeting.** I recommend that the project manager chair the meeting. He or she should formulate the agendas in consultation, with the stakeholders' view in mind and giving extra attention as a courtesy to them. But the main focus must be what is to be achieved in the meeting. The chair should control the air time, make sure no time is lost with disruptive behavior, and keep the proceedings in order. This is where the project manager's communication skills are used to the maximum. If a disruptive attendee happens to be a stakeholder, the project manager should tactfully move to the next topic of the agenda.

- **Other contributors to the meetings.** While the project manager is the chair, he or she must make sure that everyone has sufficient time to present their issue, to discuss it, and to offer a solution or report. Normally, this would be the job of a project team person, such as a task leader. Stakeholders can contribute by letting the items on their wish list be known. They can also help to answer the business questions, objectives, or changes in the company's business plan, and what impact these might have on the project.

- **Reinforcing meetings.** A lot is discussed during the initial kickoff meeting. Since memories are short, people tend to forget objectives, plans, and other details. I recommend that you say your point, say it again, and then say what you said. After that, you hope that what needs to be remembered is remembered.

- **Meeting dynamics.** All kinds of personalities will attend these meetings. Some will have bigger egos than others; some will be more aggressive and think they are the lords of the world. The project manager makes it clear at the beginning in the kickoff meeting that the meeting environment being sought is one in which:
  - We discuss issues, not the person.
  - Any person discussing an issue is courteous and deferential to others.

- There is to be no one-upmanship. Such behavior is neither healthy nor required in order to do a job well.
- Everyone has a right to present their views; others should respect that.
- **Progress reviews.** Starting right from the plans and schedules that are presented during the kickoff meeting, progress reports, and redflag minutes of the meetings should be published on the project's Web page and kept updated.

Tools of Communication

These communication tools are available:

- **Kickoff meeting.** Both sides should attend this event: the project teams and the customer personnel. While this event is a business meeting, an informal dinner with an opportunity to socialize can create a good start. The project leader chairs the meeting, but the executive sponsor should be given due courtesy and deference. The business items to be covered in this meeting are:
  - Who is who and what are their roles in the project
  - E-mail addresses and phone numbers of attendees as well as absentees
  - The different groups with whom you will communicate
  - The frequency of your messages
  - The methods you will use to deliver information
  - Initial project plan and schedule
  - The project budget
  - How you will control the project while emphasizing the roles of:
    - Scope/change management
    - Quality management
    - Risk management
    - Test plans and test procedures from strategy to customer acceptance

    Once again, social and get-to-know aspects should be kept in full focus and be given half of the total time. We have used as much as 10 to 12 hours on this aspect for large global projects.
- **Face-to-face meetings.** These meetings should be held whenever possible, involving local personnel from the project team and the client teams. A well-equipped conference room with full audiovisual aids is always nice. If this is not available, try to improvise. Out-of-towners may attend via video conferencing.
- **E-mails and Internet communications.** Encourage frequent e-mails and Internet-based collaboration methodologies. These bring down the barriers to communication. A supportive environment that does not

penalize an occasional wrong message will do much to foster the free flow of information and red flags.

- **Setups Required for Meetings:** These are
- Conference rooms and audiovisual equipment as per the project schedule
- Mailing and telephone lists
- Times for periodic conference calls as per the project schedule
- Booking the times on the calendars of major stakeholders

Communication Environment

From the project's very inception of a project, there must be a communication environment that is conducive to:

- Clear communication between the project manager and the team
- Clear communication among the project manager, project team, and their customers globally
- Clear communication among the project sponsor, project champion, project manager, and all other stakeholders
- Well-understood communication among all the listed people led, of course, by the project manager
- Free-flowing communication where no one hides any relevant facts or red flags
- Creativity. The environment must foster creativity. If not, long and even short projects can get very boring.

The project manager is constantly challenged to keep the team and every member of the team creatively engaged, so they do not get bored and tune out. One symptom of boredom is seen when people fail to contribute to meetings; another is deteriorating attendance.

Example of a Global Communication Environment

The *Wall Street Journal* published an interesting article about its global team of 50 working at three international locations.[9] The highlights of their communication methodology, as managers and experts of effective and productive global teamwork, include:

- Having an effective understanding of the task
- Clarifying roles and responsibilities
- Setting firm ground rules
- Getting to know other team members
- Communicating often

Test Plan and Test Procedures

If you build the systems, you need to test them. With the increased complexity of software systems, especially if they are mission critical, systems need to be tested to verify that they have zero defects and will not fail. If this aspect is not verifiable, it will impact quality, and hence place the risks beyond toleration levels. However, before this (defect free systems) can be accomplished, tests should be planned and procedures put in place, and the test plan should be executed at different stages of the software buildup. Next we explore all aspects relating to the test.

V Model Life Cycle of Test

The V model is a proven, industry-standard framework that defines the standard development life cycle. It gives equal weight to testing rather than treat it as an afterthought[10]. Gartner Group's V model diagram is an adaptation that describes the process so well that it is presented here without any alteration and with due credit to the Gartner Group[11]. The V model requires that each deliverable be verified in an attempt to identify defects as early as possible and to ensure that specifications are complete and correct. The model specifies that activities in one stage must be completed before moving on to the next stage. The model saves time and money in development while increasing the result quality and delivery reliability. (See Figure 8.3.)

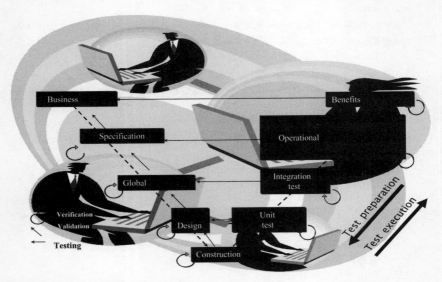

FIGURE 8.3 V Model Testing in the Life Cycle of Software Development
Source: The Gartner Group, V Model Test Approach.

Testing entails:

- Determining what the reasons are for testing
- Understanding what structured testing is
- Testing and verification at the design stage
- Testing within a system implementation/upgrade stage
- Testing within a system maintenance environment stage

Why Test?

Tests are performed to control the risks and costs that can arise from not testing, which could send the project over budget by uncontrolled development or send the effort off the implementation trajectory. Project timetable control is achieved through proper testing and by eliminating missed deadlines. The aim is to discover errors before it is too late to remedy them, and before they affect changes to a long-term project timetable. The other reason for doing proper testing is to improve system quality and performance, thereby eliminating risks to the business. Testing eliminates risks that otherwise could be damaging to business, production, business image, and they also trigger low to zero acceptance.

Structured Testing

Instead of ad hoc testing, a structured test plan lays out a process that entails test planning and test procedures at all applicable stages of the project. It defines the participants and the scope of the test activities. This will ensure that testing provides a means to continuity and completion.

Advantages of structured testing are:

- Continuity of the process and hence better risk management
- Better quality
- Efficiency that goes beyond quality and risk
- Better risk, quality, and efficiency management leading to better cost management
- Controlled system stability: besides quality, risk, efficiency, and cost, structured testing generates user confidence
- Clustered testing knowledge, due to better learning
- User acceptance, due to confidence generated bythe system
- Scalable, due to all of the previously listed advantages

Test Team

The testing team's experiences and activities are given in this section.

- Testing expertise
  - Functional: on the modules to be implemented.
  - Performance: with single-module and integration testing with input variables being the number of users and the main output variable being the response time.
  - Simulations: hard or soft simulation for autotesting.
  - Installation: during this phase either limited testing or full testing.
  - Usability: how user friendly is the user interface: Is it intuitive or is too much knowledge required to use the system?
  - Fail the system: expertise to create conditions that will fail the system; results are to be reviewed with the development staff to alleviate the weaknesses.
  - Reviews and inspections: at various stages of the project as per the guidelines.
  - Setting up quality and testing organizations.
  - Testing approach: test plan and test procedure (involving what to test and how much to test).
  - Advice on software quality issues: should be capable of translating the errors or deficiency found.
  - Training of the users and the team in some or all aspects; users can be expected to do some testing on the system.
  - A test center with the subject vendor could be beneficial if the organization does not have the setup ready.
- Testing team's activities
  - Regression testing
  - Test analysis
  - Project support to management
  - Test coordination
  - Coverage extension/completeness check
- A list of expected results follows:
  - You find the most critical production errors before going live.
  - The continuity and stability of the production and acceptance systems is under better control.
  - Projects benefit from more experienced testers with organizational experience.
  - You can continuously increase your scope, both within and outside of the system.
  - User feedback indicates high satisfaction.

How Testing Should Be Done for Various Stages of the Project

Key considerations:

- Validation and verification
- Implementation/upgrade project
  - Generic (split data and navigation)
  - Start with critical processes
  - Focus on reusability
  - Secure user acceptance
- Automatic testing
  - Only on "stable" systems
  - In case of substantial maintenance effort
- Test maintenance
  - Reuse project testing scripts
  - Regression tests: ensured continuity and quality
  - Load and performance testing

Later in this chapter we provide further details about the integration test procedure and the final integration test concept and approach with regard to the way tests ought to be performed.

What Happens after Go-Live?

Key elements after going live include:

- Vendor upgrades
- Hot packages/popular packages
- Functional releases
- Corrective changes
- Changes in interfacing systems
- Performance testing and monitoring:
  - Performance is a major issue in a live system.
  - Test the performance impact of all major changes.
  - Regularly/continuously monitor the performance of your live system.
  - Variables driving the above testing for performance is for testing:
    - New functionality
    - Intensity of use
    - Database growth
    - Number of users

Testing Tools

Key considerations:

- Team should be experienced in testing
- Regression testing is a must
  - Manual testing is acceptable if changes are rare and/or low risk
  - Use computer aided test tools (CATT) if you can manage with a limited record and playback test data set
  - Use Mercury corporation's tools if you want end to end (E2E) easy maintenance and extensive reporting facilities
- Keep an eye on the validity and maintenance on your test documentation

Final Integration Test Concept and Approach

FINAL INTEGRATION TEST OBJECTIVE   The objective of the final integration test is to ensure that the system's solution has met business requirements and can run the business. However, you cannot yet say that the system is ready to go live, since the performance test has not been completed. The performance test is executed during the final preparation phase.

FINAL INTEGRATION TEST CONCEPT   Final integration testing is accomplished through the execution of predefined business flows, or scenarios, that emulate how the system will run the business. These business flows, using migrated data from the preexisting systems, will be performed in a multi-faceted computing environment, third-party software, system interfaces, and various hardware and software components. This environment builds the necessary level of confidence that the solution is complete and will perform in the business.

EVOLVING FROM FINAL CONFIGURATION TO INTEGRATION TESTING   Final integration tests need to be an evolutionary process driven from previous testing efforts. The test cases and procedures that were used for baseline and final configuration need to be reviewed and evolved to an integrated test. These selected cases can be combined to represent a business process flow, such as a revenue cycle or a material acquisition cycle. Problems encountered during these efforts also need to be tested under an integrated environment. The final integration test cannot be viewed as independent; it is a capstone effort that brings together, and builds on, all previous testing efforts.

Integration testing should be allotted approximately 25% of the total time used during the realization phase for configuration and testing.

Test Data for Integration Test

Common data are critical elements in an integrated test. It is almost impossible to demonstrate integration without using the same data. Thus, a chart of accounts, business partners, materials, and the like must all be defined and properly configured as a part of the integrated test. Similarly, documents and control information (company codes, plants, organizational hierarchy, etc.) must function properly during the integrated test. A good deal of planning is required to conduct these tests, just like planning to go into production. Successful completion of integrated tests is one of the precursors for going into production.

Responsibilities

As knowledge transfers from the system's business process experts to the project team and approaches an apex, responsibility for the integration test becomes that of the business process users and power users. This responsibility instills a sense of ownership with the business process users and should make it easier to get their acceptance at the end of the phase.

There is a change in the makeup of the testing teams between the configuration cycles and integration testing. As the testing is now cross-functional, the test teams for each business process must be made up of members from each enterprise area being tested. This will ensure that all processes are properly tested.

Integration Test Approach

Final integration testing focuses on cross-functional integration points as well as end-to-end business processes. A well-defined final integration test plan starts with the testing of the cross-functional integration points and ends with the end-to-end testing of critical business processes identified within the business blueprint. To accommodate this approach, three integration cycles have been defined:

Integration 1: The purpose of this cycle is to test all cross-functional integration points for high-frequency and high-impact business processes and to finalize the entire system configuration. Doing this includes only the steps necessary to get data to cross from one function to another of a given module. It is not necessary to test an entire business process (end to end) at this time. The time allotted for this iteration is 50% of the total for integration testing, although careful and successful completion of this test should ensure that the remaining integration testing is relatively problem free. As with configuration cycles, all issues that occur during integration 1 testing must be added to the issue log and should include recommended solutions. Examples of integration points are creation of delivery notes in sales and distribution to be passed to materials management for warehouse processing, running of material requirements planning (MRP) in materials management to automatically generate production orders in production planning, and creation of customer billing documents in sales and distribution to be passed to finance for payment receipt processing.

Integration 2: The purpose here is to test, from start to finish, critical business flows as defined on the business blueprint. Completing integration 2 constitutes the freezing of the system for production and the completion of the knowledge transfer process between the system's business process experts and the project team. In integration 2, the entire business process from beginning to end across all enterprises is tested. Again, any issues that occur during this testing must be added to the issue log. Similarly, any issues that are resolved during testing should be closed in the log. An example of an end-to-end scenario is the taking of a sales order, the passing of the demand to manufacturing, MRP, manufacturing of the product, receipt into finish goods, shipping to the customer, invoicing, billing, and receipt processing.

Integration 3: This is the performance test involving integration 2, which stresses the system to observe its behavior with respect to response time and stability.

Levels of Testing

A testing overview is presented next.

- **Unit testing** tests the minimal software component or module. Each unit (basic component) of the software is tested to verify that the detailed design for the unit has been correctly implemented.
- **Integration testing** exposes defects in the interfaces and interaction between integrated components (modules). Progressively larger groups of tested software components corresponding to elements of the architectural design are integrated and tested until the software works as a whole.
- **System testing** tests an integrated system to verify that it meets requirements. This area sometimes can be subdivided into:
  - Functional testing.
  - Nonfunctional testing.

- **System integration testing** verifies that a system is integrated with any external or third-party systems defined in the system requirements.
- **Acceptance testing** can be conducted by the end user, customer, or client to validate whether to accept the product. Acceptance testing may be performed after the testing and before the implementation phase.
- **Alpha testing** is simulated or actual operational testing by potential users/customers or an independent test team at the developers' site. Alpha testing is often employed for off-the-shelf software as a form of internal acceptance testing, before the software goes to beta testing.
- **Beta testing** comes after alpha testing. Versions of the software, known as beta versions, are released to a limited audience outside of the company to ensure that the product has few faults or bugs. Sometimes beta versions are made available to the general public to increase the feedback field to a maximum number of future users.

  Although alpha and beta are referred to as testing, they are, in fact, user immersion. The rigors that are applied during these testing stages are often unsystematic, and many of the basic tenets of testing process are not used. The alpha and beta period provides insight into environmental and utilization conditions that can impact the software.
- **Regression testing** is performed after modifying software, either for a change in functionality or to fix defects. This test reruns previously passing tests on the modified software to ensure that the modifications have not unintentionally caused a *regression* of previous functionality. Regression testing can be performed at any or all of the listed test levels. These regression tests often are *automated*.

Case Example

I was working at a national hardware company in 1980s and was in charge of new systems development project to develop cash registers and back-office minicomputer systems. The boss asked me about my test plan and test procedure. After some thought, I concluded that what he was talking about was how we would do testing and what we would test. He was talking about a formal methodology for testing, something that I had not used before. This formalism in testing methodology became very handy in my career.

Later, at the Route 128 technology company in Boston area where I was head of systems, my one branch dealt with mission-critical systems. These systems were computer-controlled DDC (direct digital control) systems. With them, we would have to test the entire system not only

(Continued)

(Continued)

for the individual components but for the entire integrated system to ensure that each real-time stimulus would create the desired response. Here integrated testing was of utmost importance; an error that would stop the manufacturing process would cost $50,000 per minute. This problem was solved by creating the simulation panels with small lights that would go on or off depending on the manually created input condition causing the output condition to turn the lights on or off. We constructed these test panels for each part of the process to be tested. Only after successful simulation testing was the system allowed to interface with the process. Here again, stringent step-by-step component testing to integration testing was done with dummy production materials.

At another company, I served as the chief consultant to help build a lights-out factory. The eventual customer was the U.S. Navy for the Trident missile program. The system was a mission-critical DDC system. Here the challenge was different: Human lives were at stake, not merely money. We followed the steps to testing but with utmost caution and rigor. I wrote a program named Concon (Continuous Control) that was fundamental to the working of this computer-controlled facility. The program produced output signals to modulate the analog variables in the desired directions. During initial testing on the first bake furnace, I heard a whistle, indicating that the temperature in the furnace was rising. This would result in the furnace lid to coming off, a dangerous situation. This situation would occur if Concon was not working correctly. I shut down the furnace manually, and the rest of the testing was completed successfully. Concon became so fundamental to the control of the plant that even when my consulting contract expired, I was retained on call if Concon had trouble. I am proud to report that throughout the life cycle of this lights-out factory, I was never called because Concon always worked as it should have. Because the program had gone through enough testing, it always worked as planned. Such was the power of test plan and test procedure that I had learned very early in my work life.

Training

Implementation of global and complex programs is a hard and tortuous task. It is the one on which success or failure depends. Hence, training needs to be planned and acted on during all phases of the project. Deb Shinder has a fine article in *Tech Republic* that thoroughly covers the general aspects of training.[12]

Training Program

In our context, training needs to be planned for these steps:

- Strategy formulation
- KPI definition
- Benchmarking
- SCOR carding
- Workflow modeling
- Blueprinting
- Solution architecting
- Gap analysis
- Detailed design
- Configuring
- Development (if any)
- Testing
- Change management
- Quality management
- Risk management
- User training
- Performance measurement and performance tracking

Project team people need to be trained on an as-required basis in the above tasks as they pertain to the business processes. End users need to be trained in the usability and system modules. A global system is an undertaking in which every part of the organization and the project team needs to be adequately trained. Therefore, a spreadsheet should be prepared that shows who needs to be trained in the different areas. The final number of people who need to be trained can be determined only after the project scope is defined. The generic scope for each major module is shown in Table 8.1.

Repeat the spreadsheet process for each major module whose functionality is under consideration.

An expert project/program manager may be able to train his or her team as well as the user teams in the tasks from strategy formulation to risk management. But for implementation skills and system/modules, vendor expertise is the best source of information.

TABLE 8.1   Team Training Matrix

Task	Configurors	Project Team Super Users	Occasional Users	Daily Users	Super Users
Strategy formulation	X	X			
KPI definition	X	X			
Benchmarking	X	X			
SCOR carding	X	X			
Workflow modeling	X	X			
Blueprinting	X	X			
Solution architecting	X	X			
Gap analysis	X	X			
Testing	X				
Change management	X	X			
Quality management	X	X			
Risk management	X	X			
Implementation skills	X	X			
System/module Level 1	X	X	X	X	X
System/module Level 2	X	X		X	X
System/module Level 3	X	X			X

Bibliography

Change Management, Bambooweb Change Management, bambooweb .com/articles/c/h/Change-Management.

Change Management Best Practices, www.auditnet.org/docs/cmbp.pdf.

Campanella, J. *Principles of Quality Costs*. ASQC Quality Press, Milwaukee, WI, 1990.

Dvorak, Phred. "How Teams Can Work Well Together from Far Apart/ Theory & Practice," *Wall Street Journal*, September 18, 2007.

Gartner Group. *V Model Test Approach*, Stamford

Hash, Joan S. *Risk Management Guidance for Information Technology Systems,* Computer Security Division, Information Technology Laboratory, National Institute of Standards and Technology, February 2002.

Juran, M., and F. M. Gryna. *Quality Costs, Quality Control Handbook,* 4th Edition. New York: McGraw-Hill, 1988.

McCredie, Jack, and Dan Updegrove. *Enterprise System Implementations: Lessons from the Trenches.* net.educause.edu/ir/library/html/cem/cem99/cem9943.html - 47k

"Quality Model Mania," *Computer World,* March 8, 2004.

Watkins, John. "Testing IT: An Off-the-Shelf Software Testing Process." Computers. Google 2001.

Shinder, Deb. "Plan Your End-User Training Strategy Before Software Roll-Out," *Tech Republic* (March 2006).

CHAPTER 9

Performance Management

Introduction

In my practice, I had a number of meetings with "c"-level executives who had implemented large-scale business software initiatives. They all complained that their billion-dollar spendings did not give them actionable tools, triggers, and reports with which to better manage business performance. Upon closer examination of implementation strategies, we found some or all of these issues:

- The key performance indicators (KPIs) of interest had not been identified.
- The KPIs had not been configured to get up to the business warehouse.
- Scorcards had not been set up.
- Triggers and reports were not generated, or they could be generated only in roundabout ways.

In about the same time frame, large business software vendors were launching their offerings via the Strategic Enterprise Management (SEM) tool set. Recognizing this trend, John Van Decker at Meta Group wrote in 2002: "Companies should consider leading business performance management solutions that support a closed-loop life-cycle process and focus on metrics-based performance management. The goal should be developing actionable business plans to guide future results."[1] This chapter covers the performance measurement, performance tracking, and performance control features that make up performance management.

Principles of Performance Management

To control, you must have an objective function, then measure the state of the variable, get the deviation between the objective value and the measured

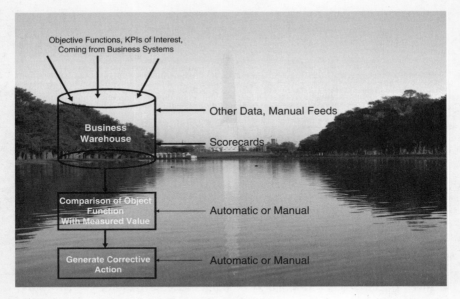

FIGURE 9.1 Principles of Performance Management

value, and finally generate the modulation signal that will correct the deviation. All this can be done in an open-loop or closed-loop fashion. If the process being watched cannot be automated, human agents can be deployed.

In the nonautomatic process control environment, the essentials come with a tool set that provides an automated means to present, access, and analyze performance. The SEM tool provides graphic views of:

- Performance objectives and measures (overview with status)
- Trends (period graphs)
- Comparisons (scorecard comparison/trend graphs)
- Drill down/where used
- Interface to Business Warehouse (BW) for more analysis
- Capabilities to document performance assessments

Figure 9.1 provides the basic principles of performance management.

Preparing to Implement Performance Management

If you are convinced by now that you should implement a performance management solution set, consider these issues:

- **Buy or build.** If you are the average information technology person, you may be tempted to build your own system. Resist the temptation. In my opinion, every single one of the large vendors provides its own solution, each of which will do more than an adequate job.
- **BW, SEM, analytics tools.** As a minimum, you should have the vendor-provided capability of Business Warehouse, strategic enterprise management, reports, and triggers.
- **KPIs and value drivers.** This is where you have to focus attention with an eagle eye. The numbers of KPIs and value drivers can be immense. You cannot look for all of them, and you must not waste time on dissecting and analyzing low yielders. Concentrate on heavy hitters. For example, the supply chain domain alone has upward of 96 KPIs. However, the most important of them is inventory carrying cost. Concentrate on that and study all the variables in your operation that contribute to inventory. Figure 9.2 provides groups of areas, such as Financial Analysis, Project Analysis, Miscellaneous KPIs, Production Volumes and Values, Health Environment and Safety (HES on the figure), and Surveys and Benchmarks. These areas are used to create the information delivery architecture in the BW. This format presents the data groups into an easily understandable architecture.

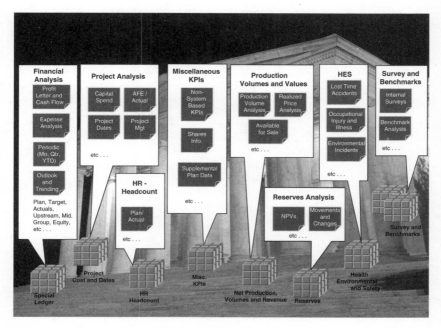

FIGURE 9.2 Performance Delivery Architecture

Generating the Corrective Signal

Imagine for one minute that the information delivery architecture represents the entire physical enterprise. In this case, it becomes a system with thousands of closed loops in the manufacturing/make stages and thousands of the open loops from sourcing to distribution. In order that they can be controlled precisely, these open loops behave very differently from the closed loops. Although state of the art understands the KPIs and value drivers, the mathematical relationships are not well understood. Hence, do not expect to generate a precise signal to eliminate the deviation. However, what you can get from the system is an actionable trigger, a report, and a trend.

Bibliography

Bansal Sam., *Multi Planner Closed Loop Cascaded Control Systems,* Chapter 1, Computer Integrated Manufacturing, Alcoa Laboratories, 1987.

CHAPTER 10

Summary

With helpful suggestions from my editor, I fine-tuned the book's title to *Technology Scorecards: Aligning IT Investments with Business Performance*. To me, the essence of this book is how to estimate and exploit business value from technology. But in the context of the title, it is how to use scorecards to align information technology investment strategy with business performance and how to use them to drive performance. In my long career, I mostly worked on projects for their entire life cycles. So it was not a case of making the technology work and moving away to greener pastures. I had to stick around to deliver the business value that the stakeholders wanted even if their objectives had changed midway. Literature and conversations with "c"-level executives more often than not indicated that their software project technology initiatives did not deliver business benefits. Motivated by this kind of situation and my successful record of delivering optimum bottom lines, I set out to write this book.

Part I dealt with the reasons for project failures; the main culprit cited was the unclear definition of objectives and measurable key performance indicators (KPIs). It defined scorecards and also discussed how the book is organized.

Part II provided functional content, including key performance indicators for some of today's important domains, such as strategic enterprise management, supply chain management, and product life cycle management. Here the KPIs and their interrelationships with the KPI drivers and KPI values shed a great deal of light on what to tweak to get what value, and also if the given value is available or not with the subject technology. The information here can be valuable for stakeholders when formulating ideas that can act as the basis of a new initiative. This part can be viewed as the "promise" part of the technology.

Part III concentrated on SCOR card methodology and on strategy formulation based on the creation of business value, which is driven by the business objectives. It also discussed business process redesign and the human factors that are important throughout, from strategy to implementation. It covered the need for correct planning during the earlier stages, such as during project strategy formulation, and issues like change, quality, risk, and test. Clients used to request that all of these aspects be included so they could understand the scope and benefits obtainable from the undertaking. This part can be viewed as the "deliver" part of the technology. The author welcomes feedback, and can be contacted at drsambansal@gmail.com.

References

Chapter 1

1. "Danger Signs on the Road to Success," *Chaos News Letter,* August 17, 2001.
2. Standish Group, "Project Success Rate," *Software Magazine,* January 15, 2004.
3. Jurgen H. Daum, "Strategy—A Holistic Approach: Adding Value Through IT Investments," Sapinfo.net.
4. Antone Gonsalves, "Gartner Backtracks on Earlier IT Spending Growth," *Information Week,* October 13, 2008.

Chapter 2

1. Sam Bansal, "Simulation in the Life Cycle of Manufacturing Systems," Inria, Paris, France, October 1995.
2. Sam Bansal, "Practical Applications of Models and Their Benefits, Evolution of a New Paradigm," *Journal of International Federation of Automatic Controls* (October 1994).

Chapter 3

1. *Takt* refers to the rate of customer demand, calculated by dividing the available production time by the quantity

Chapter 4

1. Michael Abramavici, *Status and Development Trends of Product Lifecycle Management Systems,* Ruhr University Report, 2005.

Chapter 5

1. Nicholas Carr, "IT Doesn't Matter," *Harvard Business Review* (May 2003).
2. Dorine Andrews and Susan Stalick, *Business Reengineering* (Saddle Brook, NJ: Prentice Hall, 1994); A. W. Scheer, *Business Process Engineering* (Berlin: Springer Verlag, 1994).

Chapter 7

1. Code of Practice for Project Management (2002), AllPM.Com, (February 2005).
2. Leyton W. Collins, "Interpersonal Skills and the Effective Project Manager," allPM.com (June 2003).
3. Phred Dvorak, "How Teams Can Work Well Together from Far Apart/Theory & Practice," *Wall Street Journal,* September 18, 2007.

Chapter 8

1. Bambooweb, *Change Management*, bambooweb.com/articles/c/h/Change-Management.html.
2. *Change Management Best Practices*, www.auditnet.org/docs/cmbp.pdf.
3. Ibid.
4. "Quality Model Mania," *Computer World,* March 8, 2004.
5. J. Campanella, *Principles of Quality Costs* (Milwaukee, WI: ASQ Quality Press, 1990).
6. J. M. Juran and F. M. Gryna, *Quality Costs, Juran's Quality Control Handbook, 4th ed.* (New York: McGraw-Hill, 1988).
7. Campanella 1990.
8. Juran and Gryna 1988.
9. Phred Dvorak, "How Teams Can Work Well Together from Far Apart/Theory & Practice," *Wall Street Journal*, September 18, 2007.
10. en.wikipedia.org/wiki/V-Model_(software_development).
11. V Model Test Approach, Gartner Group, Stamford, CT.
12. Deb Shinder, "Plan Your End-User Training Strategy Before Software Roll-Out," *Tech Republic* (March 2006).

Chapter 9

1. John Van Decker, "Business Performance Management," www.bpm partners.com/documents/BusinessesJoinBusinessPerformanceManage mentConsortium.pdf. Meta Group, Stamford, CT, 2002.

Index

"f" refers to figure; "t" to table.